Women in Early Modern Britain, 1450–1640

CHRISTINE PETERS

First published 2004
PALGRAVE MACMILLAN
Houndmills, Basingstoke, Hampshire RG21 6XS and
175 Fifth Avenue, New York, N.Y. 10010
Companies and representatives throughout the world

PALGRAVE MACMILLAN is the global academic imprint of the Palgrave Macmillan division of St. Martin's Press, LLC and of Palgrave Macmillan Ltd. Macmillan® is a registered trademark in the United States, United Kingdom and other countries. Palgrave is a registered trademark in the European Union and other countries.

ISBN 0–333–63358–X hardback
ISBN 0–333–63359–8 paperback

This book is printed on paper suitable for recycling and made from fully managed and sustained forest sources.

A catalogue record for this book is available from the British Library.

A catalog record for this book is available from the Library of Congress.

10 9 8 7 6 5 4 3 2 1
13 12 11 10 09 08 07 06 05 04

Printed in China

Contents

Introduction

It has become customary for books on early modern Britain to begin with eloquent pleas for the study of Britain. Citing the agenda set by Pocock and others, Britain is presented as a more valid geographic and cultural unit of historical investigation, and the writing of British history as an imperative strategy to counter the Anglocentric focus of much historiography of the period.[1] This book will not begin by making any such plea. In terms of the history of women, Britain is not a natural unit, but neither are the geographical boundaries of England, nor for that matter of Scotland or Wales.

That this is so is not due to that frequent observation that there is no shared history of women, a statement that is palpably untrue for any period, and only tenable if we demand of a shared history that its subjects have a single focus of identity. The concept of gender as the way in which society constructs and defines the relationship between men and women implies a shared history shaped by common culturally accepted parameters, which people unconsciously assimilate and to which they are expected to conform. Although transgressions occur, they entail a social censure that is rooted in an understanding of the nature of the sexes and their appropriate behaviour and draws its strength from the assumption that this is divinely ordained and, as an illustration of God's design, also biologically natural.

In broad outline, gender assumptions were similar in England, Scotland and Wales. Women were weaker vessels, a reference that encompassed not only their physical frailty, but also their more emotional nature. Such notions buttressed a patriarchal society: being less rational than men, women should submit to the authority of their husbands and masters, who were expected to guide and control their natural inclinations.

1

The resulting code of female behaviour was aptly summarised by the trio of precepts, current both in the mediaeval and the early modern periods: women should be chaste, silent and obedient.

Social reality did not, of course, live up to this ideal. Such assumptions were fissured by male insecurity about female sexuality, and by the uncomfortable possibilities that some women could be more rational than their partners, or wield more economic power. Gender was a cultural code that provided reference points, and a way of measuring one's role, but it was also a code that had to be negotiated. Such negotiation occurred on an individual level, but local and regional outcomes were also significant. Legal, religious, economic and demographic circumstances all had an important role to play in shaping the nature of female experience in different localities, and it is in this sense that there is no history of women in Britain, or in England, Scotland or Wales.

At first glance, legal structures seem to be the most influential and to reinforce ideas of the separate experiences of the three areas of Britain, but the patchwork of local custom and of adaptation to local demographic and economic circumstances suggests need for caution. However, there were some clear contrasts. Different inheritance practices meant that the independent heiress and dowager had no place in Welsh society, that daughters inherited half shares according to Norwegian law in Shetland, but that in the rest of Scotland practice was more flexible.[2] Inheritance customs that excluded daughters from a share in the parental property reduced the possibilities for a single woman to be economically independent and added to the attractions of servanthood, which encouraged the migration of more women than men from the countryside to the towns of England. Local customs that made a widow forfeit her customary landholding on remarriage shaped women's choices in ways that could differ from manor to manor, and contrasted with the pressures in favour of remarriage for the widow of a guild member or burgess. It was also possible for women to exploit legal differences to their own advantage. Welsh women marrying English husbands were able successfully to claim inheritance rights according to both Welsh and English law and thus enjoy greater rights to land and moveable goods than their English counterparts, even if such actions did not always command approval. Different jurisdictions could also determine that offences would be differently treated: until the abolition of 'foreign law' in 1611 a witch could only be fined in Shetland, but in Scotland she could be strangled and her body burnt.[3]

Changing economic fortunes were also important. They dictated whether women, along with the unfree, would be squeezed out of the marketplace, or be forbidden from practising various crafts on the spurious excuse of their lesser strength, as occurred amongst the weavers of Norwich in 1511.[4] In contrast, the introduction of new industries could render women's work suddenly more financially productive, reversing the usual situation in which women's wages were a fraction of men's. The production of high quality lace in East Devon transformed the possibilities of female economic independence, and altered marriage patterns, but was almost unique in so doing.[5] Elsewhere, new crafts were less remunerative. This was true, for example, of the lower quality lace production in Bedfordshire, and of marram grass plaiting in Anglesey.[6] In all areas, the alewife suffered from the advance of technology and capital that allowed the brewing with hops of large quantities of beer, but with significant differences in chronology.[7] Shifting emphases on arable and pasture farming affected female economic roles and status, whether as a result of the process of enclosure for pasture in England, or of the change from mixed subsistence farming in the Scottish Highlands to a closer engagement with the market and a reliance on cattle droving.[8]

The variety of economic and legal frameworks in which women constructed their lives reinforces the view of the inadequacy of national units for capturing female experience. Upland, lowland and urban areas may have more in common with each other than national units, but even this approach has its problems. Urban experience in the declining towns of Wales where, at least until the mid-sixteenth century 'Acts of Union', the legally defined 'Welsh' and 'English' had different opportunities and privileges, was distinctly different than in the rapidly expanding metropolis of London, or even in the smaller scale, but flourishing, urban centres of the east coast of Scotland, the capital Edinburgh, and the dramatically growing new arrival in the west, Glasgow. Even in the pastoral uplands there was significant variation. The movement of livestock to shielings for the summer months, traditionally by women, was gradually eroded as pressure of population moved the line of permanent settlement to higher altitudes. This trend was more advanced in Wales, Cumbria and Northumberland than it was in the Scottish Highlands.[9] North of the border, changes in clan organisation, and in attitudes to feuding and the associated raiding of livestock, were beginning to have an impact towards the end of the period. For all these reasons, the classic image of communities of dairymaids living alone in shielings or *hafodau* in the summertime became increasingly rare. Whole communities could move to summer pastures with their flocks, as was the practice of the inhabitants of Lismore in the 1630s. In Highland Scotland, especially as cattle raising displaced dairying, the possibility of sorning or

feuding meant that valuable cattle resources could not be left at the shieling under the care and protection of women alone: at Glenisla in 1608
watchmen were employed to guard the herds.[10]

In religion, it might seem that national units make the most sense. Most
obviously, there were national churches, and the Churches of England and
Scotland survived the Union of the Crowns in 1603. But, once again, this
only gives a broad framework. Whilst Wales and England ostensibly shared
the same process of official Reformation, the receptivity of the inhabitants
to protestantism differed markedly. Catholic recusancy, continued belief in
the powers of holy wells and a marked reliance on the beneficent services
of wizards and cunning folk, appear to have been more entrenched in
Welsh society than in England, even in those areas in which adherence to
catholicism remained strong. Such contrasts have a particular bearing upon
the history of women due to the close affinity of women with piety and with
supernatural power.

Historians have set out various arguments to explain gender patterns
of adherence to competing religions, but take as their starting point the
early modern assumption that the nature of women was that they were 'to
piety more prone'. As ritual specialists, and as innately emotional beings
with an affinity for the religious, changes in religious practice and doctrine fundamentally affected women's role and their conception of their
place in society. As a result, and confusingly for those who expect pre-
dictable outcomes, women could become, even if perhaps for different
reasons, stalwart adherents of both protestantism and catholicism. Some
of these outcomes were due less to the different processes of Reformation
in the constituent parts of Britain, than to the evolution of distinct devotional traditions in later mediaeval catholicism. Broadly speaking,
Continental influences produced in Scotland a style of piety focussed on
the eucharist and on the reserved host displayed in the monstrance.[11]
England, by contrast, saw the gradual spread of a style of Christocentric
devotion that emphasised the wounds of Christ and the suffering of his
Passion, whilst in Wales devotion to the Virgin Mary remained the dominant feature of catholicism.[12] Within this, there was plenty of room for
variation at the parish level. As with the Reformation itself, some parishes
were more receptive to new trends than others.

The modern stereotype of the female witch is a product of accretions.
Small details, like the pointed black hat favoured at Halloween parties and
the witch's black cat, were the product of the late-seventeenth-century
decline in the belief that powers of witchcraft could be exercised by poor
old women, dressed in old-fashioned hats. More importantly, feminist

appropriation of the 'witch hunt' as the cruel manifestation of early modern misogyny, has, until fairly recently, blurred recognition that a significant, and varying, proportion of those persecuted were men, and that, as Larner noted with reference to Scotland, 'witch hunting was not woman hunting'.[13] Indeed, witch beliefs can only be understood as part of a wider framework of belief in the world of healers, wizards, cunning folk, fairies and other spirits. In Wales, as noted earlier, the reputation of male wizards as practitioners of beneficent magic and assistants in the recovery of lost or stolen goods withstood protestant criticisms, and may have been stronger than belief in the power of maleficent witches.[14] In the Highlands of Scotland, where the word 'witch' and the idea that a witch made a pact with the devil were Lowland imports, a different view of the gender implications of witchcraft prevailed. In the Lowland version, the idea of the diabolical pact fostered fantasies of the witch having sex with the male devil and reinforced the view that the devil's agents would be weak, lustful women. In the Highlands, male witches could be answerable not to the devil, but to the elfin queen.

At this point it would be possible, despite the relative infancy of the history of women and of gender for this period in Scotland, and, even more so, in Wales, to continue to delineate striking contrasts. Attention could be drawn to the way in which the bardic traditions of Gaelic Scotland and of Wales offered the possibility of a climate more congenial to female authorship and self-expression than was the case in the more literate Scottish Lowlands and in England.[15] Religious variety offered the possibility of different interpretations of female role models, whether different emphases on aspects of the cult of the Virgin Mary and the saints, or the Calvinist assertion of the culpability of the adulterous Bathsheba prevalent in Scotland whilst English comment placed more emphasis on male responsibility and need to exercise their supposed capacity to control their passions. Origin myths offer another interesting area of investigation. The story of Scota and Gathelus, the originators of the Scots and the Gaels respectively, was unique in Britain, but not in Ireland, in its stress on the female rôle both in giving birth to the race and as doughty, merciless warriors. The accompanying politically motivated rewriting of the English Arthur legend in fifteenth-century Scottish romance stressed Arthur's treachery and duplicity and treated them as natural consequences of his illegitimate birth, instead of recounting the exploits of the knights of the round table in terms of courtly love.[16]

Yet it is time to halt this brief sketch of some of the legal, economic, religious and ideological contrasts and to assess their implications for the writing of a history of women in early modern Britain. Such a summary runs the risk of suggesting that the only history that can be written is an attractive kaleidoscope of women's experiences. Yet this image is in fact more apt than the frivolous connotations of a brightly coloured children's toy might suggest. The patterns formed by shaking the kaleidoscope are formed within limits, the culturally accepted assumptions of gender, and each coloured fragment only makes sense when juxtaposed with others. Moreover, as with the kaleidoscope, there are a multitude of patterns to view and recurring motifs to describe and explain. The kaleidoscope will not produce a British history, but when studied carefully it may produce a history of women in Britain.

Chapter 1: Marriage, Kinship and Inheritance

In early modern England the family was seen as the microcosm of the state. Following an Aristotelian tradition, the authority of the king depended on a corresponding recognition of the authority of the husband in the household. Monarchy, hierarchy and patriarchy, it was assumed, would stand and fall together. It was this analogy that determined that the murder of a husband would be viewed as more heinous than the murder of a wife. The former counted as petty treason, whilst the latter carried a lesser penalty as murder but both offences were considered to be offences against the king. In Scotland, and to a much lesser extent in Wales by this period, such acts were offences not against the king but against the kin. Where kin structures prevailed and bloodshed was dealt with according to the rules of feud, the idea of the family as a petty monarchy could have much less resonance, and wives retained much stronger ties with their natal kin. Scottish and Welsh women kept their family names upon marriage not as a gesture of independence, but as an indication of their less than complete absorption into the kindred, or 'surname', of their spouse.

As these contrasts suggest, the distinctive nature of the family and marriage in the various parts of Britain in this period was shaped by the competing claims of the kin and the state. The gradual advance of the state at the expense of the kin, manifested primarily in policies of anglicisation or lowlandisation, had important repercussions for gender as well as for governance. Women's experiences in England, Scotland and Wales in this period were far from unvaried or unchanging, but it is important to note that practice did not converge inexorably towards an

English model, even when acts of state prescribed it: the Welsh 'Act of Union' (1536) theoretically replaced native Welsh law with the law of England, but social pressures meant that marriage practices and property rights were less affected than the lawmakers intended.

The Church also had less ability to impose its practices on lay society in this period than one might expect. In many areas of Britain, especially at the beginning of our period, the practice of solemnised church wedding could not be taken for granted. In Scotland trial marriages may have been the norm in Highland areas and not unknown elsewhere. The easy dissolution of unions and the relative respectability of concubinage was a characteristic feature of Welsh society and extended to the clergy, many of whom kept concubines openly. In England, the situation was ostensibly more under ecclesiastical control, despite Lollard criticisms of liturgical rites, but the practice of spousals, which could make a valid marriage outside the Church, and the need for a godly campaign to discourage bridal pregnancy, suggests that the influence of the Church was incomplete.

Given this diversity in marriage formation, it is hardly surprising that there was similar variety in the freedom involved in choosing a marriage partner, even if in this case social status may have been more important than geography. It seems likely that strategies of marriage alliance amongst the elite of Scottish clans would have more in common with those deployed by the nobility and gentry elsewhere in Britain for whom concerns for the 'house' were similarly predominant than with those of the lower social orders.

However, historians of Scotland maintain that in a clan society characterised by feuding and the making of bonds of manrent, marriage was in fact the weakest form of alliance. More generally, differences in landholding would seem to affect the importance of women as family pawns in a marriage market. Most obviously, the fact that Welshwomen's fortunes were in goods, not land, meant that they would not be sought after as attractive landed heiresses. The commercialisation of Scottish clanship may have, perhaps paradoxically if this is seen as modernisation, increased the importance of marriage alliances. At the lower social level, attempts by local authorities to prevent pauper marriage had greater resonance in England where the poor law system was more developed.

Similar contrasts can be suggested in the possibility in this period of women actually choosing not to marry at all. Estimates of the proportion remaining single in Scotland and Wales are not available, but by the late sixteenth and early seventeenth centuries as much as one-fifth of the population of England did not marry. In explaining these patterns, economic structures must be important, especially the availability of work in service or the rare possibility of lucrative female employment, but these need to be balanced against the strong opinion that the single woman, even if not a whore, damaged the economic well-being of honest married couples and their children.

Finally, for those who did marry, legal structures, the possibility of their circumvention, and social expectations, shaped women's experience. They determined whether a wife could be expected to make a will disposing of those goods that would come to her on her husband's death whilst still under couverture, whether it was socially acceptable for a Welsh woman to pursue a claim for English dower in addition to her traditional share of the marriage goods, and whether wives had an effective right to their paraphernalia, their personal clothing and jewellery. Although, as the author of *The Law's Resolution of Women's Rights* (1632) maintained, all women could be considered as either married or to be married, the experience of what it meant for women to be married differed greatly in the various parts of Britain and was moulded by economic, legal and attitudinal developments during the two centuries under consideration here.

Marriage as an institution seems to have been weakest in Scotland, although historians, such as Anton, have argued that the assertion that trial marriages of a year and a day prevailed in Scotland and that husbands were able to put their wives away at will is a slur on Scottish practice. In his view, this misinterpretation arises from a modern misunderstanding of the practice of handfasting (a form of betrothal) common throughout Britain.[1] However, although it is possible that such practices may subsequently have encouraged a strong tradition of handfast marriage, the practice of trial marriage is not simply a figment of the modern historian's lazy imagination. Martin Martin in his 'Description of the Western Isles of Scotland' (*c.*1695) maintained that

> It was an ancient custom in the islands that a man should take a maid to his wife, and keep her the space of a year without marrying her; and if she pleased him all the while, he married her at the end of the year, and legitimised these children; but if he did not love her, he returned her to her parents and her portion (i.e. tocher) also; and if there happened to be any children they were kept by the father: but this unreasonable custom was long ago brought into disuse.[2]

The accuracy of this description, at least for parts of the Highlands, in the early seventeenth century, and presumably before this, is supported by a clause in the 'Statutes of Iona', which were agreed between the Crown and Highland chieftains in 1609. The first article declared that 'marriages contracted for a certain number of years' should be 'proscribed and the offenders should be considered, reputed and punished as fornicators'.[3] It is unlikely that this provision had much immediate impact, and even after the reissue and amplification of the 'Statutes' in 1616 it may have remained a dead letter, but it is of greater interest as a description of prevailing practice than of effective reform. However, since the 'Statutes' mainly aspired to bring the Highland areas of Scotland more into line with the Lowlands, it is possible that by this date the practice of temporary marriage was no longer widespread in the Lowlands. Although mediaeval and early modern historians alike have correctly warned against assuming the existence of a sharp Highland/Lowland division, awareness of such differences was increasing, especially after the Union of Crowns (1603). There was also a realisation of diversity within the Highlands. As James VI recognised in his *Basilikon Doron*, and in his agreement of the 'Statutes of Iona' with chieftains from the Western Isles, the Isles and the western seaboard were more tenacious in maintaining traditional practices.[4]

The continued adherence to such marriage practices was due to the strength of Gaelic traditions and their compatibility with the clan system, but it was also assisted by the weakness of the Church in some areas, even in the early seventeenth century. When the Rev. Farquhar Macrae was invited to preach the gospel in Lewis by Kenneth Mackenzie, Lord Kintail in 1610, he found that many of the inhabitants were ignorant of religion and that he had to baptise everyone under 40 years of age, and to marry 'a vast number who lived there together as man and wife, thereby to legitimate their children, and to abolish the barbarous custom that prevailed, of putting away their wives upon the least discord'.[5] Yet it would be mistaken to portray the Highlands, or even the Isles, as being outside the purview of official religion whether catholic or protestant. Rather, a pragmatic attitude to religion and marriage was adopted. Cornelius Ward, one of the Franciscan missionaries working in Kintyre in 1624–25, told his superiors that the success of the catholic mission depended on his being able to dispense from matrimonial impediments. Faced with a situation in which the local minister granted divorces for adultery and allowed such couples to enter new marriages, catholic missionaries could not compete on equal terms.[6]

Pragmatism had also been the feature of marriage alliances in an earlier period before such decisions were complicated by the existence of rival religions each claiming to declare the word of God. Marriages performed as part of the settlement of feuds or to enhance the power of a clan frequently involved a breach of the rules of the Church on consanguinity or affinity. Such political desires did not, though, cause members of the *fine* (clan elite) to disregard the Church completely. Dispensations were sought from Rome, but it was recognised that the need to consolidate a political alliance might require the establishment of the marriage before papal authorisation arrived. The contract drawn up for the marriage of Donald Ewin Allanson with Agnes Grant, daughter of John the Grant, specified that the couple were to be married in the face of holy kirk, but, if the dispensation had not arrived by 15 days after Martinmas, Agnes's father was 'bound and obliged to cause his daughter Agnes Grant and the said Donald to be handfast and put together for marriage to be completed'.[7] Such solutions were politically understandable, especially considering the lengthy delays that could arise in gaining an answer from Rome, and the expectation that most requests would eventually be answered favourably. Apart from the question of the marriage being within the prohibited degrees, the replacement handfasting ceremony created a marriage that was valid in the eyes of the Church, even if no cleric was present: a valid marriage only required the exchange of words of consent in the present tense by the couple; and consent expressed in the future tense could be turned into a valid marriage by subsequent sexual intercourse. It was this position that rendered the attempts of the Church to bring all marriages within an ecclesiastical framework intrinsically weak.

The Church could live reasonably comfortably with marriages that anticipated the arrival of a dispensation, but trial or temporary marriage presented far greater doctrinal problems. Catholics, and to a lesser extent protestants, took from scripture the view that marriages created by God could not be pulled asunder by men on the excuse of incompatibility. However, the voicing of such concern is hard to detect. This silence might suggest that the practice was, in fact, rare, but, as we have seen, this involves accusing Martin Martin of indulging in fantasy and fiction. It is more likely that the practice was too integral a part of Gaelic custom for a challenge to it to seem very worthwhile.

A comparison with Wales tends to lend support to this conclusion. Oddly perhaps, considering the more lasting vitality of clan structures there, Scotland lacks the detailed legal prescription of traditional practices concerning such fundamental matters as marriage and settlement of the feud, which survives for Wales. Classic Welsh law exists in thirteenth-century compilations, and thus only partly reflects Welsh practice in the period under discussion, but it was not completely abolished until the 'Acts of Union' in the reign of Henry VIII, and may have continued to shape expectations and practice after this date.

Welsh law does not offer a clear case of year and a day trial marriage as described by Martin, but it does draw a clear distinction between the status of the wife in the first seven years of marriage and that thereafter, and suggests that marriages could be dissolved easily. For the first seven years the wife was not considered to be fully married, and had no equal stake in her husband's moveable goods. If the marriage came to an end during the first seven years through no fault of the wife, she was entitled to *agweddi*, a payment calculated according to the status of her father, not of her husband. Interpreted by some as a security for the wife against desertion,[8] this arrangement is, perhaps more accurately, seen as a means of forcing the woman to live honestly and to avoid all suspicion of unchastity, whilst giving the husband the possibility of renouncing his wife at whim, even if at a small cost. After seven years, the woman was considered to be 'married' and to have her own share of the marital property. Separation thereafter cost the husband half of his moveable goods whatever the cause. Thus, although the Welsh system was not strictly one of trial marriage, it could come quite close to it. In later mediaeval marriage contracts marital separation with the division of goods in the usual way (*modo debito*) was envisaged as a distinct possibility.[9] The flexibility of Welsh marriage practice was also strengthened by a highly tolerant attitude towards illegitimacy, which was given legal force by the custom of *cynnwys* which allowed sons born out of wedlock to be legitimised by their fathers and to inherit.

Scottish practice is unlikely to have corresponded to these Welsh provisions exactly, any more than it did to those in Gaelic Ireland, an area with which there were closer economic and cultural contacts.[10] But in all three areas, recognition of illegitimate succession went hand in hand with a system that was more favourable towards marital separation than was the case in England. Moreover, this system not only incorporated the illegitimate son into the family, it could also render the distinction between wife and concubine almost imperceptible. When Lewis David ap Ieuan Lloyd of Llanfihangel Genau'r Glyn in West Wales made his will in 1612, he bequeathed to 'Catherine verch Gruffyth ap Ieuan Bedo my concubine a third of all my goods and chattels, and likewise the third part of all my household stuff'. In doing so, he ensured that his concubine was to be treated exactly as Welsh law would have prescribed if she had been his wife. Lewis David also left other legacies to his legitimate and illegitimate children, making it clear that he had previously been married but had seen no need to ask his concubine, Catherine, to become his wife.[11] However, men whose wives were still alive could be less content with such solutions and be prepared to risk ecclesiastical censure for bigamy in order to have their concubine publicly recognised as their wife. In 1447, for example, Ieuan ap Gwilym Goch of New Radnor, a married man, was presented for the clandestine marriage he contracted with his mistress Duthegy in Weobley church.[12]

In Wales pressures to remain unmarried were, according to an anonymous writer at the end of the sixteenth century, at least partly economic. He bemoaned the fact that it was customary for every man and woman to pay a tenth of their goods to the curate performing their marriage ceremony, or to come to some other settlement, but a fine of only 2s per year was demanded of adulterers and cohabiters. The conclusion seemed obvious: this disparity 'causes matrimony to be little set by and much refused'.[13] Like the fines and 'cradle crowns' paid by Welsh clerics for their concubines and children, the Church was effectively licensing what it was supposed to define as fornication. However, to view such decisions as merely the outcome of a fine economic calculation is probably misleading. The paradox in Wales was that, alongside a tolerance of irregular unions, there was a strong insistence in Welsh law on the need for a wife to be a virgin at her wedding and to behave with appropriate decorum throughout the marriage. As a consequence, women slandered for fornication could attempt to claim damages for loss of marriage prospects. In the Court of Great Session held at Carmarthen in 1607 an unmarried woman, Joan ferch John, brought a case against a carpenter who had called her his concubine and alleged that she had had a child by him. However, this was the earliest such case known from the plea rolls of this court, which was created by the 'Acts of Union' and dealt with a significant number of actions for slander from 1570 onwards.[14] In subsequent years similar cases were few and far between. This partly reflects a culture in which female participation in litigation was not widely accepted, but, as the contrasting histories of Catherine and Duthegy suggest, it was also significant that whether concubinage entailed loss of prospects was far from clear. For both reasons, submitting such a plea to the courts was a risky option for women.

The status of the illegitimate in Scotland is harder to determine, but there are signs that it differed little from the situation in Wales, even if the Kirk was pushing in an opposite direction to that of the Church in Wales with its two tiers of fines. Concubines were clearly acceptable amongst the clan leadership, and at the highest level the issue of succession was smoothed by the practice of the clan chief nominating his successor, the *tainistear*. At the level of the peasantry, a fluid system of family succession was probably characteristic of the classic clan system in which the chief rewarded his followers with land to consolidate the power of the clan. But with the process of the commercialisation of clanship in which chiefs increasingly came to act as landlords, rules of succession to property became more significant and this may have been to the detriment of the illegitimate. Many tenancies were still held technically at will, giving no guarantee of hereditary succession, but there were also kindly (i.e. 'kin-ly') tenancies. The idea of hereditary 'kindness', whether applied to rentals or tacks, may have encouraged a preference for the claims of the tenant's legitimate, rather than illegitimate, offspring. But, since the 'kindness' could be bought and sold, this effect may have been rather short-lived, especially in areas such as that around Glasgow and Paisley where a flourishing land market in peasant holdings soon developed.[15] The spread of feuing, which gathered pace as a consequence of the Reformation, encouraged nominated succession, and did not necessarily disadvantage the illegitimate child if this was the wish of the parents. Indeed, before the Reformation the granting of a life rent to a woman and a feu to her son had been the standard way in which clerics provided for their illegitimate offspring.[16] Without a reason for a change in attitudes towards illegitimacy, the changes in conditions of tenure in this period were easily flexible enough to provide for offspring born out of wedlock.

The fairly weak support for legitimacy in conditions of tenure in Scotland contrasted with the normal position for customary holdings on English manors where illegitimate children were not normally recognised as heirs, and widows could be deprived of their rights if they had not been married at the church door. Partly as a consequence of this, the Kirk had much more difficulty than the Church did in England in persuading individuals to solemnise their union in church. It seems likely that this tenurial background encouraged a tolerant attitude towards illegitimacy, at least among certain sections of society, which made them more capable of withstanding the efforts of kirk discipline to modify their behaviour. When he came to describe his travels in Scotland between 1614 and 1618, Richard James remarked that in the Highlands the stool of repentance in the church was usually 'well stuffed' with men and women dressed in white sheets performing penance for whoredom, but he was sceptical that this had much effect on attitudes. As he saw it, the large numbers involved were due to 'it being a thing usually for all of the younger sort to have as they will not say their whores but their women, because they commonly do not prostitute themselves to everyone'.[17] Performing penance for the 'many bastards' that resulted was accepted with resignation, and in the knowledge that careers were open to the base-born at home and as foreign mercenaries or merchants. But the existence of opportunities for illegitimate sons – our sources seldom discuss the fates of illegitimate daughters – was not the only factor encouraging the formation of marriages which were not solemnised in church. Part of the problem lay in the simple fact that, even in the eyes of the Church, simple exchange of consent constituted marriage.

Throughout mediaeval Europe churches had been struggling, with varying degrees of success, to hold onto this definition of the formation of marriage whilst bringing the control and regulation of marriage under the supervision of the ecclesiastical authorities. Most effectively, the Church had harnessed its campaign to two issues which were designed to appeal to a lay audience: the legitimation of heirs and the security of property rights for widows and their children; and the elevation of marriage as a sacrament, to provide a lay equivalent of the much praised sacred virginity. The first, as we have seen, had limited impact in Scottish and Welsh society in this period, but did much to shape English assumptions above the ranks of the landless. The second lay behind the insistent concern of churchmen and lay elders in Scotland that, although exchange of consent by the couple (handfasting) created a valid marriage, it was nevertheless not fully christian. Such concerns were not the effect of the Reformation, which in any case sought to redefine the meaning of all sacraments including that of marriage, although the apparent strengthening of church discipline gives that impression.

The resolution of the Aberdeen kirk session in 1562 is often quoted in support of the laxity of marriage practices in Scotland, and occasionally mistakenly thought to support arguments for trial marriage or marriage for a number of years. The session's concern was with handfast marriages that were not followed by solemnisation in church and it was determined that penalties should be imposed on those who did not amend their ways:

Because sundry and many within this town are handfast, as they call it, and made a promise of marriage a long time ago, some seven years, others six years, others longer, others more recently, and still will not get married and complete that honourable union, neither for fear of

God nor for love of their partner, but remain and continue in manifest fornication and whoredom.[18]

Despite the knowledge that such marital unions were valid, the session at Aberdeen, infused with godly protestant zeal, was responding to prevailing marriage practices in a way that differed little in principle from the earlier strictures of Andrew Forman, Archbishop of St Andrews, 1516–21, who maintained that the exchange of vows *per verba de futuro* followed by intercourse, which created a canonically valid marriage, was 'an evil custom or corruption which, by instigation of the enemy of the human race, had increased in this his diocese of St Andrews to an extent deserving condemnation'.[19]

Although few pre-Reformation church court records survive to substantiate the claim, Archbishop Forman's campaign probably made little impact on the behaviour of the laity of his diocese. The reformed kirk faced a similarly uphill struggle, and perhaps an even more difficult one. It had chosen even harder ground upon which to fight than that chosen by the archbishop since handfastings were less likely to be clandestine arrangements and could have the approval of parents, kin and friends. It was also unclear what was the best strategy. One option was to deprive handfastings of all vestiges of ecclesiastical respectability in the hope that the loss would be felt and would encourage couples to proceed to a church ceremony soon afterwards. Accordingly, the Aberdeen kirk session six years after its inconclusive programme of exhortation and punishment ordained that 'neither the minister nor the reader be present at contracts of marriage-making as they call their handfastings'. Soon afterwards, the General Assembly meeting in 1570 opted for a clerical takeover of handfasting. All such betrothals should take place in church 'according to the order of the reformed kirk' and, lest the kirk should be seen as sanctioning fornication before the wedding, sureties should be taken by the session 'for abstinence until the marriage is solemnised'. This was an ambitious policy, and one that was unlikely to succeed, even if it perhaps stood its best chance in a realm in which the system of reformed discipline was more effective than in most. The reversal of policy by the General Assembly in 1575, when it was stated that there should be 'no further ceremonies used' before the actual solemnisation of the marriage, was similarly problematic. Finally, kirk sessions opted for the more limited, but at least pragmatic, aim of taking cautions when the couple asked for banns and declaring them forfeit if the bride turned out to be pregnant before marriage.[20]

Discipline in this final form did nothing to entice those who had been censured by the session of Aberdeen for their long-term handfast unions into the church, but it may have done something to limit premarital sex amongst those sections of society that viewed the kirk with more favour and who came to see a church wedding as a symbol of respectability. In Scotland progress against irregular marriages was slow because, as was the case everywhere, the Church was handicapped by its own definition of marriage, which allowed it to take place entirely within a lay domain. But, despite the zealousness of the Kirk, a more severe handicap was the nature of Scottish society itself in which structures of kinship and land-holding, although evolving, left less room for the ecclesiastical authorities in the organisation of marriage and the definition of its legitimacy and that of its offspring.

That this was so can be further suggested by a comparison with England where the Church was much less industriously active, but where socio-economic changes fostered, almost by accident, the situation that the Aberdeen elders strove to achieve in their community. English society did, of course, start from a different base. As has been noted, inheritance procedures were more likely to favour the legitimate, and certain rights, especially of widows, in manorial custom could be held to depend on endowment during the marriage ceremony at the church door, and the concerns of the nuclear family prevailed. However, against this back-ground of general acceptance of church marriage, some dissenting voices could be heard. The Lollard movement made few discernible inroads into Scottish and Welsh society, but was much more significant in England.

Persecuting ecclesiastics were most concerned by Lollardy's critique of the sacrament of the eucharist, but its later lay adherents extended this to formulate a more generalised attack on the value of church ritual in conferring sacramental grace. Such outward gestures were merely com-memorative signs. Symbols were useful to prompt memory, but they did not themselves call down God's grace. This was true of the water of baptism and of the eucharist, but must have seemed all the more true of marriage, as even the not completely corrupt Church recognised this in theory, although it attempted to encourage contrary practice. Judging by figures of patchily carried out persecutions, the Lollards were not a powerful force, but, to the extent that they articulated the layperson's common sense rationalisation of the Church's teachings, these views may have been more widespread and need not have prompted denunciation of their holders as heretics by their neighbours. This is particularly so in the case of marriage, which was only occasionally mentioned in the surviving interrogatories. The few pieces of evidence for a Lollard marriage service describe a domestic ceremony indistinguishable from the general practice of lay handfasting, and such ideas were not necessarily corrosive of church wedding. Provided one did not put confidence in outward forms as conferrers of grace, there was, as Bishop Pecock perceptively realised in his attempt to bring the Lollards back into the catholic fold, no reason why such practices could not serve as acceptable outward signs.[21] In a context in which church wedding was not generally accepted, Lollard views could have consolidated lay opposition to ecclesiastical attempts to enforce it, but in England by the fifteenth century this was no longer the case.

This was partly because there were strands in late mediaeval piety, compatible with Lollardy but also more widely accepted, that suggested that the special status of marriage would continue to strike a deep chord. The evolving Christocentric piety, which focussed on the passion and wounds of the adult Christ, also appropriated the idea of the sacraments which were seen as originating from Christ's Crucifixion. In an iconographical development limited to England and Wales, the seven sacraments were graphically portrayed as the outcome of the wounds in Christ's side, feet and hands.[22] Even more powerfully such depictions were the obverse of another vivid image in which blasphemers or Sabbath breakers inflicted wounds on Christ or dismembered his body. Reinforcing the notion of marriage within Christ's church was not the main intention of these images, but they played their part in continuing to ensure that unsolemnised handfast marriages would be a minor feature in England, even when it seemed possible that protestant denial of the sacramental value of marriage could have undermined acceptance of the church wedding ceremony. This was no idle threat, incredible though it now seems: the government was amazed that the exclusion of marriage from the list of sacraments in the Ten Articles (1536) caused a vocal minority to believe that marriage had been abolished.[23]

The strength of the church wedding ceremony in England was largely because spousals themselves were in decline.[24] In the early 1620s when Henry Swinburne wrote his *Treatise of Spousals* this was already evident, although the ceremony may have lingered longer in the north and west than in the south and east. By the time of its reprinting in 1686, the editor was apologetic: spousals were now 'in great measure worn out of use' but there were enough legal similarities between spousals and marriage for the new edition to be commercially viable. The decline of spousals occurred contrary to the wishes of protestant divines, who saw scriptural sanction for it in the betrothal of Mary and Joseph. Men as diverse as Greenham, Cartwright and Griffiths welcomed the possibility of a decent delay between the recognition of mutual affection and sex so that, in the words of the latter, 'the couple might not rush like brute beasts into the marriage bed', and sought to incorporate betrothal into the ecclesiastical sphere. The campaign was a failure, but not for the same reasons that had dashed the hopes of those who had supported a similar position at the General Assembly of 1570. It occurred because in England economic developments and changing attitudes combined to undermine the function of spousals.

At the beginning of the period the ceremony of handfasting involved three key elements: the exchange of consent by the couple, the transfer of marriage goods from the parents to their daughter, and a feast or drinking for family and friends who also acted as witnesses. For women spousals marked a key point of independence. Unlike their brothers who received their inheritance when they reached a specified age, only at marriage did a young woman gain control over her property. Such independence was, of course, largely symbolic and was usually temporary: the bride surrendered control of her property to her husband when they were married at the church door. But it was not insignificant, even if few women would have envied Ann Gardyner of Great Wolford (Warwickshire) who died in 1538 before the church ceremony and was able to make her will as a single woman and to bequeath a portion of her marriage goods to her 'husband before God'. Spousals, more than the later church wedding ceremony, was the woman's day. As in more recent Mediterranean societies, the displaying of the marriage goods to neighbours, and to kin and friends of the groom, demonstrated her family's status and defined it in terms of the thrift and domestic prowess of the bride and of her mother and sisters.

The development of an increasingly cash-based economy undermined this system, but did not in itself cause the decline of spousals. Of course, it was much less interesting for neighbours to know that the bride's dowry was worth say £4, than to examine the collection of goods, many of which may have been home produced. But the spread of cash did not compel families to abandon the tradition of spousals, or preclude continuing to assemble collections of marriage goods. That families chose to do so was partly because the ability to provide money rather than goods conferred status. The loss of a ritualised focus for the bride-to-be was also not clearly detrimental since the move to cash portions was also accompanied by a trend towards giving portions to daughters not on marriage but at a certain age. For many such women the temporary independence between handfasting and church wedding could become real economic independence between the ages of majority and of marriage.

Interpreting the decline of spousals in terms of an increasingly money-based economy and shifting attitudes towards the economic endowment of daughters makes sense of both the geography and chronology of the practice of spousals. The north and west were areas in which both of these factors spread less rapidly. They were also, as Adair notes, areas in which illegitimacy levels were higher,[25] but this is a less important part of the explanation. The practice of spousals was not necessarily a licence for premarital sex. In a Somerset church court deposition of 1562, a woman's refusal to have sex with her 'husband' is reported in the following terms: 'Be you not my wife? Why should you refuse me?' 'I am so ... but what will people say, because I am not married.' Furthermore, if Swinburne's description is to be believed, even cohabitation and sexual intercourse did not always go together: 'in some places the Woman after these Spousals, presently cohabited with the Man, but continued unknown till the Marriage day'. In the practice of spousals, as well as in the reasons for their decline, there could be no clearer indication of the differences between English and Scottish practice.

Whatever the processes of marriage formation in the different parts of Britain, the possibility of individuals choosing their own marriage partner was acknowledged, at least in theory. Nevertheless, the links between marriage, property, inheritance and political alliance meant that this was often not as straightforward as the Church's definition of marriage as the exchange of mutual consent would suggest. Studies of church court depositions, especially in England, have concluded that couples had a great deal of freedom. Although promises of marriage would often be made conditional on the party obtaining the agreement of family and friends, historians have been struck by the informality of the circumstances in which marriages were formed. There is, however, need for caution here. Those cases reaching the church courts were disputed contracts, in which, typically, another woman alleged that a man had made a previous contract of marriage with her, and may represent only about 3 per cent of marriages.[26] Obviously, contracts made in more informal circumstances were most likely to provide opportunity for dispute: it would be difficult for anyone to wriggle out of a publicly witnessed ceremony of spousals. Nevertheless, it seems likely that at most levels of society there was a fair amount of freedom in the choice of marriage partner, but that this was shaped by family expectations. Parents did, after all, frequently hold the purse strings, and in England, where marriage was normally neolocal, the new couple had to be able to afford to set themselves up in a household of their own.

At the level of the social elite, the situation could be very different. Brides brought property, whether the landed estates of English heiresses or the equally valuable goods of the Scottish bride's tocher, and could cement alliances between families. Marriage was always both an economic and an emotional transaction, but the balance could shift according to family circumstances. In England, where the demographic situation meant that as many as one in five, or perhaps one in six, landed families would fail in the direct line in each generation, heiresses were fairly common. The combination of wealth and status meant that such women normally married into other landed families for whom marriage alliances were the main means of extending their estates. Male new-comers, by contrast, were usually only able to acquire landed status by purchase rather than by advantageous marriages. For women just below the ranks of the elite marriage offered more prospect of upward social mobility. Wealthy bourgeois fathers offering attractive dowries could secure husbands for their daughters from the more impecunious ranks of the landed elite, or those who had recently fallen upon harder times.[27]

In England elite marriage alliances were primarily concerned with securing economic and social status for particular branches of a family. In Scotland, where the clan system remained strong, marriage decisions could be subordinated to the need to strengthen the power of the clan. Strategies of female endogamy meant that by discouraging women from marrying outside the clan their marriage goods were not lost to the wealth of the clan as a whole. Marriages could also be used to build alliances between families and could form part of the settlement of blood feuds. It is, however, less clear how important these two considerations were in structuring the marriage decisions among the clan elites in the early modern period. The largest available sample of marriages of a clan elite relates to the Macphersons, but depends on a clan genealogy which was originally orally transmitted. Additionally, historians of feud and of forms of alliance such as bonds of friendship and bonds of manrent have concluded that alliances created by marriage were the weakest.[28]

The Macpherson genealogy, despite concerns about the accuracy of a document describing an oral tradition, should not be completely disregarded. Encouragingly, where details can be checked with genealogies of other clans, they usually correspond. But the analysis of these marriages only supports the thesis of female endogamy as a strategy within some *sliochdan*, rather than of the clan as a whole. Of the over 300 marriages recorded in this source, more than one-third (119) occurred within the clan, and of these, 40 involved marriage partners from the same *sliochd*. The smaller *sliochdan* exchanged equal numbers of men and women, but the most important provided more women to the other two *sliochdan* than it took from them, suggesting that only the more important *sliochd* could afford a marriage strategy that did not balance the inflow and outflow of wealth. From this basis it is, of course, a large leap to suggest that such considerations structured the making of marriages between clans.

The female endogamy strategy assumes that the prime significance of elite marriage is an economic transfer. There is, of course, something in this. Clan power was maintained by a cycle of feasting and feuding, and the tocher of a bride could provide a healthy supplement to the resources of the groom's clan whilst diminishing that of the bride's. When, for example, the Clanranald *tainistear*, John Macdonald of Moidart, married Marion, the daughter of Roderick MacLeod of Dunvegan in 1613, her tocher consisted of 200 cows and a fully tacked out galley of 24 oars and three sails.[29] But, if the economics of tochers was the only issue, Roderick MacLeod, and the largest of the three Macpherson *sliochdan*, would have been acting extremely imprudently. A MacLeod husband should have been found for Marion, and the most powerful *sliochd* should have learned a lesson from its weaker neighbours.

Clearly, there is a need to reassess the view of historians that marriage was a rather ineffective form of alliance. It was one, after all, in which families invested heavily. Moreover, there is a paradox that the historians most strongly influenced by anthropological 'peace in the feud' arguments and concerned to clean up Scotland's reputation for anarchy and lawlessness, should downplay the role of marriage alliances which anthropologists identify as the principal means by which blood is taken out of the feud. In his classic study of the Sudanese Nuer, the anthropologist Gluckman concluded that marriage weakened the unity of each vengeance group. Conflicting loyalties made it difficult to pursue vengeance against the kin of one's wife, and encouraged resort to arbitration. This theory gains further support from the Albanian case where the blood most emphatically remained in the feud. Here brides were sought from far away and contact with the bride's kin was deliberately kept to a minimum. Moreover, feud was a male concern in which women should take no active part and were not even seen as legitimate targets of vengeance. Feud was a matter of blood. What counted were relations of consanguinity, not of affinity.[30]

Of the two types, early modern Scotland was closer to the Nuer than to the Albanian, although it seems to have differed from both in being more unstructured. Retributive violence, a matter of honour, was indiscriminate, as also were acts of sorning or raiding. When, for example, William Ros entered Andrew Haynes's house in Glasgow in 1576 he found no one there except his wife and the nurse of his children, and attacked the nurse by stabbing her under her breast with his knife.[31] When women, and even temporary employees, are victims, we should expect some role for kin by marriage, as well as by blood, in the pursuit and settlement of feud. Commentators on clan and feud in Scotland who believe that marriage created the weakest tie of alliance do, of course, concede that it played some role, but the observation of another Scottish historian that when women are finally included in political history it is to suggest that they had no real significance is not far from the mark.[32] For Wormald, forms of alliance came in three strengths: bonds of manrent, bonds of friendship and bonds of marriage. The latter brought two kindreds into juxtaposition but did not impose mutual obligations of kinship on the husband and the male relatives of the wife. Relatives by marriage could assist in feud and were less likely to be one's enemies, but they had a choice of action in which loyalty to their own kindred usually came first.[33] However, if marriage alliances were really so weak, it is hard to see why families did not rely on the first two forms, which created reciprocal obligations for no initial economic outlay. Looking at some of the evidence more closely, it is less clear that marriage alliances were always the weakest link.

Part of the problem is how the strength of marriage alliances should be assessed. Clearly, they did not always prevent conflict, but to expect this may be to misunderstand an important part of their purpose. Unlike bonds, which could be agreed for a fixed number of years, ties of affinity were recognised as enduring. A story told by Sir John Wynn of Gwydir about two feuding families in Wales also applies to the Scottish situation. The feud between Howell ap Rees ap Howell Vaughan and his brother-in-law Evan ap Robert ap Meredith could support the argument for the weakness of relations of marriage, but the feud came to an end some time after the death of Evan ap Robert 'for his three eldest sons were the sons of Howell ap Rees ap Howell Vaughan's sister'. In the next generation, bonds of affinity seemed a good reason for calling the feud to a close.[34]

It is therefore important to look more closely at the kind of alliance created by marriage. In both Scotland and Wales, married women traditionally kept their own family name indicating that they were not fully assimilated into their husband's kin. Moreover, in Wales, although apparently not in Scotland where detailed regulation was not a feature, a married woman's *galanas* (blood price) was always calculated in terms of the status of her natal family, but the *sarhaed* (insult payment) depended on the status of her husband. This lack of full assimilation, as shown by the use of patronymics, is used by Wormald to explain why marriage was the weakest form of alliance. But it may actually explain the opposite. That a woman is not assimilated into her husband's kin in this way keeps visible the fact that she is of a different surname. It may be true that the marriage imposes no clear obligation on the husband and the men of the wife's kindred, but the children of the marriage may be conscious of their link with both surnames. This is especially the case in a society like early modern Scotland in which surnames implied important bonds of loyalty. As Wormald notes, bonds of manrent and friendship did not need to be made between parties sharing the same surname, except among the Kennedies, a clan in which claims to headship were unclear and contested. In the letter written by Adam Bothwell, Bishop of Orkney, to his brother-in-law Archibald Napier of Merchiston (1568) it is true that there was 'a careful distinction between "your house", or kindred, and "friends" who included the writer, related by marriage'.[35] But Bothwell's sentence, 'Always I beseech you as you love your own weal, the weal of your house, and us your friends that would your weal. ...', contains nothing to support the view that the assistance of such 'friends' by marriage was less reliable than that of those friends whose friendship derived from a bond of friendship or a bond of manrent.

The second part of the case for the weakness of marriage in creating alliances rests on the relationship between them and bonds of manrent. Wormald, in her study of the latter, assumes that when the two alliances were used in conjunction, it was the bond of manrent that was being used to shore up the deficiencies of an alliance based on marriage.[36] As will be clear from the argument developed so far, the evidence for this prioritisation is not overwhelming. It is clear that a marriage alliance could seem to be the best way to cement risky or precarious contracts. The indenture drawn up in 1482 between Lauchlane Mackintosh and Donald Angus Mackintosh provides a good example. According to the terms of the contract, Donald was to take the Castle of Kilravock by force from Hugh Rose, baron of Kilravock, who was deemed to have no proper title, and then hold it as constable for Lauchlane. Nevertheless, the indenture was not considered to be a sufficient safeguard for this arrangement, Donald presumably wishing to be sure of Lauchlane's support should Hugh Rose try to regain possession. Consequently, it was agreed that, for further security of contract, Donald would marry Lauchlane's daughter Margaret as soon as the castle was taken.[37]

Marriage alliances often formed an important part of the agreed reconciliation of feuding families, suggesting their strength rather than their weakness. Although there is no precise statistical analysis of assythments, bonds of manrent were only very rarely used in such circumstances. Such bonds could be used to prevent the escalation of incipient conflict, but were seen as less appropriate in damping down the flames. This, in Wormald's view, does not undermine the argument for their strength, but rather reminds that their efficacy depended on the voluntary nature of such agreements. However, assythment was an agreed compromise conducted with the option of the continuation of the feud constantly in the background and thus a process scarcely distinguishable from the drawing up of a bond of manrent when relations were tense. Marriage, it would seem, was preferable because it formed a stronger and more enduring alliance of families. Although somewhat repellent to modern sensibilities, the practice of marrying the daughter of the victim to his assailant made perfect sense to contemporaries. It not only provided a protector for the woman whom the feud had deprived of her natural protector, it also provided a safeguard against future conflict that was not limited to the lifespan of the contracting parties. Marriage therefore was not the weakest form of alliance. Instead, like the surname, it drew strength from the fact that the reciprocal obligations of support did not have to be drawn up, but were understood.

Consequently, when bonds of manrent accompanied marriage contracts, we should not automatically assume that they were shoring up the latter. Even the bonds of manrent and the marriage alliance made in the fifteenth century by the Stewarts of Garlies and John Lord Maxwell, which are adduced by Wormald in support of the weakness of marriage, need not be read in this way.[38] The first point to notice is that the first agreement made between the two parties was a bond of manrent, which was made by the Stewarts of Garlies to Maxwell in 1486 for five years. As the end of this term approached, a second bond of manrent was given, this time for seven years. This second bond of manrent was not given unconditionally: the Stewarts of Garlies reserved their service to Patrick, earl of Bothwell. At the same time, a marriage was agreed between

Maxwell and Agnes, daughter of Stewart of Garlies. Between 1486 and 1491 Maxwell's ability to command the loyalty of the Stewarts of Garlies had diminished, and it seems likely that, far from the bond of manrent being used to buttress the weakness of a marriage alliance, the marriage was agreed to strengthen the bond of manrent. This is not to say that the bond of manrent was intrinsically weak during the period when it was in force. The problem was one of ensuring renewal. When the status of a recipient of a bond of manrent was strong but faltering, and such agreements were only issued for a few years at a time, a marriage alliance could seem the ideal way of creating the expectation of renewal. The surviving record is, of course, patchy, but further bonds of manrent were made by the Stewarts of Garlies to Maxwell in 1521, 1523 and 1550. The marriage alliance did not obviate the need for bonds of manrent, but this should not be thought to undermine its strength and place in the tactics of alliance.

It seems likely that the importance of marriage alliances for clan strategies increased towards the end of this period. Until the 1590s it was still common to make bonds, but after 1600 'hardly any' were made.[39] This is quite surprising. It is tempting, but unconvincing, to attribute this change to the success of the crown's attack on feud and its justice. But there was no open attack on bonding, and it is implausible to argue that there was no longer any need for clientage relations. The reshaping of attitudes concerning feud was a gradual process and even if settlements of some types of feud now reached the law courts this did not reduce the possibility of influence by a powerful protector. Bastard feudal affinities flourished in late mediaeval England and securing judicial favour was one of the key elements in this system. The disappearance of bonds is therefore a puzzle, but one which perhaps suggests their somewhat peripheral nature. Agreed in times of heightened stress, they could seem less necessary as the clan system became more regulated.

Economic developments were primarily responsible for the redefinition of clanship, although the Crown made a series of attempts to hasten this process, beginning with the introduction of regular rents on crown lands after the forfeiture of the Lordship of the Isles in 1493. The traditional chiefly economy consisted of a cycle of feuding and feasting sustained by raids on neighbouring clans (sorning), dowries (tochers) brought by brides from beyond the clan, and the levying of food and hospitality (*cuid oidhche*) for the chief and his companions from members of the clan. As Macinnes and Dodgshon have argued, the sixteenth and seventeenth centuries saw the development of a more commercially oriented clan society. The introduction of fixed rents instead of *cuid oidhche* and the development of the long distance cattle trade with the Lowlands placed clanship on a different basis, even if many of the same attitudes prevailed. The chronic indebtedness of many clan chiefs was due to their less than commercial outlook. Giving loans according to 'feasting and feuding' principles ensured support but was likely to result in financial insolvency. There were, of course, different chronologies of feuding, rents and commercialisation in the western seaboard and isles, the rest of the Highlands, Lowlands and Borders, and not all were prepared to adopt the new ways. But those that refused to do so were increasingly outflanked by their neighbours. The Macgregors continued the traditional practice of sorning, but whereas in the sixteenth century the Campbells of Glenorchy dealt with this by the procedures of feud, by the seventeenth century the Macgregors found themselves classed among the broken men and caterans outside the law by clans who were now playing by different rules.[40]

As a consequence of these changes, marriage alliances took on an extra significance. In a situation in which increased resources could not be gained respectably by sorning, and the need for wealth was only partly compensated by the transformation of *cuid oidhche* into regular rent payments, a bride's tocher provided a much needed injection of wealth. Nevertheless, despite the increasing commercial contacts with the Lowlands, it remained the case that the elite of Highland clans continued to seek brides from within Gaeldom. Only clans like the Frasers of Lovat, located on the periphery of the Highlands, contracted a significant number of marriages with Lowland families.[41]

The border between Wales and England was also a barrier to marriage formation amongst the elite, although more intermarriage probably occurred, particularly between the gentry families of North Wales and those of Lancashire and Cheshire. In forming such alliances English cultural prejudice was mingled with economic concerns and, in some cases, the desire to dispose of otherwise unmarriageable daughters. The remoteness of Wales was considered an obstacle, as illustrated by the responses given to the attempts of Sir John Wynn of Gwydir to find an English wife for his son John who was studying at Lincoln's Inn *c.*1604. Sir Baptist Hicks, silkman and moneylender of Cheapside, and Sir Henry Bainton both declined due to the remoteness of Wales. Hicks added a further complaint: in his view such a marriage was also impossible because the Welsh were more irreligious than the English.[42] Such prejudices did not only operate in one direction. In 1615 Sir John Wynn wrote to his son-in-law Sir Roger Mostyn, who was also seeking an English bride for his son, and commented that 'it is more easy to have good brides in this country [North Wales] being simple and not having vices, than in England where a great deal of virtue is taught but they incline to vice more, because of the liberty the English fashion allows to women'.[43] Marrying one's son to an English bride could confer status upon a Welsh gentry family, but some fathers at least were concerned that it might not be conducive to domestic and family harmony. Furthermore, as will be discussed in more detail later, such marriages involved a different type of marriage settlement and rights for the wife in her widowhood than Welsh custom prescribed.

In Anglo-Welsh marriages, in general, the English party was economically in the strongest bargaining position. This explains why the most common pattern was for English women to marry Welsh men rather than vice versa, except in Lancashire, and especially Cheshire, where both types of intermarriage were more likely to occur. Such English confidence could cause offence in Wales where slights to family honour were felt as keenly as anywhere else. In 1614, Thomas, the son and heir of Sir Roger Mostyn, was one of the most eligible young men in North Wales. Negotiations with Sir Richard Molyneux of Sefton, Lancashire, initially seemed promising but were subsequently broken off when it became clear that the only one of his daughters that Sir Richard was prepared to marry to a Welshman was the one with a limp. As Sir Roger commented to his father-in-law, she 'has a slight limp which I believe he thinks is good enough for Wales ... If he insists on the youngest, I certainly think it best to break off in good fashion, for although in her youth she may bear it well, yet with the bearing of children, and as she grows older, it will seem greater with every day that passes'. Not all English families were so disparaging of a Mostyn alliance, but suitable marriages do not seem to have been easy to arrange: it was not until nine years later in 1623 that Thomas was finally married to Elizabeth, the daughter of Sir James Whitelocke, Chief Justice of Chester.[44] Despite the wranglings in their formation such alliances were often successful, and many English brides soon assimilated Welsh culture. According to Lewis Morgannwg, Barbara, the daughter of Robert Bret of Somerset and the wife of Sir George Mathew of Radyr, became proficient in Welsh.[45]

Marriages across the Anglo-Scottish border have been much less studied, but more work has been done on the intermarriage of the aristocracy following the Union of Crowns in 1603. For James VI and I, marriage was a metaphor for the union of Scotland and England: 'I am the Husband, and the whole Isle is my lawful Wife'. But he also wished it to have more than metaphorical significance, and recognised that intermarriage between the nobilities of both kingdoms was a desirable means of making the union a reality. This aspiration met with less enthusiasm from the aristocracy. William Cavendish, the son and heir of the first earl of Devonshire, was virtually bought by James in 1608 as a husband for the 13-year-old 'pretty red-headed wench' Christina Bruce, the daughter of the earl of Kinloss. In fact, the only Anglo-Scottish alliances that aroused enthusiasm were those between the Scots serving in the King's Bedchamber and English women. Since the Scottish near monopoly of the Bedchamber was for the English a serious political grievance, the attractiveness of such marriage alliances is obvious. But the majority of Scottish noblemen did not seek an English marriage for themselves or for their heirs. Between 1603 and 1642 only 23.5 per cent of marriages involving Scottish peers or their heirs were to English women, and most Scottish noblemen continued to find wives in their locality. Even great magnate families like the Gordons did not seek English brides.[46]

Pressures to subordinate personal desires to family strategies were the, perhaps occasionally unwelcome, privilege of the social elite whose marriages made a significant political statement or accomplished significant transfers of property. By contrast, it is often assumed, marriages of the poorer sections of society, and especially the landless, were characterised by freedom of choice. But, if inheritance expectations imposed less restraint, it is far from clear that such people enjoyed complete liberty. In Scotland, the *First Book of Discipline* (1560) stated that it was the duty of the couple to ask the permission of their parents before marrying, and gave them the right of veto. This was a stronger position on parental control than adopted in the rest of Britain, but it was still relatively mild compared to the policies of the Catholic Reformation in Europe. Scottish parents were advised that their veto should not be given lightly or for worldly reasons, and, in the event of disagreement, the minister or civil magistrate was to arbitrate and was to consider the affection of the couple as important. There were occasional attempts to give parents more control. At the Synod of Lothian (1581) it was declared that 'all marriages without parental consent, proclamation of banns or in other ways lacking the particular solemnities prescribed by the kirk be decreed null', but this much more radical position had little effect in practice.[47]

In England, the control of marriage of the lower orders of society was much more likely to be motivated by economic concerns. As Hindle has pointed out, there were significant institutional restraints on the marriages of the poor, ranging from the provisions of the 1563 Statute of

Artificers to objections to the banns of poor couples on the grounds that such marriages were imprudent and would increase the burden on the parish poor rate.[48] These policies had two aspects. The first was a concern to prevent untimely marriages as in the clause of the Statute of Artificers, applicable within England and Wales, which specified that the minimum age that individuals could leave their apprenticeships and get married was 24 for men and 21 for women. This was actually less repressive than it seems. The ages given were in fact slightly below the mean ages of first marriage in England at this time, and the measure was designed to ensure the completion of training to allow the new family, headed by a journeyman rather than a labourer, to subsist on a reasonable income. It was also, of course, a measure that in practice affected men more than women, since few women were formally apprenticed. The second concern focussed more directly on the economic insufficiency of the couple, especially as they were likely to soon become burdened with children and become an extra charge on the parish poor rates. For the parish elite concerned partly to protect their own pockets, but influenced also by their expectation that economic calculations would shape the marriage choices of themselves and of their children, entering upon marriage without a sufficient economic base was improvident and irresponsible. Penny bridals were, therefore, one focus of their concern. At such gatherings, the gifts of the guests provided almost the only economic resources of the newly married couple. Local elites in parishes like Kendal (Cumbria) and Halesowen (Worcestershire) in the 1570s shared the same concern as the Edinburgh authorities in 1636 who attempted to control penny bridals because such occasions were riotous and a motive for the marriage of indigent people who would subsequently become beggars or a burden to the city with their wife and children. They were, however, unable to proscribe such events completely and settled for limiting their excesses. Henceforth, no one was to give more than 20s Scots at a penny bridal and no more than 24 guests were allowed to attend.[49]

Other attempts to prevent pauper marriage by members of the parish elite seem more draconian, but it is hard to gauge the frequency of such practices. There was a fine line between the expectation that prospective couples would take the advice of family and friends before marrying and the interference of parish busybodies motivated by a concern to reduce the poor rates. The parishioners of Aldington (Kent) were 'sore against' Alice Cheeseman's proposed marriage in 1570 because they 'misliked' her proposed husband, but this, perhaps kindly meant, expression of concern also included the threat that she would be expelled from the parish if she went ahead with the marriage.[50] Some individuals clearly felt that poverty was an impediment to marriage, but the case of William Jackson, rector of North Ockenden (Essex), suggests that parishioners were not always prepared to follow the lead of their minister, and could even present him to the church court for his tactless handling of the matter. When in 1636 Jackson asked the banns 'of a poor couple', he departed from the usual canonical formula by prefacing the standard request for objections with the comment that the pair 'would marry and go begging together'.[51]

The scattering of cases makes it difficult to be certain whether such practices were widespread, but, as the reaction of the parishioners of North Ockenden suggests, there are reasons to err on the side of caution. Moreover, even in a parish so clearly in the hands of the godly as Terling (Essex), social control was not exercised without discretion. The records yield one case in which a labourer presented in the church courts for fornication in 1617 claimed that when the banns had been asked 'the parish would not let them marry'. There may, of course, have been more. Certainly, the number who could have been disqualified by their poverty in Terling was substantial. But there is reason to pause for thought. Presentments for bridal pregnancy combined moral concerns and those of burdening the poor rate since the practice of premarital sex increased the incidence of illegitimacy. Were strict social control being exercised, we would expect a high percentage of the pregnant brides recorded in the parish register to be presented for bridal pregnancy. In fact, from 1570 to 1640 just over 40 per cent of pregnant brides were prosecuted in the courts, and even in the decades when prosecution was most intensive, from 1620 to 1639, over a quarter of pregnant brides still escaped any form of discipline.[52]

Whatever the incidence of institutional controls on pauper marriages in the parishes of England, it seems clear that such practices cannot have prevailed in all parts of Wales where the same poor law provisions were in force. In Anglesey, as an anonymous author complained in c.1613, it was the custom for every married couple to go begging in the year after their marriage, irrespective of whether their own resources were sufficient. The groom went begging for seed and corn at sowing and harvest time respectively, and the new bride, accompanied for the sake of decorum by an elderly woman, went begging from the beginning of June until mid-August for cheese, wool, hemp and flax.[53] Where such customs were still strongly entrenched, appeals like that of the minister of North Ockenden that the marriage should be stopped because the couple 'would marry and go begging together' can have had little resonance.

Demographic factors played only a marginal role in preventing marriages taking place. Arguments based on skewed sex ratios in particular areas, especially urban communities, which attracted more female than male migrants as servants, are ultimately unconvincing given the degree of population mobility. Instead, such situations contributed to delaying the age of marriage and form part of the explanation of the late marriage pattern typical of northwest Europe. The strongest case for migration patterns affecting the possibility of marriage can be made for Scotland, where emigration accounted for a much larger proportion of the population than it did in England or Wales. It is estimated that emigration to Poland, Scandinavia and Ireland accounted for an annual loss of *c.*2000 people, and, assuming that most migrants were young men, it is likely that almost 20 per cent of young men left. However, although migration to Scandinavia was mainly of mercenaries, that to Poland, and especially to Ireland, involved both men and women. Most of the migrants to Poland were small merchants, pedlars and tradesmen, but in 1624, James VI's Scottish subjects at Danzig complained to him about the new decree in the town which ordered the 'removal of all strangers' and blamed it on the recent arrival from Scotland of 'exorbitant numbers of young boys and maids, unable for any service'. Female migration to Ireland was probably more significant, although it still lagged behind that of men. No detailed lists of inhabitants on the Scottish proportions in Ulster survive, but there is no reason to think that the sex ratio differed much from that on the listing of an English proportion in Ulster in 1622 where there were 1.5 women for every two men. All this suggests that to extrapolate from the figure of the emigration of almost 20 per cent of young men annually that one in five young women would fail to find a husband is a gross exaggeration. The actual imbalance must have been much more modest.[54]

Failure to marry may have been a matter of choice as much as a necessity. Although early modern society was suspicious of the sexual honesty of the single woman who lived alone, the unmarried life could seem an attractive possibility to some women and an acceptable choice in the eyes of their parents. Robert Colville of Cleish specified in his will that his son Robert was to ensure that his sister Elizabeth would 'marry such a one that fears the Lord according to her degree and estate' and was to pay her tocher of 4,000 merks. Thus far, the will was unremarkable but Colville continued, 'and if it shall happen that my said daughter leads a single life and is not moved in her heart to take a husband, in that case my son shall maintain her during her life in all necessaries according to her estate'. It was clearly possible in the sixteenth century for the daughter of a laird who had the expectation of a substantial tocher to be given the option of not marrying if she was so 'moved in her heart'.[55]

For Elizabeth Colville, the option of remaining unmarried did not entail complete independence: she was to be looked after by her brother throughout her life in a manner befitting her status as the daughter of a laird. For many other single women of lesser social status, similar solutions were also possible. In 1559 on his deathbed George Cumpayne of Halesowen (Worcestershire) made provision for his daughter Eleanor, who was then unmarried. Eleanor was given a chamber next to the fire in his house in Hill, a garden, an acre of land, 3s 4d annually, a cow called Fillpayle, a mare, bedding, the best pot and pan, six sheep which were to be kept with the rest of the family's sheep and also, at the death of her mother, a pasture. These careful provisions suggest that George envisaged this as a long-term arrangement, and one that, since there is no reference to her suffering from any disability, presumably reflected her choice. Whatever the reason, Eleanor continued to live semi-independently as a single woman with the assistance of her family in Hill until her death in 1592. Eleanor was not alone in attracting family support for continuing in the unmarried state. On her death in 1554, Margaret Moclowe of Rowley (Staffordshire) divided her house precisely between her two daughters, Agnes and Eleanor, who were clearly expected to live separately and independently. Margaret's decision may have been partly because of her poverty, her goods totalled just 26s 4d, but wealthier testators who could have placed unmarried daughters under the control of male relatives chose not to do so. Silvester Syche of Chaddesley (Worcestershire) was able to name his brother William as one of his executors and had goods worth £47 2s 6d, but stated that his four unmarried daughters were to share his house in Cakebole. Taken together, these examples suggest that, whether out of necessity or choice, it was perfectly acceptable for single women to be given a semi-independent livelihood under the family roof, and for households to be formed that consisted only of never married women.[56]

These case histories come as something of a surprise. The extent to which early modern women were defined by their marital status – daughter, wife or widow – has led historians to assume that all women were expected to marry. Support for such a view can indeed be found. The author of *The Law's Resolution of Women's Rights* (1632) stated that all women 'are understood either married or to be married', a legal perspective that assumed that all members of the weaker sex were under the authority of their father, master or husband. Local authorities were also concerned to reinforce this understanding, and tried to prevent unmarried women living and trading alone. However, such cases also show that many women who had taken up positions as servants and had migrated to urban areas were not satisfied with remaining in the dependent position of a servant. Living alone and working as a brewster or a huckster could appear preferable, even if it was not envisaged as a permanent lifestyle.

Many examples of such attempts at regulation can be found and a variety of justifications given. For example, in 1589, the Manchester court leet ordered that no single woman should be permitted to keep any house or chamber, or sell ale or bread, or work at other trades. In this case, the explanation given was economic: trading by single women was 'to the great hurt of the poor inhabitants who had a wife and children'. In Edinburgh flight from service underpinned the authorities' concern. In 1530, and periodically thereafter, it was noted that as soon as a servant woman earned five or six merks in service to a good family, she left her master and mistress, took a house of her own and began to make her living as a brewster or a huckster. Their prescription was drastic: henceforth no servant woman was to leave service, or take a house of her own, unless she was married on pain of banishment. The Edinburgh authorities were not alone in Scotland in adopting this strategy. The Stirling records for 1601 include a reference to one Marion Alexander who 'confesses she brews ale in a house on her own and sells it, the which trade she is commanded to abandon because she is a single woman living on her own, and is ordered to enter honest service'.[57]

The recurrence of these provisions in some sets of records suggests that authorities were dealing with a trend that they could not completely control. Some of the reasons for this can be seen more clearly in the evidence from Coventry. An ordinance of 1492 forbade single women under the age of 50 and in good health to take or keep a house or chamber by themselves or with any other person, and ordered them to go into service until they married. Despite the fact that this pronouncement was issued in the context of a campaign against prostitutes in the city, it provoked considerable opposition from honest women, and presumably also from their families. In the Michaelmas leet of 1495 the age limit was reduced to 40 and any single woman was permitted to rent a chamber from an honest person who would be held responsible for her conduct. Otherwise, the single woman was to enter service or else suffer imprisonment or banishment from the city. Although the city fathers clearly feared the moral risk of having masterless women dwelling alone in the town, many of the important inhabitants were also aware that there were honest women who posed no threat to the city by living alone. The position of such women was acceptable, provided that the idea of women being, however slightly, under the authority of others (interestingly it is not male authority that is specified) could be maintained.[58]

The authorities' acceptance of the single woman, albeit sometimes grudgingly given and in conflict with economic and moral concerns, did not, of course mean that the life of the unmarried woman was very economically viable. Spinning is the activity that we associate most readily with the single woman, although in fact the general use of the word 'spinster' to describe an unmarried woman was an eighteenth-century development. In the sixteenth century commentators were clear that a livelihood could not be gained from spinning alone. As John Fitzherbert observed in 1534, 'a woman cannot get her living honestly with spinning on the distaff, but it stops a gap and must needs be had'.[59] Nevertheless, many single women relied on such low paid work to the extent that in Edinburgh the authorities declared that spinning and carding should be reserved for the married. Other employments were, of course, available, but wage labour was seasonal and precarious, especially as the sole source of income for women as female wage rates were lower than those for men. Eking out an existence from these various sources was not impossible, but it was scarcely a situation that made not marrying an attractive option. The poverty of Marslye verch Rees was not untypical. In her will, proved in the archdeaconry court of Brecon in the reign of Elizabeth, she asked the vicar to give all her worldly goods to her niece, and this amounted to three items of clothing and some household goods of a total value of £1 19s.[60] But it is also, of course, true that married couples burdened with children could experience similar levels of poverty.

The attraction of the single life was not so much economic as the degree of independence it conferred. As the heroine of the ballad 'A fairing for maids' (1639) advised her audience,

Whilst you are single there's none to curb you:
Go to bed quietly and take your ease.
Early or late there's none to disturb you,
Walk abroad where you [will] and when you please.
A single life is free from all danger:
Then, maids, embrace it, as long as you may,
And never yeeld to neighbour or stranger,
    For when you are bound, then you needs must obey.[61]

But for most women, as for the ballad heroine, such independence was only seen as a temporary possibility. This was even the case in areas where female employment was particularly lucrative. The making of high quality bone lace in the area around Colyton in East Devon provided a good livelihood for women, but seems to have postponed women's entrance into the married state rather than encouraging them not to marry.[62] Nevertheless, it was also true that, although the lure of urban life could make service an attractive option, even more attractive for many was a lifestyle that gave more independence, whether the choice was to live as a single brewer or huckster, or to assume a semi-independent lifestyle in part of the family home. Even within the constraints of servanthood women with some economic means could bargain for a more advantageous position. In Elizabethan Denbighshire, for example, a young girl, who owned a cow, pewter, clothes and some sheets, hired herself and the use of her animal and moveable goods in return for preferential treatment in board and wages and the use of piece of pasture.[63]

The cumulative effect of such decisions and preferences was to make it increasingly easy and acceptable for women to remain unmarried throughout their lives. Many, even if not all, of the c.20 per cent of men and women who never married in England in this period may have done so from choice, and this became increasingly likely as time went on. By the 1680s, ballads had picked up on this trend. Unlike the heroine of 'A fairing for maids', the female protagonist in 'Tobias' observation' (1687), told her suitor that 'she had no fancy to be made a Wife', and advocated the single life as a permanent 'delight' which avoided the possibility of slavery in marriage.[64]

Options for single women were probably broadly similar throughout Britain. Urban decline in Wales, rather than the lack of economically independent single women, explains the apparent absence of urban regulation. Will samples included unmarried women. In the archdeaconry of Cardigan, 1600–40, of the 40 women who made wills two were spinsters.[65] In contrast, the position and economic security of married women and widows differed significantly according to prevailing local customs and legal traditions. In all areas, the married woman was seen to be under the authority of her husband, but different rules governing marriage settlements shaped the experience of widowhood and the frequency of remarriage.

In Scotland, as in England and for those in Wales to whom English law applied, a tocher or dowry in money, land or goods was provided by the bride or her family. In return, the husband granted his wife her dower when they were married at the church door, or when, according to a Scottish Act of Parliament in 1503, the existence of the marriage was known by common repute. This was usually assumed to be a third of his assets, and that it became known as terce in Scotland underlines the fact that this was the usual fraction. Indeed, it was generally the case that a wife could not be endowed with less, but that she could be given more. In Scotland the nature of the widow's third was also more clearly defined, and it was explicitly stated that the principal dwelling should not be included. The idea, as Marshall notes, was not that terce should sustain a wife in her widowhood, but that it would enable her to find a new husband.[66] A widow's right to her husband's lands was also influenced by the form of tenure. Manorial customs varied and tenants of customary land on English manors could be obliged to recognise the widow's right to half, or even all, the holding for her natural life, or for the duration of her chaste widowhood. For example, in the manor and lordship of Castlemartin (Pembrokeshire), according to the customs drawn up in 1592, a wife 'remaining a true widow' was to have all her husband's lands and tenements before his heir.[67] The same custom prevailed in Ombersley (Worcestershire) whilst at Wolverley and Tardebigge in the same county the widow only had a life interest in half of her husband's customary lands.[68] In Scotland both rentals and tacks could recognise the life interest of widow. The widow was often able to keep a tack after the death of her husband, and if the tack had been granted to the couple jointly, she kept it by right. On the death of a rentaller, the normal practice was for the widow to enjoy the rental for her lifetime, and for the heir to be rentalled in his father's place without regard for any other wishes on the part of the widow. Moreover, according to a privilege known as 'St Mungo's widow', it was the practice on the estates of the Archbishop of Glasgow to grant the widow a life interest in the holding even if the rental had only been in the husband's name.[69]

For the Welsh in Wales whose marriage settlements were governed by Welsh law until the 'Acts of Union' and to some extent thereafter, the main difference was the general inability of women to hold land. In some areas mediaeval attempts to change this situation had met with some success. Edward I's Statute of Rhuddlan (1284) stated that 'whereas women in Wales have hitherto not been dowered by their husbands, the king permits that henceforth they shall be dowered'. This permissive, rather than coercive, strategy had an effect in some areas. There is evidence from Anglesey and Flintshire in the fourteenth and fifteenth centuries of Welsh widows leasing their dower lands. But, other parts of Wales, especially the Marcher Lordships, continued to adhere to Welsh practice, as shown, for example, by the 1391 extent of Bromfield and Yale, which stated that on lands held by Welsh tenure the wife was not to be dowered. Welsh custom prescribed that a wife was to receive a third of goods and chattels of which her husband died in possession, and that if there were no children the wife was to get a half rather than a third. The custom of North Wales was even more generous, granting the wife half of her husband's goods even if there were children.[70]

In practice, the position of widows was more complex than this outline suggests as new forms of landholding and marriage settlement became more common. The spread of the Welsh mortgage (*tir prid*), a form of lease which did not violate the principle that family land was inalienable, meant that it became possible for Welsh women to claim that the interest in such leases was part of their husband's goods rather than his lands, as shown by the fact that he had the right to devise them by will.[71] Some of these claims appear to have been accepted, but there was resistance to conceding the general legal principle. It is this that probably explains the, otherwise puzzling, comment in George Owen's account of Pembrokeshire in the reign of Elizabeth: 'Also there goes a report of a custom for women to have the thirds of all their husbands' goods and leases, and many have it without denial, but recently this custom has been sore shaken and now languishes very weak and is hardly likely to recover'.[72] Early in the seventeenth century, the attempt by Welsh widows to gain control of their husband's leased lands by the custom of North Wales in the courts in London met with failure.[73]

Of greater importance for women in Wales, as well as those in Scotland and England, was the spread of jointure. Jointure meant that the bride and groom were put in joint possession of piece of land, from which on the death of her husband the wife drew a fixed annuity for her maintenance. Whether jointure benefited the widow depended on the relative strengths of the families of the bride and groom at the time of the making of the marriage contract. A small jointure compared to the tocher indicated that the groom's family were dictating terms, and could be less attractive than the amount that would have been due to her as terce had no jointure been arranged. The same considerations applied in England, where it is calculated that in the sixteenth and seventeenth centuries there was a distinct movement in favour of the groom. The average jointure in the 1560s was a fifth of the bride's dowry, but by 1700 it was an eighth or a tenth. In Scotland, the change was more gradual, and in the late seventeenth century jointures were typically a fifth or a sixth of the dowry.[74]

The spread of jointure in Wales, unlike in England and Scotland, probably improved the position of Welsh widows because dower was less established there. In guaranteeing an annuity attached to certain lands, jointure gave elite widows some control over freehold land which in itself conferred status due to the link between freehold and gentry status. Also, in contrast to the traditional Welsh position in which the widow received her share of the goods but only had the formal right to remain in the house for nine days after her husband's decease, such contracts usually gave widows a place to live. Even more advantageously, the establishment of jointure did not mean that the widow would not receive her share of moveable goods according to Welsh custom. In practice, there was less improvement in the Welsh widow's position than the legal provisions suggest. Most widows relying on Welsh rights alone probably managed to keep a roof over their head beyond the prescribed nine days of the thirteenth-century law codes. Even if her children were not too keen on the idea, her share of the household goods gave the widow significant bargaining power, especially since, unless there was only one child, the widow's share was greater than that of any individual child.

Since jointure involved the acceptance of English practice by the Welsh, it was resorted to more frequently by some families and in particular circumstances. The Mostyns of Mostyn, for example, began to draw up marriage contracts involving jointures by 1540. By far the greatest pressure for a settlement to include a jointure was the practice of mixed marriage. Jointures were always part of marriage settlements between English women and Welsh men in the early modern period, but families that accepted this necessity in catching an English bride for their sons were less willing to do so for the marriages of their daughters. Sir John Wynn of Gwydir arranged prenuptial jointures for the wives of the three sons whose settlements he supervised, two of whom acquired English brides, but not for his two daughters who were married in 1597 and 1608 to Welsh gentlemen. For Swett this behaviour suggests that reliance on Welsh custom could be seen as being in the widow's best interests, but this interpretation seems unlikely. As long as it was accepted that English customs of jointure, and also dower, did not preclude a widow receiving her share of goods according to Welsh custom (which remained legal until its abolition in 1696), a purely Welsh settlement cannot have been in the daughter's best interests. The diversity of contracts drawn up by the same families indicates changes in bargaining power with different sets of prospective in-laws. The later sixteenth and early seventeenth century was, as Swett notes, a period of change and ambiguity in provision for widowhood which 'contained both risks and opportunities for women', and the outcome depended increasingly on the ability of her family to strike a good deal.[75]

Some power was also in the hands of the widow, but this was much harder to exploit whilst remaining within the limits of decorum. The case of Elizabeth Bodvel, the younger daughter of Sir John Wynn of Gwydir, illustrates this clearly. When her husband, Sir John Bodvel, died in 1631, the terms of his will were unusual. He bequeathed all his lands and goods to his wife and their two daughters for a period of ten years after which they were to be given to his son and heir. Such a scheme was not conducive to family harmony. By 1633 Elizabeth's brother Richard was suing her in the Court of Wards and claiming that she was depleting her son's inheritance. Elizabeth's response was not to focus on the issue of the alleged depletion, but to put forward a case for her entitlement to more than the testamentary provision. As she argued, she also had a right to a dower of one third of his lands for her life and to half of his goods according to the custom of North Wales. The case was eventually settled by arbitration: the testamentary provision was overturned, and Elizabeth gained her dower and goods according to Welsh custom. As the court concluded, only a prenuptial jointure, and not a testamentary provision, could block a dower claim. That this was the legal position makes it all the more surprising that so few Welsh widows pursued a claim for the dower to which they were entitled. But to do so ran the risk of social opprobrium. In the midst of his legal dispute with his sister, Richard Wynn wrote about her to their brother Owen, 'her carriage is so odious to all good men that I am ashamed to answer truly to such questions as a number ask me'. Had it not been for Sir John Bodvel's highly unusual testamentary provisions, it is quite likely that Elizabeth would have been satisfied with her goods according to Welsh custom and would have ignored her claims to an English dower.[76]

Such female quiescence was contrary to the stereotype. In bemoaning the decay of the Welsh custom of widow's thirds in his native Pembrokeshire, George Owen added that the situation was likely to continue 'except the women of our country would erect an Inn of Court and study the law to defend their common cause, wherein I think they were like to profit, for that there are of them many ripe wits, and all ready tongues'.[77] As the attempt by Welsh widows to establish their legal right to leases as part of their husband's goods mentioned above suggests, such statements were more than simply an opportunity to reinforce the stereotype of women as gossips. Female influence was, however, often more effectively asserted within the marital partnership than by the widow in competition with the heirs of the deceased. A striking example of this concerns a woman's right to make a will during the lifetime of her husband. The standard legal position was that the woman and her goods were under the authority of her husband during the marriage. Married women could make wills, but only with their husband's consent. Nevertheless, in Scotland, although the same principles applied in theory, in practice the wife was allowed to test upon third or half of the goods with the consent of the husband who was expected to agree to this. As the lawyer Sir James Balfour wrote in his *Practicks*, which he completed in 1583,

> A woman clad with a husband and thereby in his power and subjection, may dispose and give no thing in her last will without his consent and authority, because she herself, and all her goods, are at the disposition of her husband. Nevertheless, the husband does an honest and godly thing if he permits and grants to his wife licence and power to make a testament of that part of the goods and gear which would have belonged to her if she had happened to outlive him.[78]

When this is contrasted with the situation in England where wives rarely made wills, it is perhaps unsurprising that as early as 1498 Don Pedro de Ayala, the Spanish ambassador at the court of James IV, should have commented that Scottish women were 'absolute mistresses in their houses, and even of their husbands, in all things concerning the administration of their property'.

The fact that in Scotland, unlike England, canon law remained dominant until the Reformation explains to a large extent the contrast between the position of wives in the two kingdoms. Canon lawyers in England had maintained that, although the wife's personal property passed to her husband on marriage, it was fitting that he should allow his wife to make provision for her soul out of that part of his property that would have passed to her if she had outlived him. From the thirteenth century, common lawyers challenged this position, arguing that wives could not bequeath what they did not own. By the 1440s, it was rare for a wife to make a will, and in 1540 the Statute of Wills, which permitted most freehold land to be devised by will, explicitly excluded married women. The practice of wives making wills became a little more frequent during the seventeenth century, but this did not represent a challenge to the common law principle. The numbers were still small, only six wives made wills in

Oxfordshire between 1561 and 1640, and the seventeenth-century increase can be largely explained by the development of trusts and the idea of separate estate which gave married women property of their own to bequeath.[79]

However, the importance of canon law cannot be a complete explanation. Both Scottish and English husbands had the possibility of granting permission to their wives to act as testators, but the burden of expectation upon them seems to have been greater in Scotland, and may reflect a greater importance of the wife's tocher. The importance of expectations can be seen particularly clearly in the case of a wife's right to her paraphernalia, that is to say to personal items such as clothes, jewels and linen. In England the removal of claims to paraphernalia from ecclesiastical jurisdiction to equity courts probably meant that such claims were less likely to be defended, and it would seem logical to assume that the practice declined along with that of married women making wills. Nevertheless, some women continued to believe that they had such a right. Widows compiling inventories of their deceased husband's goods omitted those that they considered belonged to the female sphere, or that they had brought with them from a previous marriage. The inventories of a Lincolnshire couple, William and Sarah Foxe, provide a good example. In 1603 the inventory of William's goods amounted to £33, only £8 of which was accounted for by household stuff. Sarah's inventory, made three years later, totalled £40 and no longer included any animals or husbandry gear, but household goods worth £35 were now listed. It seems quite unlikely that Sarah would have acquired such a substantial increase in household goods during three years of widowhood, and more probable that she, and the neighbours who acted as appraisers for her husband's inventory, considered them to be her own goods. It is difficult to ascertain how widespread such practice was. In general, the reservation of goods of the wife is only visible when contested by creditors, and it is, of course, in these circumstances that the strategy was most desirable. In 1618 Agnes Crow from the Isle of Ely was accused of only declaring £19 of the couple's £39 assets, and the nature of the goods withheld suggests that she may have considered them to be hers by right. These included a blanket of red woollen cloth with velvet trimming, which was valued at £3 and used for carrying children to church for baptism, an old side saddle, bedding, table linen and 15 stone of hemp.[80]

In Scotland, the right to paraphernalia was more contested in the courts, and a series of cases clarified the principles that should be followed. In 1582, a case brought by the Mistress of Gray against her husband resulted in the decision that he should restore to her 'certain chains, rings of gold, and certain other things, which belonged to the ornament of her body and were part of the wifely sphere'. Pressure from creditors meant that this legal victory would not be uncontested. In Davidson v. Maccubin in 1610 gifts of a paraphernal nature that were made before or during a marriage were deemed attachable for a husband's debts.[81] As in England, though, it is less clear how extensively such principles were applied in practice. In Welsh law no principle coincided exactly with that of paraphernalia, but the wife's right to her *cowyll*, or morning gift, was inalienable and could not be forfeited even if her husband's desertion or dismissal of her was justified by her fault. The extent to which a woman had control over her paraphernalia within the time of the marriage was more disputed. As Balfour summarised the Scottish situation, no woman could sell or give away any of her husband's goods, and she required her husband's approval to dispose of any items of her paraphernalia. Nevertheless, although it sat awkwardly with the legal principle, lawyers had to recognise that some exception had to be made for 'alms given moderately'. The idea that upon marriage a woman and all her property was subsumed under the authority of her husband was weakened by the duty of charity incumbent upon all christians and envisaged by contemporaries as a particularly female virtue.

The author of *The Law's Resolution of Women's Rights* (1632) commented that married women's 'desires are subject to their husband, I know no remedy though some women can shift well enough'. From the perspective of a male lawyer this statement may be thought to refer to illegitimate female influence, persuasive pillow talk, or outright duplicity. In 1624 a gentleman, Stuckley Lewis of Anglesey, complained that the night before his marriage to Alice in 1603 she had secretly drawn up bonds to her daughters from her previous marriage with the intent 'to defraud and defeat' her new husband and to deprive him of all the personal estate. The case was defended by Alice's daughter Ellen, the wife of Robert ap Hugh ap Robert, Alice being no longer alive.[82] From this distance it is impossible to know who was being duplicitous. It is not impossible that after the death of his wife her husband seized his opportunity, and it is certainly the case that, in safeguarding the economic position of her daughters, Alice was acting with the caution contemporaries, both men and women, expected from a remarrying widow. The same was probably true when a widow withheld her paraphernalia from the inventory of her deceased husband's goods or when a Scottish wife made a will disposing of the goods that would have come to her if her husband had died first. That women could 'shift well enough' was a recognition that social practice and attitudes diverged from the core legal principle of female subjection.

This is not, of course, to say that the legal position was insignificant, or to dismiss the importance of notions of patriarchy and subjection in the early modern period. Contemporaries could struggle with reconciling these theories with concerns for equity and feelings of empathy. This was most evident in the difficult case of what to propose when the husband fell far short of the expectations of the behaviour and qualities of a household head. What was the wife to do who was married to an improvident husband who wasted his family's goods through excessive drinking or gambling? Early seventeenth-century Puritan moralists, such as Gouge, who saw the patriarchal family as divinely prescribed, were nevertheless convinced that the wife had a duty to protect her children and argued that, when the behaviour of the husband endangered this, she should assume economic authority in the household, but gave no licence to the wife with no dependent children.[83] Lawyers were also sympathetic to the plight of such wives, but were more reluctant to renounce the principle of the subjection of the wife and her property to the authority of her husband. In Chancery, c.1639, the case of a woman with 'an improvident husband' who had 'unknown to him, by her frugality raised some monies for the good of their children ... being otherwise unprovided for' was initially considered favourably, but the verdict was subsequently reversed on the grounds that it was 'dangerous to give a woman power to dispose of her husband's estate'.[84] Such attitudes were also possible in Scotland, despite the fact that women generally seem to have enjoyed a greater degree of economic independence there. In several cases considered by the burgh court of Elgin in the 1540s husbands came forward to complain against their wives who had sold and depleted their goods imprudently. In each case the court was sympathetic ordering a proclamation to be made at the tollbooth that henceforth no one should buy, sell or receive from the wife any goods belonging to the couple, and that if such transactions were made the goods should be returned to the husband without compensation to the purchasers.[85] Parallel examples of communal intervention are unknown from English records, but the cases of these women, and that of the wife with the improvident husband considered by Chancery, provide a reminder of the potential economic weaknesses of the position of women that will be considered more fully in the next chapter.

Chapter 2: Work and the Household Economy

One of the most significant historical reinterpretations of the history of the family has been the recognition that, in England at least, the nuclear family was the norm in the mediaeval and early modern periods. At marriage the couple expected to form a new household unit. Assumptions that the traditional 'world we have lost' differed significantly from the 'world we have gained' have been overturned by a more subtle analysis of the surviving evidence, which pays closer attention to the changes in family structure according to the life cycle. A nuclear family could become extended on the death of a father, when the heir and his family could occupy the holding with the widow jointly, but such arrangements were temporary, and often short-lived. However, although these solutions may be of marginal significance for demographers, they should not be ignored by the social historian. Like the practice of some families choosing to make semi-independent economic provision within the family for an unmarried daughter, they influenced the nature of female experience. Moreover, the possibility of such outcomes differed according to circumstance. Studies have shown that the size and structural complexity of family forms differed in urban and rural areas and according to social status. Manorial customs or urban gild regulations could encourage or discourage the remarriage of widows, and the fact that service in England was envisaged primarily as a life-cycle phase rather than as a lifetime occupation also affected the process of household formation.

The consensus of views that has emerged concerning family structure for early modern England and, with some vestiges of disagreement, for the later mediaeval period has no real counterpart in studies of Scotland

and Wales. This is largely due to the lack of equivalent documentary evidence, whether in the form of manorial records or census listings. However, there is enough evidence to suggest that it would be rash to assume that similar patterns prevailed in all parts of Britain. Most obviously, it appears that the practice of servanthood, which in England enabled most couples to amass sufficient resources to establish a separate household on marriage, was less established in other areas of Britain. In parts of Lowland Scotland the practice of farms employing married couples (hinds) reduced the opportunities for life-cycle service for unmarried young people. In Pembrokeshire agricultural labour was supplied by single farm workers (*gweision*) and by married labourers living in tied cottages. Moreover, the custom of bidding or bridals may indicate, as Roberts suggests, that service was less common and did not normally provide a sufficient financial basis for marriage.[1] Although there are scattered references to communal attempts to control bridals in parts of England, it seems that such practices were seen as distinctively Welsh by the sixteenth century. In Chester, a city in which Welsh presence was quite noticeable, when the authorities wanted to limit such practices they did not hesitate to refer to them as 'Welsh weddings'. The begging customs of newly weds in Anglesey mentioned in Chapter 1 also suggest that service played a less important role in the economics of marriage formation there.

The contrast between England and Wales is hard to explain, but a number of possibilities can be suggested. Although much of Wales was quite anglicised even before the 'Acts of Union', those deemed legally Welsh still suffered some disabilities and urban opportunities may have been more limited. In England it was service in urban areas that was particularly significant, especially for women. The towns of the late mediaeval north, for example, experienced extensive female immigration resulting in skewed sex ratios. Moreover, although Welsh towns were reasonably vibrant in the fourteenth century, the fifteenth and sixteenth centuries represented a period of decline that must have reduced the opportunities for service and that may have been as significant as any remaining discrimination along ethnic lines.

Whatever the explanation, it seems that Welsh families, including those of higher social rank, were more prepared to contemplate sheltering the newly wed couple under the parental roof than was usually the case in England. In 1542 the terms of the indenture drawn up on the occasion of the marriage of John ap David ap Howell, son and heir of David ap Howell of Bersham in the lordship of Bromfield, to Jane, daughter of

John Puleston the elder of Wrexham, specified that,

> the said John Puleston covenants and grants to bring the said Jane
> Puleston his daughter to the church door in the same state as she is
> now, and there wed and take as her husband the said John ap David,
> and also to dress her for her wedding according to her degree, and also
> to pay the said John ap David the sum of thirty six pounds xiiis
> iiiid … and also to provide the said John ap David and Jane his wife
> with food, drink and lodging for the space of one year immediately
> following the marriage, and at the end of the year to deliver and give
> reasonable bedding to the said John and Jane.[2]

Other contracts envisaged much longer-term arrangements in which the
young couple contracted to work for the older generation. A good example is the 1611 indenture agreed between two Flintshire gentlemen,
Gruffith ap Rees ap David ap Rees of Soughtyn, and Edward ap William
ap Howell of Gwesany, on the marriage of Gruffith's daughter Jane to
Edward's son and heir Gruffith ap Edward ap William. This stipulated
that Edward would convey to his son the house in which he lived in
Gwesany in trust for Edward for his life and then to the use of Gruffith
for his life and to his heirs. The way in which the household was to
operate during the lifetime of Gruffith's father was also clearly spelt out,

> the said Edward shall during his natural life provide, maintain, and
> keep the said Gruffith ap Edward, Jane his wife, and such children as
> the said Gruffith ap Edward and Jane shall lawfully beget between them
> during the said period, with meat, drink, houseroom, fire, candle, bed-
> ding, washing, wringing, clothes, and all other necessaries befitting
> their degrees and calling, except the clothing of the said Jane, which the
> said Edward is not to provide; and the said Gruffith, in return for
> the maintenance and keep of him and of his said wife and children
> during the said period, is to work and labour as a labourer unto the
> said Edward, for him and at his commandment, and also the said
> Jane is to labour and work when she is lawfully required to do so by the
> said Edward or his wife during the said time.[3]

Some of these details seem rather surprising, and the present state of
research means that it is not clear how typical such arrangements were.
The picture it presents of the gentleman's son working as a labourer at
his father's command is at odds with ideas of gentry lifestyle in which

manual labour was eschewed, but this may have been a fairly general practice in Wales where those accorded gentry status generally enjoyed a poorer economic position than those upon whom the title was conferred in England. The extent to which the new bride was less firmly integrated into the maintenance arrangements also suggests the distinctiveness of Welsh practice. The older generation were to provide clothing for their son and any children born of his marriage, but not for the new wife and mother, and had less control over the labour of their daughter-in-law than of their son. These arrangements make sense as a further symptom of the less than complete integration of the bride into her husband's family in the first years of marriage. Provided with clothes and linen at her marriage, further provision may have been deemed unnecessary, and although the new bride was subject to the authority of her husband, complete subjection to the authority of his kin seemed inappropriate.

Whether the kind of arrangements made for the newly extended household at Gwesany were also found elsewhere in Britain is unclear. Economics, even for Edward's parents, did not dictate it. In England, similar arrangements were possible amongst families of yeoman and husbandman status, but usually occurred when only a widow survived, and in such circumstances the son, whether married or unmarried, might enjoy more household authority. The pattern at Orwell (Cambridgeshire) in which all widows were granted houseroom or maintenance seems to have been unique. More typically, about 15 per cent of widows were provided for in this way, as was the case at Kings Langley (Hertfordshire) 1498–1659 and Salisbury, 1540–1639, and in some areas the figure could be as low as 3 per cent.[4] The low frequency of such arrangements helps to explain why, when the widow and adult children were expected to live together as one unit in the family house and holding, husbands usually envisaged the widow as the dominant figure, even when the son was bound to run the farm. Thus, Thomas Byrd of Oldbury in the parish of Halesowen (Worcestershire) stated in his will in 1557,

> Unto my wife I bequeath my farm with all my other goods if she keeps herself widow. But if she does not, or if she dies before the years of the lease expire, then I bequeath my son Richard and his children the said farm. And the said Richard shall occupy the said farm under the authority of his mother. And if he will not be obedient unto his mother he shall be ex-authorised and deprived of all.[5]

Such conditions were, of course, usually only set out in detail by testators when family friction was expected. Thomas Byrd, in fact, went on to stipulate that the land should descend in the event of Richard's disobedience and lack of heirs to each of his three remaining sons and their children in turn, subject to the same condition of obedience to the widow and cultivation of the land. Where family relations were not so tense, a less hierarchical arrangement might be reached in practice.

In the ideal household as prescribed in contemporary advice literature, the roles of the husband and wife were clear and distinct. The wife was responsible for the domestic sphere, which included not only the housework but also a special responsibility for the poultry and the dairy. The husband, by contrast, operated in the public sphere, which included work in the fields and the holding of political office. In identifying such spheres, there was no clear sense that one enjoyed higher status than the other, but rather that they were appropriate to the capacities of each sex. A prosperous household required capable contributions in both spheres. As Thomas Tusser's much-printed manual of husbandry neatly summarised it: to thrive one must wive. Moreover, despite the stereotype of the remarrying widow, it was more often widows than widowers who could be found running a household single-handedly in their declining years.

Maxims like Tusser's, and advice literature in general, envisaged an ideal case set in a particular social milieu. The households they described in detail were usually agrarian and of prosperous husbandman or yeoman status in which the employment and management of servants was taken for granted. Many families, of course, did not fit this description. Although the model could be transferred fairly easily to artisan households, it was less appropriate to the growing number of journeymen families for whom rising to the status of master was becoming increasingly unlikely, and to the mass of cottagers and labourers. Nevertheless, the power of this model throughout most levels of society should not be underestimated. When the ideal prescribed that work in the fields fell within the male sphere, we need to question whether we should read female participation in harvest work or, more rarely, in ploughing as an indication of female independence and equality. Contemporaries probably did not see it that way. Households with the greatest reputation for thrift, a word at this period carrying the twin meanings of diligent industry and prosperity, were those in which each sphere made an effective contribution, and extra hands could be hired for harvest rather than crossing the gender divide within the family itself. Such attitudes were not in themselves misogynistic, but they were rooted in a gendered understanding of capacities.

It was the same idea of fitness for task that dictated that women should receive lower wages than men, or should be limited to the use of the sickle rather than the larger scythe that required greater physical strength.[6] In all parts of Britain male and female servants received different levels of remuneration for their work. The greatest discrepancies are apparent in Scotland where the youngest female servants could receive less than half of that paid to men. Two early seventeenth-century assessments of wage rates survive drawn up by the Fife justices in session at Cupar and Perth. A 'lass' was to be paid no more than £1 10s Scots per half year whereas an immature farm labourer was to receive no more than £4 Scots in the same period. For more experienced servants the gap narrowed, with men receiving £6 Scots and women exactly half that sum.[7] In England, servant women seem to have had a slightly better position than their Scottish counterparts receiving at least two-thirds of the male wage, which perhaps reflects a greater rural and urban demand for female servants. The Worcester wage assessment for 1560 attempted to establish a payment of 20s, plus 5s for livery, for a male servant in husbandry and 13s 4d, plus 5s for livery, for a female servant.[8] In Norfolk in 1613 the annual wage of a common male servant was fixed at 42s, and of a female servant over 20 years of age at 30s.[9] More specialised female servants could also improve their position. At Worcester in 1560, the woman maltmaker or deywoman was expected to receive 15s, as well as the standard 5s for her livery. Such attempts at regulation may not accurately reflect practice, but the principles underlying them are likely to have been widely shared and are broadly supported by surviving farm accounts. At Courthall Farm in Pembrokeshire in 1593 the ploughman and his wife earned 46s 8d a year, the second ploughman and the two ploughboys received 16s 8d and 8s 4d respectively, whilst the two labouring maids were paid 12s each. Payments for casual and seasonal work showed similar variation. At Courthall Farm at harvest time additional workers were employed for reaping and binding, the men at 3d and the women at 2d per day.[10] The 1560 Worcester assessment distinguished between male and female reapers. The rates without meat and drink were 6d and 7d respectively and the penny difference was preserved when refreshments were also supplied. For more menial harvest tasks there was the possibility of equal rates, although it was assumed that it would normally be women who performed these: women working as rakers, and others (probably children) were to receive 4d per day or $1\frac{1}{2}$–2d per day if food and drink was supplied.[11] In 1621 the Lincolnshire justices of the peace attempted to establish that for shearing wheat, rye or other grain, women should be paid 2d per day with food and drink, or 6d per day without (rates for men 3d and 8d), and that women cockers of barley and peas should receive 1d per day with food and drink, or 4d without (men's rates 2d and 6d).[12]

Viewed in isolation, such rates may seem grossly unfair, but such distinctions were accepted by both women and men, even if occasionally, as at Monmouth in 1454–5, both sexes could be paid the same rate of 2d per day for reaping.[13] Martin travelling in the Western Isles of Scotland in the later seventeenth century, noted that men servants were always given twice as much bread than female servants, and that the women were not offended since they recognised that the men's work was physically more strenuous. In his view, this distinction permeated society with women of all ranks eating less than men. That Martin felt that this was worthy of comment may, of course, suggest that these habits were less noticeable in his native England, where in any case wage differentials were also smaller, but such principles underpinned the different economic treatment of men and women. To an extent, though, arguments drawn from gendered notions of physical strength can appear to be a cynical ruse. When the worsted weavers of Norwich declared in 1511 that women and maids lacked the necessary strength to carry out the craft of weaving and that henceforth they should not be allowed to practice the trade, they were overturning a tradition in which female weavers had made a significant contribution.[14] No significant changes in women's strength, or in the technology of the loom, explain this regulation, but at a time of contraction in the textile industry it seemed appropriate to those in positions of power to preserve male employment. After all, the notion of the patriarchal family required that the male household head should be the principal breadwinner. However, such reactions could also be temporary. A similar ordinance was passed against female weavers in Bristol in 1461, but two years later, presumably as the economic circumstances improved, women were being advised to 'help and labour with their husbands to sustain them both and to benefit their children' and so boost the city's total cloth production.[15]

It is, in fact, largely the differences in economic development in various parts of Britain that explain variations in female economic experiences and opportunities. Weavers in Bristol, Kingston-upon-Hull and Norwich attempted to exclude women in 1461, 1490 and 1511 respectively.[16] The arguments used to justify such policies in different places and occupations may vary, but they are all responses to deteriorating economic circumstances. Interestingly, physical strength is the argument least often deployed, perhaps because the contradictions inherent in the Norwich weavers' argument were recognised. Instead, two strategies were particularly favoured. First, to proclaim a concern to protect the economic well-being of honest married men who had a wife and children to support, and secondly to identify female economic activities as creating opportunities for, and giving encouragement to, sexual licentiousness. In this process women were not the only casualties. Other vulnerable groups were also likely to be squeezed out of the market place when competition became more intense. In urban centres throughout Britain those deemed unfree, or who were not members of gilds, had fewer economic privileges. In Aberdeen unfree brewers were not allowed to sell the strongest, most expensive, ale, and when the trade was under pressure in periods of scarcity, it was the unfree who were excluded first, as in 1531 and again ten years later.

Nevertheless, it was also true that the exclusion of women from trade involved casting slurs upon their character, in terms of both their economic and their sexual honesty, which was not the case for the unfree. In a system in which urban citizenship or gild membership was primarily transmitted by marriage or inheritance, the lack of such status was more an accident of birth than a personal failing. Moreover, even when the authorities wished to clamp down on the activities of both men and women in the same occupation, the reputation of women was likely to suffer greater disparagement. In May 1580 the Edinburgh council was concerned about the risk of a water shortage in the city and ordered that burnmen and female water bearers should desist from carrying water to brewsters from the common wells. If such people required water, they, or their servants, should come and draw it themselves. Part of the reasoning behind this measure was presumably that it would encourage a less wasteful use of water, but it is also evident that the council wished to present it as part of a wider clean up operation. The measure was also commended to the inhabitants on the grounds of the desirability of ridding the city of female waterbearers who had a notorious reputation for theft, harlotry, swearing and blasphemy. The character of the burnmen was not impugned, even though defamatory terms usually associated with men, such as theft and swearing, were included in the list alongside the typically female offence of harlotry.[17]

The most visible economic activity involving women was the brewing and selling of ale. Although malting was generally a male occupation, due to the drying kilns and the amount of space needed, the rest of the brewing process was largely the preserve of women. In lists of those amerced for brewing in the fifteenth century both in England and Scotland women were usually in the majority. In Wales, where brewing for sale was mainly confined to the towns, female brewers also dominated the trade: in Clun in 1425 only one of the 27 brewers was male.[18] It was no accident that 'alewife' had no male equivalent, and that the female form 'brewster' was more commonly used than 'brewer' in regulations. Nevertheless, the alewife was a vulnerable figure in this period. There were two reasons for this. The making, and especially the selling, of ale strengthened the idea of women as the deceivers of men. The stereotypical alewife served poor quality ale in false measures and tempted men into drunkenness and immorality. Such associations conspired to diminish the social status of the alewife, and also prompted authorities to periodic attempts at greater regulation. The second development was the gradual spread of hopped beer, which displaced ale and required greater capital investment. Like the production of malt, it was beyond the reach of most women.

The strength of the negative image of the alewife was graphically illustrated in many depictions of the souls of the damned in hell in pre-Reformation scenes of the Last Judgement on the walls of parish churches. At Bacton (Suffolk) and Combe (Oxfordshire), for example, alewives were portrayed being carried off to hell, clutching their false ale measures or being fondled by demons.[19] In the tapster scene introduced into the Harrowing of Hell play in the Chester cycle in the sixteenth century, the dishonest alewife was dragged off to hell and married to demons. Literature, written for both popular and elite audiences, con-solidated this image. William Langland's Rose the Regrator and Betoun the Brewster and Skelton's Elynour Rummyng, for example, developed satirical and grotesque images of the alewife. Such stereotypes, despite their vivid nature, may however have had little role in altering the posi-tion of women as brewers. They did, after all, develop in a period in which the brewing and selling of ale was largely a female preserve. Like the assumption of female physical weakness, their significance was that they could furnish useful excuses when it seemed necessary to justify restrict-ing a trade to men. In 1639 the incorporation charter of the brewers of London explained that women 'are not fit' to sell ale or beer.[20] The real explanation for the gradual displacement of women from ale brewing lies elsewhere and in many ways epitomises the nature of women's work in the early modern period.

The brewing and selling of ale seems a natural employment for women. Like baking, it involved adapting existing domestic production to a greater scale when the opportunity arose. In the fourteenth century when the brewing and selling of ale was almost a female monopoly most female brewers produced ale for sale episodically. Using existing domestic utensils to brew slightly larger quantities of ale could provide an occasional supplement to the family income, and for many brewing was essentially a by-employment within the domestic economy. Consequently, whether brewing continuously or infrequently, the majority of brewers were married women, although it was still possible for widows and single women to supplement their income in this way. The first changes to this situation were prompted by the increase in demand for ale in the period of growing prosperity following the Black Death (1348–49) when individual consumption increased. In a process that initially appears paradoxical, the demand for more ale and the accompanying expansion in the number of alehouses resulted in the squeezing out of those brewers operating on the smallest scale, primarily widows and unmarried women. These pressures were informal and largely a matter of choice. The post Black Death period also presented women with a wider range of employment opportunities, including service in urban households, and the expansion in textile production must also have absorbed a significant proportion of female labour.

The changes in the period following the Black Death do, however, illustrate the pressures of scale, which were to help to turn alewives into alesellers. A further vulnerability was the extent to which ale production was becoming the preserve of the married. The growing practice of amercing husbands for the brewing activity of their wives may appear innocuous and perfectly in accordance with the prevailing legal position on marital property, but it also facilitated the male takeover of brewing. When local authorities moved from exacting fines from those who brewed to issuing licences to brew to a select number of individuals, it began to matter that this business was expected to be in a man's name. Even if some husbands, such as Richard Pickering, a member of the London Brewers' Company in 1544, could see an advantage in asserting that 'he commits the whole responsibility thereof to his wife', this was, as Susan Cahn points out, a new world in which men were now the managers of work which had previously been seen as part of the woman's domestic sphere. Richard's wife, Joan, was not a member of the gild.[21] The description furnished by Henry Stocker of Salisbury may have summarised the situation more aptly. He testified in 1585 that he 'mainly lives by selling and distributing ale wherein he employs his wife'.[22]

Impulses towards licensing and regulation were strongest in urban centres in which there was a need to secure a constant supply of good ale and there was the authority available to achieve it. Oxford provides a good example of this process. With the exception of Queen's, none of the colleges brewed their own ale and were dependent on the, often haphazard, provision by the town's brewers. This unsatisfactory situation from the university's point of view was reversed in 1355 when it obtained sole jurisdiction over commercial brewing in Oxford. Close supervision followed which did not initially exclude women, although by the end of the fourteenth century women were more likely to be tapsters and servants in brewing households than they were to be brewers in their own right. This trend increased as the pressure of regulation intensified and by the end of the fifteenth century the introduction of a 15-day brewer's rota made the position of the alewife untenable. Women, and also poorer male brewers, lacked the capital resources to produce the quantities of ale demanded and could not maintain a position in the rota. Oxford's experience was in many ways unique, although there are some parallels with the situation in London and in ports where the need to supply ale in bulk for troops gave the advantage to larger scale producers. But the problems encountered by the alewives of Oxford were shared by alewives throughout the country as official control of the trade increased. The licensing act in 1552 may have been less of a landmark than Bennett suggests and only adopted initially in places like Middlesex, Cambridge, Worcester and Sandwich, but it established the framework for future regulation. Illicit tippling continued, and was encouraged by the belief that seasonal trading did not require a licence, and by the reluctance of the authorities to imprison offenders. But by the early seventeenth century, the instruction to the alewives of Weymouth (Dorset) that they should buy ale from the common brewers rather than market their own supplies followed a pattern set in many communities, and, as Clark argues, a series of parliamentary acts in the mid-1620s made the licensing system seriously effective. In this new climate women retained a place, but it was a minor one. The Kent quarter session records for the years 1590–1619 mention 901 country alehouse keepers, but only just over 9 per cent were women. The situation in the northern counties is less clear, but it is probably significant that, whilst there were over 500 licensed brewers in the southern and Midland counties in the 1630s, there were only about two dozen in the north.[23]

The introduction of beer, which is often credited with displacing women from brewing, developed in tandem with these general pressures towards regulation. Initially eschewed by the English as a sour foreign import and consumed by foreigners living in London and east coast ports, beer grew in popularity during the fifteenth century. The use of hops gave beer brewers the potential to amass greater profits than were possible for brewers of ale. Hops improved the keeping and carrying qualities of the drink allowing for production and marketing on a much greater scale. It did not take long for beer to displace ale as the staple in the provisioning of troops, and domestic consumption also grew. The addition of hops also meant that a larger volume of beer could be produced from the same quantity of grain than was the case for ale. At first sight, it is not clear why female brewers could not benefit from these advantages as well as their male counterparts. The brewing of beer was essentially the same process as the brewing of ale, and it was one that some women learned in order to produce beer for the use of their own households. Slightly more work was necessary since the wort had to be seethed in the hops, but this was not the main problem. Of greater significance was the scale of operation now involved. Producing larger quantities from a single brewing required more space, more vessels for brewing and storage, and more credit to tide the brewer over between the production of the beer and the sale of the complete batch. Even without the initial monopoly of beer brewing in the hands of male foreigners, such practical constraints would have excluded women trading on their own behalf. The trade of the beer brewer, like that of the maltster, was beyond the reach of the domestic side of the household economy.[24]

The outline presented above refers to England and draws heavily on the work of Judith Bennett. In general terms, it is probably also applicable to other areas of Britain. Lynch noted that the formation of the Society of Brewers in Edinburgh in 1596 resulted in the decline of the female ale brewer.[25] But, as in England, chronology and geography are likely to have been significant. Expanding capitals and port towns provisioning troops are likely to have been affected first by the changes in scale, necessary capital investment and regulation which resulted in the alewife becoming the tapster. Even in some parts of England, for example in Devon, beer did not begin to displace ale until the later seventeenth century. It was introduced in South Tawton in 1649, and as late as 1681 there was still only ale for sale in Ottery St Mary.[26] A similarly delayed chronology was probably characteristic of much of Wales, where, with the possible exception of ports like Haverfordwest, there were no strong incentives for regulation and small-scale producers were not significantly disadvantaged.

One of the consequences of the redefinition of women as the sellers of ale produced by others was the fading of the positive image of the thrifty housewife selling surplus ale. The new focus of concern was the problem of women as the sellers of alcohol to men. This had always been part of the stereotype of the alewife, but the idea of the ale seller as a temptress, who took advantage of men who were rendered vulnerable by drink, became more important when they could no longer be chastised for producing adulterated ale and when drinking increasingly took place in alehouses rather than at home. A particularly striking manifestation of these concerns occurred in Chester in the 1560s when the mayor and council forbade all women between the ages of 14 and 40 to work as tapsters in taverns or alehouses.

> Since, in contrast with the practice in all other places in this realm, all the taverns and alehouses of this city are, and have been, kept by young women, all strangers resorting hither greatly marvel at this and think it an unsuitable custom whereby not only great slanders and dishonest report of this city has and does run abroad, to avoid this and also to eschew as well such great occasions and provocation of wantonness, brawls, affrays and other inconveniences as thereby does and may ensue daily amongst youth and light disposed persons as also damage to their masters and owners of the taverns and alehouses.[27]

Despite the rhetorical advantages of suggesting that such practices occurred only in Chester bringing the city into disrepute, the same concerns surfaced periodically elsewhere. An equivalent campaign against women working in taverns and alehouses was mounted by the Edinburgh authorities. The first ordinance issued on 10 June 1560 did not prohibit such employment, but attempted to impose higher standards of morality. Owners of taverns were to be fined £10 if a woman serving ale was unchaste but could avoid this if they handed her over to be disciplined by the baillies as soon as they learned of her offence.[28] Honest tavern owners who did not wish to run brothels had nothing to fear from this measure, but the issuing of further ordinances suggest that it proved unsuccessful. This does not necessarily mean that all taverns doubled as brothels. Those who sympathised with the occasionally unchaste, or who considered the harsh punishment that could be meted out to them to be inappropriate, may have contributed to the failure of this strategy.

Whatever the case, the council later redoubled its efforts. Moved by the fear of the wrath of God which would be unleashed upon the city, rather than by the concern for the reputation of their city amongst other cities as in Chester, the council's ordinance of March 1580 was more forceful. It lamented the increase in fornication and drunkenness in the city and attributed this to the large number of female taverners, tapsters and sellers of wine who, for their personal profit and that of their masters, enticed the youth and 'insolent people'. To counteract this, the council decreed that from next Whitsun no women, with the important exception of the wives of freemen and the widows of free burgesses, were to sell wine, ale or beer and male servants were to be employed in their place. The stated penalties for infringement were draconian. For the first offence the master or mistress was to be fined £5 and, as usual, the female servant was to suffer more harshly being sentenced to banishment from the city. A second offence attracted a double fine and a branding on the cheek for the woman so employed, whilst for a third offence the master or mistress was to be banned from trading and from the freedom forever, and the serving woman was to be whipped through the streets of the burgh.[29] Whether such measures were effective or fully implemented even in the short term is not clear. Certainly, some women with sufficient financial backing seem to have been able to avoid such harsh treatment. In November 1580 William Stewart the younger stood surety for his mother, Margaret Aitkyne, and his sister, Katherein Stewart, that they should not violate the statute about female taverners in future.[30] By the early seventeenth century a more moderate strategy prevailed. In 1608 policy reverted to the principles of 1560 and focussed on those with a reputation for fornication whilst stopping short of fining their masters or mistresses. Instead, all women who committed fornication, or were slandered of it, were to be discharged of their service to taverners and sellers of wine.[31]

The compromise position reached in Edinburgh by the early seventeenth century is just one of many possible reminders that policies designed to exclude women from certain economic activities could not always pursue a straightforward course, despite the vulnerabilities inherent in women's social position. The idea that for women the early modern transition from a mediaeval economy to a modern capitalist society represented the loss of a mediaeval 'golden age' is too simplistic. There is, of course, some validity in the thesis promoted by pioneers of women's history like Alice Clark that a more capitalist economy tended towards the exclusion of women from many areas of employment, but this usually required the conjunction of adverse economic circumstances, as in the case of female weavers in Bristol. Moreover, as Bennett has pointed out, the thesis of decline should not be defined by the process of exclusion alone, but by comparing the status of the various employment opportunities open to women at different points in time. In her view, the shift from women as ale brewers to ale sellers should not be accounted a decline: all that has really occurred is a reinforcement of the situation in which women are only able to occupy the trades with the lowest status. As brewing becomes more profitable, larger scale and requiring greater capital resources, control of it becomes a male preserve, and women are limited to the task of selling.[32]

Bennett is clearly right to draw attention to the similarities in status of women's work. But perhaps, in reacting against the views put forward by Alice Clark, and more recently Ivan Illich, we risk losing part of the picture. Bennett's downward revision of the status of the mediaeval alewife is arguably convincing – the negative stereotype cannot be completely written out of the story – but ale selling may still represent a further decline in status. It intensified the association between women, the provision of ale and whoredom. Moreover, many of the sellers of ale were not running their own businesses but were the servants of taverners and this altered the status of women in the trade. The Edinburgh authorities' exemption of the wife from the prohibition on female servers of ale and wine reflects the continuing higher status enjoyed by women working within the domestic economy. As the ballad 'Choice of Inventions' reminded, it was possible that one's wife running an alehouse might be a whore, but she could also be a faithful wife.

A man that hath a sign at his door,
    and keeps good Ale to sell,
A comely wife to please his guests,
    may thrive exceeding well
But he that hath a Whore to his wife
    were better be without her.[33]

It was much less evident that an unmarried woman working in the same environment, and without a husband's control, could maintain the same chaste status.

In fact, in defining women's economic position and status during the early modern period it becomes increasingly necessary to differentiate between married and unmarried women. Brewing simply provides the most obvious example of this. In Scotland, as in England, most brewers were married women who brewed intermittently to supplement the household economy. Seventy-eight of the 88 women amerced for brewing ale in Aberdeen in 1472 were wives, and married women were similarly strongly represented in Dundee in the early 1520s accounting for 18 out of 29 brewers. However, some places seem to have had a different pattern. In Dunfermline between 1490–1521 only eight brewsters were identified as married women and 35 appear to have been single.[34] But larger burghs, at least by the sixteenth century, made efforts to avoid this outcome. In Edinburgh, for example, an ordinance of 1600 declared that 'all unmarried women and other solitary and unfree persons without masters' were forbidden to brew or sell ale.[35]

The response of authorities elsewhere was similar, and brewing was simply seen as part of a wider group of interrelated employments from which unmarried women should be excluded. In 1584 the court leet of Manchester ordered that no single woman was to keep any house or chamber, sell ale or bread, or work at other trades and argued that the economic activity of single women was 'to the great hurt of the poor inhabitants who had a wife and children'. However, the 'great inconvenience' caused by single women was not only the increased economic competition. The problem was said to lie also in their 'abusing themselves with young men and others, not having any man to control them to the great dishonour of God and setting an evil example to others'. Other ordinances issued at the same time aimed to clamp down on the number of inmates and showed particular concern about the number of 'strange beggars and pregnant women coming unto us from other places who are a great nuisance and burden on the town'.[36]

For the authorities, the answer to such problems was to insist that single people entered service so that they would be under the control of a master. The 1563 Statute of Artificers stipulated that all unmarried women between the ages of 14 and 40 could be put to service. Nevertheless, urban authorities could struggle to enforce this. The problem was perceived to be acute enough in Southampton in 1597 to persuade the authorities to note that,

> there are in this town diverse young women and maidens who make a living out of service and work for themselves in various men's houses contrary to the statute, and we desire that their behaviour might be considered and reformed.

But authorities attempting to reform this situation faced an uphill struggle since many single women were unhappy with the constraints of servanthood. As many urban authorities noted with concern, many of those who entered service saw the attractions of leaving it when possible, and not only, as the authorities hoped, on the occasion of their marriage.

In comparison with England, the problem of the unmarried leaving service in urban areas of Scotland was more severe. Lacking such an established tradition of servanthood and similarly powerful statutory enforcement, it was much easier, especially in a fast-growing city like Edinburgh, for the unmarried to earn a living outside service. Attempts to prevent unmarried women leaving service recur in the records of the capital. Beginning in 1530, the authorities tried to prevent what they saw as the common practice of servant women and wet nurses who had saved up enough money, leaving their master and mistress and setting up on their own as a brewster, huckster or prostitute. Claiming that their main concern was the rising costs of food and drink due to regrating, they ordered that no servant woman was to leave service and take a house unless she was married, and was not to enter the brothel without licence from the provost. To strengthen these measures, anyone who rented a house to such a woman was to be fined 40s, and no brewster was to hire brewing vessels under pain of banishment.[37] Later in the sixteenth century the council renewed its efforts, proclaiming in 1546 that no regrators, hucksters, cake bakers, tapsters or brewers were to be allowed in the burgh unless they were married or widowed, and they even attempted to stipulate that carding and spinning should only be done by widows and 'failed householders'.[38] By 1600 it was realised that a simple prohibition of trade by the unmarried and masterless, in this case as brewers, would not be effective unless the definition of servanthood was tightened up. The fear that the measure would be undermined by friendly neighbours claiming that unmarried brewers were their servants suggests the extent to which an economic existence for the unmarried outside service was seen by many as socially acceptable. In an attempt to counteract this, the council decided that no one was to be defined as a servant but those who were contracted and paid for the year, or at least half a year, and who had their meat, bedding and 'actual remaining' in a house with their masters.[39]

These difficulties do not mean that regulation of women's work was ineffective, but serve as a reminder that it proved to be least effective when it was designed to control the participation of many of the poorest in what Hufton has termed the 'economy of makeshift'. When in 1573 the authorities in Leicester decided to clamp down on the 'disorderly' practices of 'evil' persons known as 'brogers or pledge women' who went from house to house selling second-hand clothing and household goods, they decided to license two men as 'brogers' who would sell such goods from their shops rather than door to door. The fate of this initiative can only be surmised, but since the ordinance prescribed no penalties for pledge women continuing to hawk their wares, and pledging articles for credit was commonplace, it seems likely that their trade continued.[40] In contrast, as we have seen in the case of weaving, gild regulation could be much more effective in making a craft a male preserve. In the 1520s women played a significant role in the craft of bonnet making in Edinburgh, even being included among its representatives, but were unable to sustain this position through the sixteenth century.[41] But other examples, significantly perhaps in the victualling trades, suggest that boundaries could be easier to breach. In 1505 the barbers' craft in Edinburgh forbade women to make and sell whisky. However, some continued to do so, and in 1557 when Bessie Campbell was presented for distilling whisky illegally, the council suggested that she apply for admission to the barbers' craft, which was presumably now thought to be prepared to accept female members.[42]

It would however, be wrong to paint a picture entirely in terms of male resistance, with varying degrees of success, to female pressure for entry. In 1397, 16 women were members of the merchant gild at Prescot (Lancashire) and the reduction to six in 1415, one in 1542 and none thereafter might look like a classic example of progressively effective exclusion. However, in 1592 the gild reaffirmed women's right to membership, and this gesture evoked no response.[43] Different readings of this case history are possible. The gild may have been hostile to female membership in the mid-sixteenth century, but have been seeking new members in the changed circumstances of the 1590s. Alternatively, and perhaps more plausibly, it is possible that a mercantile career and the associated gild membership became increasingly less viable for women who had less access to the necessary capital and credit than men. A comparison with Bennett's study of the Brewers' gild in London suggests that membership privileges for women were so limited that there was little point in women investing in them.[44] If this was the case in a gild in which the primary expertise rested with women, such considerations must have weighed more heavily in a context in which women were less likely to be engaged in a trade alone or independently from their husbands. The mechanisms of exclusion were much more subtle than simple misogyny.

A further example of this process is the mechanisms in place to ensure good trading standards, which were designed, at least in theory, to protect the consumer, although they could also have the effect of controlling competition within the trade. The penalties for breaking standards and set prices could be severe and could include forfeiture of goods, equipment or urban freedom. Women were, of course, not the only possible targets in this process, but it is also true that quality and price controls were most in evidence in the victualling trades in which, especially at the beginning of this period, women predominated. Thus, in Dunfermline in 1573 it was announced that 'the first brewster that can be apprehended selling 7d ale, her vat is to be broken, her freedom forfeited for a year and 40s unlaw paid'.[45] Clearly, the authorities hoped that dealing thus harshly with the first offender would have an intimidating effect on the rest of the brewsters in the town. However, in general such drastic penalties as deprivation of freedom and banishment from the town were seen as a punishment of last resort, rarely used, and frequently rescinded upon production of acceptable sureties to guarantee future good behaviour. The position adopted by the Edinburgh council in 1529–31 was probably more typical than the punishment threatened in Dunfermline. Brewsters who overcharged their customers were to be fined 8s and on the third offence were to bring their cauldrons or kettles to the cross where they would be pierced and rendered useless.[46] But even where more moderate policies were enunciated, it is unclear how rigorously they were enforced. The likelihood of significant discrepancies between ordinance and punitive practice makes it difficult to assess how difficult the conditions of urban working women actually were.

Certainly, there were some individuals who refused to be cowed by the authorities, even if in doing so they rarely obtained tangible benefits. In 1578 Margaret Miller of Glasgow was fined for not allowing the officers to enter and weigh her candles.[47] The protest of Gilbert Brabner's wife in Aberdeen was even more dramatic. When she was fined in 1540 by the council for selling 16d ale, she responded angrily to their interference and threw away her ale rather than see it be doled out at the market cross. Perhaps predictably, this fit of pique did not advance her cause. She was fined again and officers were appointed to distrain her for the value of the amount of ale she had wasted, and to buy the equivalent quantity of ale and dole it out. Other threats may also have been counterproductive. In 1520 four female candle makers presented for their failure to keep the assize protested that the set prices were uneconomical and that keeping the assize would force them to cease trading. Unfortunately for them, the authorities took them at their word and, rather than altering the set prices, ordered them to cease trading under penalty of 8s.[48] But some women probably felt that they had made gains by asserting their position. In the 1620s the charwomen of Salisbury refused to work for the wives of town officials unless they were put on the poor rate. In the short term this pressure resulted in an increased income, but the longer-term effect appears to have been detrimental. With poor relief payments subsidising wages, the wives of Salisbury could keep the cost of employing a cleaning woman low.[49]

Part of women's vulnerability as workers derived from the fact that regulation of their trade was rarely in their hands, even when they were the sex assumed to possess the expertise. With only a few isolated exceptions, the aletasters who established the prices and tested for the quality of the ale were men. In the marketplace too, despite the use of phrases such as 'the housewives' market', those who supervised all its aspects, including the cleaning up after the hours of sale, were usually men. In the detailed lists surviving from Manchester in the later sixteenth century the name of only one woman appears: the wife, or probably more accurately the widow, of Philip Bexwicke who had held the office for a few years immediately prior to this.[50] In this context, the decision of the burgh court of Aberdeen in 1522 comes as a surprise. They ruled that eight women, two from each of the town's quarters, should meet together on market days to agree the day's price for malt and meal with the growers from the surrounding countryside.[51]

The exceptional nature of the experiment in Aberdeen serves as a reminder that the market was far from being seen as the woman's natural sphere. Instead, many urban communities witnessed periodic attempts to exclude women from certain transactions and to define their place. The 'housewives' market' in Leicester was contrasted with 'the drapery', and in early seventeenth-century Anglesey the use of different Welsh and English measures for cloth provided an excuse for two separate cloth markets from one of which at least some women were excluded.

> Let a Country housewife upon the street sell a piece of cloth to a mercer by yard, it must be measured by the Welsh yard; and let that housewife's own husband or any other follow the Mercer close by the heels to the shop, and there agree with him for the same piece of cloth, or any part thereof, and it shall be instantly measured with the English yard.[52]

When times were hard, as in the famine year of 1438, housewives could even be excluded from the marketplace where they bought food for their families. As part of their policy of restricting the activities of female hucksters in times of dearth, the council of Aberdeen ordered that only men were allowed to purchase meal in the market.[53] Other solutions established more complicated restrictions. An undated entry in the Gild Court

Book of Dunfermline recorded that,

> It is ordained that, except during proclaimed market, no women whether clad with a husband or a widow, shall buy wool, skins or hides except black wool and black skins, and that wool, skins or hides bought in this way shall be forfeited.[54]

In buying hides and wool, women could compete on equal terms with men at market time but not when they dealt directly with suppliers. Moreover, even when women were part of a gild household they could be seen as inappropriate purchasers. In 1554 the master and wardens of the London gild of carpenters agreed,

> that no woman shall come to the waters to buy boards of timber, laths, quarters, punchions, joists and rafters when their husbands are in town upon pain of forfeiture every time they are discovered to have done so.[55]

As part of the family business, women here were not denied the expertise and the ability to act as effective substitutes for their husbands, but their presence was seen as undesirable.

The detail of some of these prescriptions comes as a surprise. We do not expect women to be prohibited from buying grain to feed their families, and are perhaps surprised at the vision of women in timber yards purchasing boards, joists and rafters in what we think of as a masculine building trade. This is not, of course, to say that the vision of separate spheres and of gendered patterns of work should be abandoned. Ideas of gender offered a vocabulary for exclusion, but did not necessarily provide a consensus: the women buying timber were not there without the authorisation of their husbands who remained in town. A more complex issue is the related question of status. The men who did the family shopping in the exceptional circumstances of 1438 did not suffer a decline in reputation, but the husband who appeared regularly at the housewives market in normal times could be seen as henpecked and unable to exert the control over his wife that maintenance of his status required.

It is also the case that the work carried out by women conferred different degrees of status and economic independence. Although probably the majority of female employments were of low status, ranging from the women employed as searchers of the bodies of suspected plague victims to the taverner's female servant with a reputation for unchastity, this was not invariably so, even within the same trade. In Chester bone lace making was associated with the poor, whilst in East Devon production of a higher quality lace put women into the ranks of the better paid, and gave them an economic independence that allowed them to postpone entrance into the married state.[56] Nevertheless, such opportunities were rare in the crafts. Women were actually able to accumulate more resources in domestic service and by becoming wet-nurses. The latter was especially the case in parts of Scotland, such as Aberdeen, where it was expected that the wet-nurse would live with the birth family. English infants, by contrast, were sent out to be nursed by poor women in the surrounding countryside. In England concern about the practice of wet-nursing centred on the belief that the child's character was shaped by the milk it suckled. Mothers who allowed their child to be nursed by another were neglecting their maternal duty and risking the moral corruption of their child. In Scotland, religious leaders were similarly to the fore in articulating concerns about wet-nursing. However, their main anxiety was not the potential immorality of the child, but that the profitability of wet-nursing encouraged the immorality of the nurse. In the sixteenth century, the minister of Anstruther Wester (Fife) warned that some women became wet-nurses 'not caring what will become of their own'. Giving one's illegitimate child to a cheaper rural wet-nurse and taking up the well paid employment of a live-in wet-nurse for an urban family could be an attractive option, and possibly the only way for a single mother to cope. In Anstruther Wester from 1583 the session attempted to regulate the situation, and, as in Edinburgh (1588) and Aberdeen (1609), warned parents not to employ wet-nurses before they had at least atoned for 'their harlotry and fornication'.[57]

For many wet-nurses the connection made between their harlotry and employment may have been justified, but this is unlikely to have been the case for all such women. A recurrent theme in this chapter has been the repeated failure of contemporaries to divorce the regulation of work from fears of illicit sexuality and of threats to the propriety of the respectable married household. The history of women and work in the late mediaeval and early modern periods cannot be told simply in economic terms. It is, of course, true that, as Bennett argues, an abiding characteristic of women's work was its poor remuneration and low status, and that recognition of female expertise offered little protection when the scale of production outgrew the concept of the complementary domestic sphere of the household economy. However, we need to place these observations in a contemporary perspective. Most wives who ceased to brew for sale episodically did not become barmaids, and could retain their status as thrifty and productive housewives by diverting their energies into surplus production of other domestic products such as eggs or butter. Moreover, whatever the economic opportunities on offer, the core of female reputation remained their housewifely skills. The history of women and work is not a 'history that stands still' nor is it a straightforward history of female oppression. Rather it is a story in which single women lose status relative to their married sisters. This was partly because they were more vulnerable to the increases in scale and supporting credit necessary for some enterprises, such as brewing. As important, if not more so, was the ease with which the sexual reputation of economically active women, especially the unmarried, could be sullied simply by association with their employment. And yet it would also be misleading to substitute a notion of the oppression of women with the oppression of single women. This is also a period in which many women actively rejected more respectable servanthood opportunities for a degree of independence. Expressions of disapproval surrounded what, for many, seemed to be desirable windows of opportunity.

Chapter 3: Disorderly Women

'Our saviour Christ was a bastard and our Virgin Mary a whore', or so at least a Worcestershire man claimed whilst drinking in a Stratford alehouse. His blasphemous outburst, which came to the attention of the authorities, reminds us of the fragility of reputation and the teachings of the Church in the early modern period.[1] If Christ and Mary could be slandered in such a way, it seems that the reputation of ordinary people must have required extra special protection. Even the reputation of Elizabeth I, the Virgin Queen, was not immune, and moreover could be used as an example to sanction illicit sex by others. When Edward Frances of Melbury Osmond (Dorset) attempted to seduce Elizabeth Baylie in 1598 he told her that the Queen had three bastards by noblemen at court and that this showed that there was nothing wrong with extramarital sex.[2] But such disruptive and undeferential attitudes were not shared by everyone. Someone reported the Worcestershire man's outburst to the courts, and Elizabeth Baylie was not persuaded by the alleged whoredom of the reigning monarch to agree to her seducer's suggestion. Similarly, women acting as witnesses in witchcraft cases, or defaming the reputation of their loose-living neighbours, cast their vote on the side of the patriarchal order with little regard for the sexual double standard it contained in order to secure their reputation amongst the honest and chaste.

It was, however, not quite so simple as this. Slanders of Christ, the Virgin Mary or the reigning monarch were extreme statements, and taking sides against neighbours who were a disruptive nuisance could have its own attractions. But what does this tell us about the importance of chaste reputation for women? Was it the case, as Gowing suggests, that women's reputation was defined by their sexual honesty, whilst men's was not?[3] And was the double standard to be taken equally for granted in the different environments formed by the expectations of clanship, by the moral and pastoral expectations of religious leaders of diverse hues, and by the legal and economic considerations introduced by the establishment of poor relief? These are difficult and complex questions, but in addressing them we must not assume that the behaviour of honest women was always subordinated to this system of reputation.

This can be illustrated most clearly with reference to dress. In an era in which sumptuary laws attempted to define what people could wear according to social status, and in which, as the Scottish parliament noted in 1567, dressing above one's status was the mark of the whore, clothing proclaimed one's identity and was used to indicate misbehaviour. Thus, in Edinburgh in 1556 the authorities ordained that no married woman or widow who was known to be a fornicator or adulterer should dress like honest men's wives who wore a little hat, under pain of banishment and the forfeiture of their clothing.[4] Similar concerns surface periodically in the later records: in 1601 widows of burgesses who fell into 'the filthy crime of fornication' were forbidden to wear the busk of a burgess' wife. Nevertheless, despite the reiteration of these codes and of the honour and shame they were supposed to confer, it is clear that women ignored them without apparently jeopardising their reputations. From the late 1620s the provost and baillies of Edinburgh attempted to outlaw the wearing of plaids as part of a campaign against Highland customs that were increasingly seen as uncivilised. However, despite the provision that all plaids worn in public should be confiscated and tarred, the practice continued and by the 1630s aroused additional fears that fashions in dress no longer proclaimed morality. In 1637 the authorities forbade

> that barbarous and uncivil habit of women wearing plaids, yet such has been the impudence of many of them that they have continued the foresaid barbarous habit and have added thereto the wearing of their gowns and petticoats about their heads and faces, and this has now become the ordinary practice of all women within this city to the general imputation of their sex, matrons not being able to be discerned from strumpets and loose living women to their own dishonour and scandal of the city.

The scope of the punishments indicate the gravity with which this was viewed by the city fathers and suggest that disregard for the outward signs of honesty was not only confined to poorer women. In addition to the by now standard provision of the confiscation of plaids worn in public, the

authorities added a two-tier system of monetary fines to be imposed upon
women who wore their gowns or petticoats around their head. For the
first offence a woman of quality was to pay ten pounds, and female servants and those of lower degree were fined 40s. A third offence involved
the possibility of banishment.[5] The conflict between the attitude of the
authorities and female concerns is most visible in Edinburgh because of
the allied concern to redefine Highland dress as uncouth, but women
elsewhere also disregarded dress conventions that were supposed to define
their honesty and marital status. In Chester, for example, the authorities
deplored the habit of wives, widows and many maids in the city wearing
white caps, kerchiefs and great broad black hats 'whereby a single woman
cannot be distinguished from a married, which disordering and abusing
of apparel is not only contrary to the good use and honest fashion used
in other good cities and places of the realm, whereby great obloquy
among strangers has and does run abroad, but also is very costly more
than necessary'. In response, they imposed monetary fines on all unmarried women who had the temerity to wear caps and on all women wearing black hats unless they were riding or going to the country.[6] In terms
of dress, at least, women of all ranks including the wives of burgesses, felt
able to disregard measures designed to safeguard their respectability.

And yet the vulnerability of female chastity was a commonplace, which
was constantly reiterated in literature and in the claims and counterclaims thrown around in slander and defamation suits. It was present
even in tales lauded by historians as rare examples of narratives in which
the wife is assumed to be chaste, such as Adam de Cobsam's poem discussed by Hanawalt. In this poem, written in 1462, a married carpenter is
given a contract to build a hall and turns down the opportunity of taking
his wife with him, claiming that he has no need to fear for his wife's
chastity during his absence. However, as the narrative unfolds, it becomes
clear that the story hinges less on the wife's natural chastity, than on the
incentive and assistance she has in maintaining it. A woman of poor family, her only dowry is a magical rose garland that will not fade so long as
she is true to her husband. Moreover, as if the inability of the wife to con-
ceal her unfaithfulness was not a sufficient deterrent, the carpenter felt
the need to improve his wife's ability to defend her chastity by construct-
ing a tower and a dungeon. In sequence the lord, the steward, the proc-
tor of the parish church and the priest all try to test the wife's chastity in
her husband's absence, but when they offer her money, she leads them to
the tower where they fall through the trap door to the dungeon below.
Here, suffering from hunger, they experience the final degradation of

being reduced to begging to be allowed to do women's work (preparing flax and spinning) in exchange for some food until the husband returns from his building contract.[7] When this was one of the most positive literary assertions of the married woman's capacity for chastity, it is hardly surprising that women's reputation was to a large extent defined by their sexual honesty, and that women seeking to defend themselves against slanderous comment most commonly sought a retraction of the label 'whore'.

This was largely due to the prevailing assumption in this period that women were by nature more lustful than men, and that women, their sexual passions having been aroused by the experience of marriage, were insatiable as widows. By the later seventeenth and early eighteenth centuries, partly as a result of the development of new medical theories, such views were undergoing a revision. In the new scheme the naturally chaste woman could be mastered and controlled by the sexually dominant man. Before this development, the greater lustfulness of women, together with the uncertainty of paternity, supported the idea of woman as temptress and deceiver and seemed to justify the double standard. But this viewpoint was not unchallenged. Those with pastoral concerns could reach different conclusions about culpability and responsibility. On the one hand, the catholic classification of mortal and venial sins suggested that gravity depended on the nature of the offence rather than the sex of the offender. More interesting, since it fostered diametrically opposed conclusions about gender and sin, was the idea that sin represented a loss of control. Following contemporary assumptions about the nature of the sexes this meant that naturally weak-willed women should be deemed less culpable than men who were thought to be more rational and to be more able to control their sexual desires. These ideas were already present in the late middle ages, but were given a sharper edge with the development of protestantism especially when zeal for godly reformation coincided with the opportunity of social control.

In the late mediaeval period these issues were most clearly discussed by authors in the context of adultery, but their arguments were equally applicable to fornication by the unmarried. In the fifteenth century, the author of *Dives and Pauper* explained that adultery was a greater sin for a man than for a woman because of man's natural superiority. The general rule for all individuals that 'the higher the degree the harder is the fall and the sin more grievous' applied as much to men and women as, for example, to the gravity of sexual sins committed by a cleric and a layman. Moreover, even if it was the wife who committed adultery, the husband was still culpable since it was the duty of a husband to be a model to his wife and to govern her. Such an assessment, the author conceded, was contrary to much popular opinion, but this was due to man's social dominance and 'shrewdness' in a situation in which more men than women actually committed adultery and in which the husband who was chaste and true to his wife was widely scorned as not being a true man. However, contrary to these assumptions, women, whose gender made them less prone to chastity, were the most accomplished maintainers of it. Women were not temptresses but rather the potential victims of malicious male seducers as Scripture made clear. Thus, Samson was already weakened by his lechery and misgovernment of himself before the episode with Delilah; lust was in David's mind before he saw Bathsheba, and in the minds of the elders who contrived to watch and proposition Susanna.[8]

Such views were clearly not dominant in the late mediaeval period, but the voice of the author of *Dives and Pauper* was not an isolated one, and his rejection of the double standard, whilst preserving contemporary notions of gender characteristics, was a rationalisation potentially available to all. Stereotypical portrayals of those suffering in hell for lechery illustrate this diversity. In texts like the *Ordinarye of Chrysten Men* (1506) or the *Kalendar of the Shyppars* (1503) male souls were mainly shown burning in hell, but in Doom paintings in parish churches it was more common (and perhaps easier) to depict the lustful woman and wanton temptress being dragged to hell. Thus at Combe (Oxfordshire) a woman was shown allowing a devil to fondle her breast, and at Chesterton (Cambridgeshire) 'luxuria' was depicted as a temptress in a low cut dress.[9] There was also a widespread view that lechery was the unmaking of a man. As Mirk explained in his widely disseminated sermon collection, lechery led not only to the loss of a man's goods, reputation and friends, but also, and more terribly, it transformed him into a 'mopish fool' who has to 'let his mistress be his master'. The male lecher lost control of his wits, and of his ability to govern and hence no longer possessed the natural male capacity for rational judgement. It is, however, less clear where the blame for this transformation was thought to lie. Men were clearly envisaged as vulnerable, as shown by Mirk's account of the answer to King Darius's question: which is strongest a king, wine or a woman? The king has power to command, but can be overcome by wine. The woman is stronger than both because she brings up the king, and, as the king's mistress, can manipulate his moods.[10] The answer presents male vulnerability as unquestionably natural, and does not seek to explore the issue of male responsibility. But the latter was, of course, central to any concept of avoidable sin and hence to preachers' concerns, even if the precise relationship between male vulnerability and responsibility was often not straightforward.

Two exempla used by Mirk in his sermons illustrate this clearly. In the first, Mirk tells the tale of a woman, who has been a man's mistress for many years, and suddenly feels moved to mend her ways, having heard a sermon that graphically described the torments of the lecherous in hell. Meeting her lover on the way home, she refuses his advances and tells him of her resolution. His answer: 'If everything was as the preachers say, then no man or woman would ever be saved, therefore do not believe it, for it is not true. But if we from now on agree together as we did before, then I will plight you my troth that I will never leave, but stay with you for ever' convinces her to resume their relationship, and has a prophetic irony for the end of the tale. After their deaths a holy man prays to learn their fate and hears their quarrelling voices coming from a black mist which has risen over the water. The woman curses the man as the cause of her damnation, and in reply he places the blame on female lack of constancy, rather than on his own lack of, even temporary, contrition: 'Accursed be you and the time that you were born, for you have made me damned for ever! For, if I had ever been contrite for my sins as you were, I would never have turned as you did, and if you had kept good covenant with him who you made it with, you might have saved both of us. But I promised you that I would never leave you, and therefore we now go together into the torments of hell that are ordained for both of us!'[11] Whilst enjoying the humour of the tale, the audience was clearly supposed to reject the man's attribution of responsibility, but this meant accepting individual responsibility rather than completely rejecting gender stereotypes. Female inconstancy, and the ease with which women can be misled by beguiling male arguments, are not questioned, but men should not use this as an excuse for their own conduct. To do so involves an abdication of responsibility, which runs counter to the innate, or stereotypical, male capacity for reasoned judgement. The second example, taken from Mirk's wedding sermon, similarly accepts female stereotypes whilst retaining an idea of male responsibility. At night a charcoal burner sees a vision of a man on a black horse chasing a woman around his fire, cutting her to pieces with his sword and throwing her onto the fire. When asked to explain, the ghostly rider recounts that in life he had enjoyed the woman 'under her husband, and therefore each night I shall slay her and burn her in this fire, for she was the cause of my sin'.[12] In this story the woman is claimed to be the cause of the man's sin, but his enforced participation in the nightly penitential task of pursuing, attacking and burning his lover suggests that he also shares in the responsibility for their adultery.

These fifteenth-century arguments presage those used by the puritan authors of the seventeenth century. Writers of godly advice literature, such as Gouge, drew the same unsettling conclusions from accepted gender characteristics and notions of responsibility. Whilst recognising the 'inconvenience' of uncertain paternity, which meant that an illegitimate son might inherit the lands of a man who was not his actual father, Gouge argued that this did not justify the conclusion that female adultery deserved stronger censure. Rather, since a husband and wife are one flesh, they should be punished equally, and, if one party was to be considered guiltier, it should be the husband.

> If difference be made, it is fitting that adulterous husbands be so much the more severely punished by how much the more it appertains to them to excel in virtue, and to govern their wives by example.[13]

Such views differed little from those of the late mediaeval period, but were perhaps more widely disseminated in the later sixteenth and seventeenth centuries as part of the expansion of print. The circulation of the works of such authors is harder to demonstrate in Wales and Scotland, but the development in both these areas of parallel strains of puritan piety, as well as the possible development of ideas expressed in the late mediaeval period, suggests that these ideas were not unknown.[14]

It is however less clear that these arguments changed the extent to which women were taught to safeguard their chastity. In her *Mother's Blessing* (1616) Dorothy Leigh advocates Susanna as a name to be given to daughters because of her exemplary chastity. For Leigh, chastity is defined in broad terms. It includes the avoidance of idleness and of all 'vain delights' like pride and vanity in dress, and their replacement with humility and christian virtues which are outwardly manifested in reading, meditating and acting upon the Scriptures. But sexual chastity was also Leigh's concern and here the point of the story of Susanna is that it reverses the assumptions inherent in the story of Eve: although Adam was beguiled by Eve, nowadays men are more likely to deceive women as the elders did Susanna. The moral is that the only way to avoid this outcome is for women to be chaste like Susanna.

> Man said once, *The woman which you gave to me, beguiled me, and I did eat.* But we women may now say that men lie in wait everywhere to deceive us, as the Elders did to deceive *Susanna.* Therefore let us be, as she was,

chaste, watchful, and wary, and keep company with maids. Once *Judas* betrayed his Master with a kiss and repented it: but now men, like *Judas*, betray their Mistresses with a kiss and repent it not: but laugh and rejoice, that they have brought sin and shame to her that trusted them. The only way to avoid all this is to be chaste like *Susanna*, and being women, to embrace that virtue, which being placed in a woman, is most commendable.

Leigh's argument is however more complex than it first appears. She is not simply turning the tables by identifying every man as a potential seducer rather than every woman as a potential temptress. The chapter concludes with the hope that 'women be persuaded by this discourse, to embrace chastity, without which we are mere beasts, and not women'. Pursuit of chastity is not merely a defensive strategy, but it is one that simultaneously humanises and feminises women. More than this, it is the only means to preserve and nurture the conjugal relationship: a woman's failure to keep chaste entails destroying 'both the body and soul of him she seems most to love'. Ultimately, the model of Susanna, in Leigh's interpretation, shows that in a dangerous world the onus lies upon women to assert their femininity and to preserve their chastity.[15]

Such conclusions partly explain why the reversal of the double standard in terms of natural capacities did not result in legislators and local authorities being prepared to state as a general principle that men should be more harshly punished for fornication than women. Nevertheless, it was possible for legislation to establish penalties that applied equally to both sexes. When the Scottish parliament turned its attention to such matters in the 1567 Act 'Concerning the filthy vice of fornication' the penalties imposed did not draw distinctions according to sex, although there was the option of paying a monetary fine for pious uses in order to avoid the degradation of public physical punishment. Impoverished first offenders suffered eight days imprisonment and two hours public exposure in the marketplace, those offending for the second time underwent double the length of imprisonment and were to appear in the marketplace with their heads shaven, and those insufficiently cowed by such treatment were imprisoned for 24 days, ducked 'in the deepest and foulest pool or water', and then banished from the town for ever.[16]

Nevertheless, equal treatment, despite being pastorally and logically satisfying, was not always easy to sustain. When authorities felt under pressure, or had no legislative lead, different strategies could be adopted. The example of Dundee shows that, even when an even-handed approach was initially adopted, increases in the incidence of fornication could result in women being held principally to blame. In 1559 the penalties for male and female fornicators were the same: for the first offence the offenders were to be admonished by the preacher and to show public repentance; the second offence merited three hours in the gyves and being ducked three times in the sea; subsequent offences attracted the penalty of banishment. By January 1562, when it was noted that 'fornication continues and increases daily in the burgh and that it does not cease with the penalty of open repentance', imprisonment for two days and two nights was added to the punishment of men and women offending for the first time. Curiously, but ostensibly for humanitarian reasons, the imprisonment of pregnant women was deemed to be perilous, and they were to be banished for a year. However, since banishment was often in practice a very temporary phenomenon, the 1562 solution soon seemed unsatisfactory. The record for 1564 dropped the gender-neutral mask and explained that 'the women who are the principal initiators of fornication' could escape punishment if they were pregnant at the time of their apprehension. Imprisonment was still considered an inappropriate remedy for this situation, although there were efforts to make male imprisonment more penitential by forbidding a man's friends to join him in carousing, eating and drinking during his spell in prison. Instead, the woman was to be taken to the market cross where her hair was to be cut off and nailed to the cucking stool as a sign of her shame.[17]

The diversity of responses, and the availability of conflicting arguments about gender and moral responsibility in both the catholic and protestant traditions, suggest that the emphasis on moral discipline promoted by some protestants during the Reformation did not necessarily mark a sharp break with the past. In their assumptions about gender there were no new ideas, but there were always a variety of possible interpretations that could be favoured by particular doctrinal positions and that could mesh with other economic concerns. This means that, despite all the arguments about puritanism and social control, the relationship between the nature of moral discipline and godly protestants, whether the zealous presbyterians of the Scottish kirk, or their puritan counterparts south of the border, is far from straightforward. Did zealous protestants change the nature of moral discipline, and how did their actions affect women?

In England it is argued that protestants, who were dissatisfied with the incomplete Reformation instituted by Elizabeth I and her parliament in 1559, initially turned their attention to cleansing the Church of the remaining remnants of popery, objecting to such observances as the continued use of the surplice, 'the popish rag', or making the sign of the cross at baptism. A smaller group also campaigned for a more radical reorganisation of the protestant church, but this presbyterian initiative ran into the sand as it failed to gain sufficient parliamentary support to make such a change seem even a realistic goal in the last decades of Elizabeth's reign. In place of these two campaigns, puritans redeployed their energies towards moral reform. The drive for further reformation was no longer to be focussed on church ritual and ecclesiastical structures. Protestantism stressed that, although an individual could not earn his salvation by his lifestyle and good works, this did not exonerate the christian from striving to live a moral and upright life. Puritans took this injunction more seriously than most, many of them obsessively examining their conscience and their sins in an exhilarating, but also crushing, cycle of hope and doubt that they might be numbered among God's chosen elect rather than among the reprobate who had no hope of salvation. However, although salvation was viewed in individual terms, this did not mean that the morality of the community was not the puritan's concern. Plenty of Old Testament examples could be cited to make it abundantly clear that God could unleash his wrath upon communities in which the activities of the ungodly remained unchecked. Moreover, it was possible that the ranks of the apparently ungodly were not entirely filled by the reprobate, but could also contain some members of the elect who were not yet aware of their obligation to God and their duty to behave in as godly a manner as humanly possible.

This interpretation is not without its problems. In particular, it fails to explain convincingly why the concern with morality was not a constant feature of the puritan movement when it was so integral to its theological position on salvation and the relationship of christians with God. One possible solution to this difficulty is the thesis advanced by Margaret Spufford, which attempts to dissolve the tight connection between puritanism and social control by pointing out that parallel waves of moral regulation took place in periods of economic difficulty and population expansion when puritanism cannot be a factor, such as the thirteenth century. This is a useful reminder that moral campaigns do not occur in a vacuum and that much moral regulation can have economic implications that render it attractive to some. But such observations do not close the question of puritanism and social control. Spufford's attempt to do so relies on an unwarranted disconnection of attitudes about morality and social behaviour from the spiritual core of religion, the individual's relationship with God.[18]

In Scotland other problems of interpretation arise due to the different nature of the Reformation. In areas of Kirk control the rapid establishment

of a system of kirk sessions at parish level, and the more chequered development of a system of presbyteries, meant that the exercise of godly discipline was a possibility from the early years of the Reformation, and that
issues of church structure and the survival of catholic rituals were less of
a diversion for the energies of the godly. The more clearly Calvinist cast
of the Kirk may also have encouraged the identification of moral discipline as a priority, and, as Lenman suggests, the development in Scotland
of covenant theology may have intensified the corporate sense of guilt
and the commitment to godly discipline.[19] The Scots Confession (1560)
recognised 'Ecclesiastical discipline, uprightly ministered as God's word
prescribed, whereby vice is repressed and virtue nourished' as one of the
three marks by which the true church could be distinguished from 'that
horrible harlot', the Church of Rome.[20] Nevertheless, the nature of such
discipline, which impressed travellers such as Richard James who commented that in the Highlands the stools of repentance were usually 'well
stuffed' with men and women doing penance for whoredom, is in need
of further explanation.[21] As Graham points out, the dominance of cases
of sexual discipline in Scottish kirk session records is not paralleled in the
caseloads of Calvinist consistories in France. Graham's conclusion that
the exercise of kirk discipline generally rejected the sexual double standard in favour of gender-neutral notions of individual responsibility also
requires discussion. He concedes that in some cases unequal punishment
was meted out to male and female fornicators, but identifies such women
as an exceptional class of 'prostitutes' or frequent fornicators.[22] However,
this creates an artificially sharp division that seems questionable in terms
of the formation and maintenance of female reputation. The honest,
chaste housewife defined herself against the sexually promiscuous
woman, and such validations only made sense if female sexual behaviour
was seen as a continuous spectrum. Nevertheless, even if Graham's
conceptualisation is rejected, it is still possible that kirk discipline placed
less emphasis on the double standard than did disciplinary efforts
elsewhere in Britain.

In considering developments in both Scotland and England, it is
important to remember that protestantism was less innovative in morality
than it was in doctrine. Broadly speaking, the kinds of moral offences pursued by elites in the period of the Reformation were those that would
have attracted some degree of moral censure from pre-Reformation
catholics. The difference lay in the gravity associated with particular
offences, the zeal with which offenders were pursued, and the incorporation of some offences, such as bridal pregnancy, which had been largely

overlooked by pre-Reformation courts. These reflections are particularly important in assessing the significance of the relationship between English puritanism and social control, which has largely been discussed by historians in terms of the competing strengths of religious and economic motivations. In reality, of course, the two were often mixed. A petition from the minister and some of the principal inhabitants of Castle Combe (Wiltshire) in 1606 complained of a woman's 'filthy act of whoredom ... by the which licentious life of hers not only God's wrath may be poured down upon us inhabitants of the town, but also her evil example may so greatly corrupt others that great and extraordinary charge for the maintenance of baseborn children may be imposed upon us'.[23] Such statements appear to make a mockery of the attempts by historians to distinguish between puritan and non-puritan forms of social control in English parishes. Even if we were to accept Ingram's view that the village elites of Keevil (Wiltshire) were less puritan than their counterparts in Terling (Essex), it is unclear why this difference should manifest itself in the addition to the menu of social regulation in the latter parish of alehouse regulation.[24] Puritans may have abhorred drunkenness, but such concerns did not lack an economic foundation. Alehouses were thought likely to foster fornication and illegitimacy and hence increase the burden of the poor rate. It was also the case that clamping down on the keepers of unlicensed and disorderly alehouses did not directly remove the evil of drink, but it did protect the livelihoods of respectable, licensed keepers of alehouses many of whom were from the ranks of the respectable elite. In another Essex parish in which social discipline was apparently in puritan hands, Earls Colne, the elite did not pursue alehouse keepers, recognising that the selling of ale was an important safety net for the poor who would otherwise become a burden to the parish.[25] If even in alehouse regulation puritan elites could come to different conclusions, was there any connection between puritanism and social control, especially in sexual morality, the area of behaviour most con-sistently targeted in disciplinary campaigns?

Consistent with his view that puritanism and alehouse regulation were connected, Ingram suggests that in campaigns against illegitimacy and bridal pregnancy economic factors were more important than religious ones in prompting local authorities to act. In his detailed study of the diocese of Salisbury, Ingram found that there was no clear correlation between the incidence of brides who were pregnant at the altar and the intensity of prosecution. In fact, bridal pregnancy occurred more frequently in the chalk/agrarian parishes than in cheese/clothworking ones, but it was in the latter area that presentment was more frequent. For Ingram this apparent paradox can be resolved with reference to the greater economic pressures in cloth areas that made elites more sensitive to the problems of poor relief and thus more inclined to regulate what they saw as irresponsible sexual behaviour.[26] Underdown, on the other hand, would presumably see Ingram's statistics as supporting his view that puritanism struck deeper roots in woodland areas than it did in arable ones.[27] Wrightson's objection that this would appear to put Terling, the model of puritan social control, into the wrong camp as an agrarian parish, in fact helps to clarify these divergent views. Terling, though an agrarian parish had more of the social characteristics of woodland communities. The increasing commercialisation of agriculture, presumably to serve the London market, resulted in wheat production displacing barley from the last quarter of the sixteenth century and by the seventeenth century probably half the adult males in the parish had no land except a cottage plot. Terling resembled the artisan, wage labour structure of Underdown's woodland areas more than the classic model of the agrarian manor. However, of course, placing the emphasis on the presence, or absence, of pronounced social stratification does more to make sense of the geographical pattern than it does to determine whether there was anything particularly puritan about such regulatory activity.[28]

To answer this, focussing on the prosecution of bridal pregnancy may be helpful for several reasons. First, of all the targets of moral regulation in the Reformation period, this was the one that would have seemed most innovatory to contemporaries. In Spufford's thirteenth-century example the payment of leyrwite for women who fornicated or bore a child out of wedlock comes close to this. But leyrwite payments, as a seigneurial exaction from the unfree, had become largely obsolete during the later middle ages and had fallen out of use even earlier than merchet or marriage fines. In parts of Wales, especially in the Marches, *amobr* fines continued to be levied by lords and combined the concerns of merchet and leyrwite. However, although there was a strong view in Wales that a woman should be a virgin at marriage, it is unclear whether an *amobr* fine was paid for bridal pregnancy. In England, at least, bridal pregnancy seems to have aroused little concern before the later Elizabethan period. Nationally about one fifth of brides were pregnant at the time of their marriage, and the proportion could be much higher in some areas: in Lamplugh (Cumbria) in the early seventeenth century 60 per cent of brides were pregnant.[29] To a large extent such variation depended on the strength of different spousal, or betrothal, customs and the frequency with which unforeseen economic developments disrupted the timing of marriage. But, whatever the incidence, bridal pregnancy was not usually assumed to be a source of shame. Pregnant brides were not the objects of charivari rituals and defamation cases were almost never in terms of bridal pregnancy despite the frequency of fornication allegations. In part, of course, the latter was because such accusations were incontrovertible at the time, but if they had the capacity to shame we would expect them to be used retrospectively as part of a general attempt to damage someone's sexual reputation. Secondly, with bridal pregnancy, as also with illegitimacy, it is possible for places with good surviving parish registers to assess what proportion of pregnant brides were actually pursued by the authorities, and thus whether elites in particular parishes were more or less tolerant of such behaviour.

The first thing to note is that in all the parish case studies examined by historians, there was never a case of a zero tolerance policy. Even in cases of illegitimacy which were much more likely to attract official censure, some mothers escaped presentment. In Terling, for example, the authorities proceeded against 83 per cent of women who bore bastards between 1570 and 1640. The proportion of pregnant brides prosecuted was always lower. In Terling during the same period only 40 per cent of those who could have been presented to the courts actually were. In Steeple Ashton, Keevil and Wylye (Wiltshire) the percentages range from 38 per cent to 57 per cent for the first three decades of the seventeenth century.[30] A variety of explanations for this selectivity seem possible. Favouritism is perhaps the most obvious, and presumably played some part, but it seems unlikely that it accounts for such leniency. In Earls Colne, for example, pregnant brides among the village elite were more likely to be targeted than those among the poor in the later Elizabethan period.[31] A more plausible explanation is that local elites recognised the possibility of mitigating circumstances, especially when economic factors had disrupted the expected timing of marriage. If the point of presenting cases of bridal pregnancy was to discourage feckless fornication that might result in illegitimacy such distinctions made sense. But it is hard to see in this pattern of presentment anything specifically puritan. Herrup has shown that a recognition of mitigating circumstances was a feature of court decisions in cases of theft in Sussex and explains this by amassing mainly puritan quotations stressing the sinfulness of all mankind and the need to be tolerant of human frailty. However, the statistics showing that the courts were more lenient when theft derived from need, as in the case of someone stealing a loaf of bread to feed the family, than when it arose from a desire for substantial profit, as in the case of horse stealing, suggest that this was a viewpoint shared by most protestants. The jurors of Sussex were hardly uniformly or predominantly puritan.[32] Moreover, it appears that the prosecution rates for bridal pregnancy in the supposedly contrasting parishes of Keevil and Terling were broadly similar. However, it is possible that the case for puritan zeal producing a different pattern of presentment can be made by adopting a more fine-grained approach. In Terling the proportion of pregnant brides presented changed with time: 35 per cent in 1580–99, 28 per cent in 1600–19 and 73 per cent in 1620–39. What is striking about these figures is that the highest percentage does not correlate with the period of the greatest economic difficulty and highest rates of illegitimacy, but rather with a period of relative stability. It seems no accident that the third period coincided with the arrival of more stridently puritan ministers in the parish who strengthened the resolve of the godly group amongst the elite, but it may be as significant that they were helped in this by the fact that by this date bridal pregnancy occurred mainly in social groups below the elite.

The word 'puritan' was a term of abuse, but it seems unlikely that this was particularly due to the role of puritans in promoting campaigns of sexual discipline. Individuals, given favourable circumstances, could intensify such efforts and distort the usual correlation between such campaigns and economic tensions in stratified communities. However, most of the time godly elites dealt with sexual misconduct in the same way as their less godly protestant neighbours. If puritans were to be disparaged it was probably more for their attacks on popular festivities such as maypoles, a feature apparently lacking from both of our most quoted parishes, Terling and Keevil, or for the hypocrisy that was assumed to lie behind their self righteous religiosity. As far as women were concerned, the late sixteenth century did mark a new period as the institutionalisation of poor relief and severe economic difficulties encouraged local elites to hold bridal pregnancy up to scrutiny and censure. However, the significance of this should not be overestimated. Pregnant brides were usually spared the full rigour of public penance by the church courts. In the dioceses of Salisbury and Ely, and in the archdeaconries of Chichester and Leicester, for example, offenders were allowed to confess wearing their own clothes or semi-privately in front of the minister and churchwardens. In contrast, some courts in the diocese of York imposed full public penance dressed in a white sheet. Whatever the form of penance adopted, presentments for bridal pregnancy seem to have had little effect. The general decline in the actual incidence of bridal pregnancy in the early seventeenth century can be traced both in parishes in which presentments were rare, such as Broad Chalke (Wiltshire), and those in which it was increasing, such as Steeple Ashton in the same county.[33]

Rates of illegitimacy also experienced a similar decline irrespective of the intensity of prosecution. Discipline of mothers of bastards was, however, more far reaching. Secular courts could order brutal shaming punishments: in 1599, for example, the Essex justices ordered that Frances Barker, the mother of an illegitimate child, should be carted and whipped until her blood flowed.[34] Ecclesiastics adopted subtler, but probably no less effective, strategies of withholding church ceremonies from unrepentant mothers or their newborn children. But such tactics did not always gain wholehearted support even amongst puritan clerics. Ralph Kirke, curate of Manchester, who was puritan enough to describe the surplice as 'a Rag of the Pope', was presented by his parishioners in 1604 because 'he christens diverse bastard children and churches their mothers without confessing their faults and when the parish clerk requested him to register their name and to set down a "b", or some such like note or mark for a bastard, in the margin, he answered that he would not, giving as his reason that when the child is christened it is no bastard'.[35] This case is of interest in a number of respects. There was never any directive that parish registers should distinguish illegitimate children, although many keepers of them chose to do so. The parish clerk and the parishioners who presented their curate to the consistory court of Chester may have been considered by contemporaries as puritans. Certainly they fit the intolerant stereotype, but it was their curate, the puritan who objected to the surplice, who held the doctrinally more consistent position. However reprehensible a sin bearing a bastard was, the child that was born was an individual in relation to God. As some contemporaries realised, puritans could divide between those concerned with ecclesiastical ritual and with moral regulation, even if some shared both concerns.

Another tactic in the attempt to regulate illegitimacy, and perhaps provide some maintenance for the child, was to insist that the mother of an illegitimate child should name its father and to make this a condition of reconciliation and admission of the child to baptism. In some jurisdictions we can see this concern, or at least the level of success, increasing over time. In the archdeaconry of North Wiltshire the fathers of bastards were specified in about 60 per cent of cases in the 1590s and this rose to about 80 per cent by the 1620s.[36] Although the context of illegitimacy was not specified, Bishop Middleton's unusual article for the diocese of

St David's in 1583 may have had the recognition of paternity at least partly in mind. He instructed his clergy to ensure that 'the father of the child that is to be baptised be present at the baptising of his said child, during the whole action of baptism'. He was certainly concerned to specify that no 'common whores and wicked women' should be allowed to give thanks for their safe delivery in childbirth until they were examined and permitted to do so by the ordinary.[37] The latter was a more frequent expectation and had the merit that non-compliance affected the mother rather than her child. Churching, understood by protestants as a ritual of thanksgiving for safe delivery in childbirth rather than a ritual of purification as claimed by the catholic church, was a popular ceremony. The chrisom book from late Elizabethan Salisbury shows churching rates of 75–93 per cent and making churching conditional on penance was probably an effective strategy.[38] This was either performed in advance, or, as Whitgift's articles for the diocese of Worcester in 1577 suggested, incorporated into the churching ceremony which should take place on a Sunday or holy day with the woman dressed in a white sheet.[39] Given the view that churching retained its popularity not least because it was a women-only rite associated with feasting and celebration, the first of these options was presumably normally considered preferable by the mothers concerned.

Withholding churching from mothers of illegitimate children or notorious fornicators was evidently a tactic that affected women more than it affected their male partners. With this exception, it is less clear how far ecclesiastical authorities deliberately fostered the maintenance of a double standard. However, as Hindle points out, part of the distinctiveness of the late-sixteenth and seventeenth-century campaigns to regulate morality was the close alliance between ecclesiastical and secular jurisdictions, which resulted in an increased emphasis on physical punishments, such as whipping. There was also a tendency for such punishments to become more severe. In Essex the punishment of unmarried mothers at the end of the sixteenth century changed from a few hours in the stocks, to a moderate whipping at the cart's tail, to a public whipping until their backs were bloody.[40] Such punishments could be administered equally to men and women. At Glastonbury (Somerset) in 1617, for example, Nicholas Ruddock and Katherine Canker were whipped through the High Street with 'two fiddles played before them ... to make known their lewdness in begetting the said bastard upon the Sabbath day, coming from dancing'. But in other cases the woman seems to have been singled out for punishment: in 1630 a woman, whose name was recorded only as Joan, was 'whipped up and down the market street between twelve and one o'clock ... stripped from the neck to the girdle' for her harlotry.[41] Since fathers were not named in all cases of illegitimacy, some gender imbalance in prosecution was inevitable, although in periods of economic difficulty the authorities could intensify their efforts to reduce this. In Wiltshire in the 1620s and 1630s, for example, a higher than average percentage of fathers of baseborn children were whipped for their offence.[42]

The institution of bridewells or houses of correction was part of this same punitive trend, and increased the possibility that women would be disproportionately punished for bearing children out of wedlock. The 1576 bridewell statute gave magistrates a fair amount of discretion, but recurring parliamentary debate resulted in a much clearer statement in 1610. From this date, justices of the peace were supposed to incarcerate in bridewells all unmarried mothers whose children were chargeable to the parish. The implementation of the Act varied regionally, especially since many local authorities were tardy in the building of the bridewells necessary to support such a policy. However, it is clear that the availability of such places of detention was not the only determining factor. In Somerset, where two houses of correction existed at the beginning of the seventeenth century and a third was added in the 1620s, the authorities did not respond to the 1610 Act by imprisoning women, but continued to sentence offenders of both sexes to whippings or periods of time in the stocks. In Lancashire, in contrast, the statute rapidly produced a change in policy after the establishment of the Preston house of correction, the only one in the entire county. King suggests that this was not because there was a stronger commitment to the sexual double standard in Lancashire than in Somerset, even if the consequence of placing women in houses of correction was actually to strengthen it. Instead, the different strategies were based on concerns to ensure that the illegitimate child was maintained at the least cost to the parish. The period in which local JPs had been able to exercise discretion had produced different solutions that shaped the response to the 1610 Act. In Somerset where maintenance was expected from both parents incarceration of the mother made less sense than it did in Lancashire where the burden of maintenance fell on the father and imprisonment of the mother could be viewed as appropriate, and relatively inexpensive, moral discipline. Not all men avoided imprisonment in this system, but, of the small percentage of men who were confined, only a tiny minority were being disciplined directly for their sexual immorality, and these were men accused of fathering a string of bastard children. The majority faced a spell in the local house of correction for their failure to provide sureties for the payment of maintenance, a point that further strengthens King's interpretation.

The contrasting treatment of men and women makes quite stark reading. In the counties of Hertfordshire, Lancashire, Somerset and Warwickshire of the 203 women punished in the late Elizabethan and early Stuart period for having an illegitimate child, 60 per cent were imprisoned and 35 per cent were whipped. During the same time span, of the 135 men prosecuted, 4 per cent were imprisoned and 25 per cent were whipped.[43] However, it is important to note that in general this system was not so harsh, or one-sided in gender terms, as this description may suggest. The number of bastardy cases considered by the justices was only a small fraction of those that came before the church courts. For most parents of illegitimate children, performing ecclesiastical penance in a white sheet was the most likely consequence of their actions.[44] Moreover, it is also clear that women potentially had a great deal of power over the men they knew. The mother of an illegitimate child was pressurised in childbed by the midwife to name the father, and this may often have been an unpleasant additional trauma. But it was also possible for a scheming or malicious woman to saddle a man who was not the father of her child with a significant economic burden of maintenance, typically 40s per year in the early seventeenth century. In general, the woman's identification was taken as decisive by the authorities, and, even when they were in some doubt as to its validity, the desirability of preventing the burden of maintenance falling on the parish caused them to cast such scruples aside.

In Scotland parish poor relief was less institutionalised and burdensome, but it became a more significant factor in some urban areas, as, for example, in early seventeenth-century Edinburgh. Here in 1608 the authorities ordered that a mother of an illegitimate child who did not identify the father was to be banished, and if she named a father who was unable to maintain his child all three were to suffer the same fate.[45] Such policies were, however, unusual. Possibly more frequent, although not always explicitly stated, were the attempts of the local kirk to at least secure an acknowledgement of paternity and reconciliation. In Aberdeen in 1562 the preacher was instructed to baptise an illegitimate child only if the father was present and made open repentance for his fault. Since baptism often occurred before the mother had completed her lying-in after childbirth, cautions were to be taken to ensure that she would perform her penance afterwards.[46]

As these examples suggest, there was a similar alliance between ecclesiastical and secular authorities north and south of the border. Kirk sessions worked closely with secular courts when a physical punishment was deemed appropriate, and from their inception sexual offences were their staple concern, normally accounting for at least half of the cases considered. The parish basis of the system of kirk sessions meant that local elites were able to exercise moral discipline with a greater intensity than was usually possible in England and Wales. However, this may not have been to the particular detriment of women. In Graham's view this system of discipline was largely gender-neutral. Although there were cases in which women were treated more harshly, these can be dismissed as involving notorious prostitutes. However, as mentioned briefly earlier, this division of female sexual offenders into two discrete categories is untenable. In part, this is a problem of evidence: identifying prostitutes is impossible in records in which commercial transactions for sex, even if perhaps present, are not revealed, and even a more general definition of a separate category of frequent fornicators runs into difficulties. But more fundamentally it is a conceptualisation that ignores the possibility of more subtle gradations of reputation and the way in which female identity is measured against the extremes of this spectrum, whether the chaste, honest woman, or the shameless, infamous harlot. Of all the sessions examined by Graham, Canongate provides the clearest evidence of differential treatment of men and women for sexual offences. Incorporating a large part of what may be considered as sixteenth-century Edinburgh's red-light district, this might seem to support Graham's thesis. In particular, it was women, rather than men, who were routinely banished from the gate for sexual offences. In many of these cases the women are labelled as harlots, which we might think we could read as a synonym for Graham's 'prostitutes'. However, the same label could also be applied in the record to cases in which such a description seems inappropriate; a servant woman sexually exploited by her master, or a stable couple who had an illegitimate child and intended to marry.

The case of David Pearson and Isobel Mowtray provides a good example of a couple inhabiting the grey area between the even-handed treatment meted out to those who experimented sexually before marriage, and the gendered response to identified harlots. In October 1564 they both admitted an illegitimate child. Isobel was ordered to leave the burgh within 48 hours 'under pain of scourging', whilst David was ordered to spend four hours in the branks which he subsequently commuted to a payment of 40s. Isobel's banishment seems particularly severe,

as does her inclusion in the list drawn up at the end of the session register of 'The names of the principal harlots'. In practice, both these aspects
were mitigated; Isobel's later readmission to the kirk and her marriage to
David were envisaged, and, despite being listed among harlots, she was
one of the few in the list not to be explicitly described as such.[47] Her position clearly was not identical with a woman like Jonet Tod who was
expelled from St Andrew's in 1598 and described as 'a common harlot ... not worthy of christian society'.[48] Nevertheless, the treatment of Isobel
demonstrates how the presence of harlots could influence the response
to less promiscuous women and act against the tendency of the Kirk to
advocate equal treatment of man and women in sexual cases.

The situation in Canongate may have been extreme, owing to the con-
centration of harlots that normalised harsher treatment of female sexual
offenders, but what is significant is that female sexual reputation was seen
as a continuous spectrum. Reputation was clearly defined, but it was also
perilously easy to slip between categories. Moreover, as the example of
Dundee mentioned earlier suggests, at times of heightened concern,
urban authorities could make the application of a double standard general policy. Consequently, women were forced, and probably also
expected, to be more careful of their sexual reputations than men. In this
context it is no surprise that women's appearances before the kirk session
were more likely than men's were to be for sexual offences. The significance of this cannot be explained away by the observation that women
were accused of a narrower range of offences. Such patterns also focussed
the construction of female reputation on the sexual sphere. However,
since in Scotland handfast marriages were tolerated in practice even by
the kirk session, the implications of this were slightly different than those
prevailing in England. In Scotland, as also in Wales, illegitimacy, was not
so stigmatised as in England where bastard bearing was considered more
gravely than fornication in the courts. But a crucial part of this Scottish
perception was the regularisation of the union, which meant that
toleration of handfast marriages and illegitimacy could be consistent with
a heightened concern with female reputation and the labelling of the
whore.

Since the session's response was tailored according to the reputation of
the accused, it is significant that women were more likely than men to
acquire tarnished sexual reputations. Two early seventeenth-century
cases from the records of the kirk session of North Leith illustrate this
process clearly. The fornication committed by John Erskine and Janet
Gray was considered to be particularly reprehensible by the elders since

it had taken place on the golf links and, more importantly, at 'the time when the hand of god was so heavily among us with the plague of pestilence'. As a result, John Erskine was ordered to sit for three days upon the public place of repentance and on one of these days in linen cloths. As for Janet, described in the session register as 'alias scourged lady', the session decided that 'because she is so infamous...therefore other punishment be given to her' and, when the session finally caught up with her, she was ordered 'because of her infamy to stand in the jougs the next sabbath from the time of morning prayers until the forenoon sermon is over, with a paper upon her head with this inscription A SHAMELESS AND AN INFAMOUS HARLOT'. The importance of reputation determined that in the eyes of the session Janet Gray would be seen as the worst offender, and that the worst punishment was a day in the jougs (rather than three appearances on the stool of repentance) with a notice definitively labelling that reputation.[49]

The case of Helen Hewisone provides a parallel example, but also one in which the relative impermeability of male reputation by acts of sexual misconduct can also be seen. Hewisone, a woman apparently of less notoriety than Gray, was reported to the session in June 1610 for being on a ship with Walter Livingstone, the ship's boy, on the sabbath at night 'in a slanderous manner'. The session ordained that she was to perform public repentance the next sabbath at the kirk door with a paper on her head 'declaring her impudence and shamelessness'. The session demanded repentance from Walter Livingstone, but no similar declaration. More significantly, in demonstrating the extent of Helen Hewisone's loss of reputation, the same meeting considered the case of Adam Patersone who was accused of saying to Walter Livingstone that 'he had got but his leavings of Helen Hewisone'. In an unusual move the session ordered Patersone to make public repentance 'to set an example to others not to make vaunt of their evil deeds'. Despite implicitly accepting the truth of Patersone's claim, the session did not order him to do repentance for fornication with Helen Hewisone, but it did act against the vaunting of evil deeds of fornication. In labelling Helen Hewisone's reputation, the session could countenance letting the two men off more lightly, and, in the case of Patersone, could consider boasting of evil deeds to be more heinous than fornication with a woman of ill reputation.[50] An important aspect of the double standard as it operated in Scottish kirk sessions was not simply the relative ease with which a woman's sexual reputation could be tarnished, but the extent to which a woman's ill repute could exonerate some, or all, of the guilt of her male partner.

Ecclesiastical discipline meshed much more closely with secular discipline in Scotland than in England and Wales since offenders were not reconciled to the kirk until they had satisfied the demands of the civil magistrate. Secular discipline, seen most visibly in the case of burghs, was to a large extent able to work out its priorities autonomously, although it was also guided and/or constrained by the specifications of Acts of Parliament and the stance adopted by secular courts. In 1562, for example, the elders of Aberdeen specified that adulterers would be carted and banished, and went on to note that, although by the law of God the punishment for adultery should be death, the magistrates had no power to implement the death penalty 'for the princes have not received God's law in that part: therefore they can do nothing else but purge their town of rotten members'.[51] Such aspirations, in fact, had little chance of success. The attempt of the *First Book of Discipline* (1560) to persuade magistrates that they were obliged to follow Scripture and sentence adulterers to death had not been warmly received, and even its authors in 1560 realised the need to elaborate what should happen 'if the civil sword foolishly spare the life of the offender' and envisaged the possibility of readmission to the Kirk of the excommunicate if sufficiently penitent and reformed.[52]

In the case of fornication, opinions were generally closer. The most important statement was the 1567 'Act concerning the filthy vice of fornication', but this should not be read uncritically as a statement of the disciplinary practice prevailing from this date. Despite their evident concern about sexual immorality in their areas, magistrates could be less than diligent in ensuring that the terms of the Act were applied. In Edinburgh on occasion, as in April 1587, pressure to do so could come from the kirk session, which encouraged the magistrates to declare that the baillies should execute the act of parliament against fornicators rigorously.[53] Whether their response was anything more than a diplomatic declaration is unclear. Certainly, two years later, and probably on their own initiative, the authorities, noting that their burgh was 'greatly defiled with the vice of fornication', took steps to close a loophole in their application of the Act. Since fornication was committed within the burgh by inhabitants and also by outsiders, the statutory penalties were now to be imposed on the latter as well as the former.[54] The Edinburgh authorities were not, however, uniformly dilatory in their pursuit of discipline, and even after the passing of the 1567 Act could issue their own provisions that exceeded its measures. Their 1578 statute of harlots was, as usual, proposed as a response to 'the daily increase of the horrible vice of fornication for lack of sharp

punishment' and established that 'all the harlots that shall be apprehended in vice hereafter are to be carried in a cart through the town and
banished from its bounds for as long as the provost, baillies and council will'.
Summary despatch of harlots caught *in flagrante* had an obvious appeal,
even if it was not quite what the parliamentary legislators had intended. It
also alleviated the problem, which was noted as severe in February 1581,
of the number of prisoners, 'some for adultery, some for incest, who are
poor and likely to perish from hunger'.[55]

Adultery, at least on paper, was met with much more severe discipline,
even if offenders generally escaped the death penalty. In Dundee, as in
Aberdeen, banishment was prescribed for the first offence, whereas
according to the 1567 Act this penalty was only available for the third and
subsequent offence of fornication. Tenants of Alloway, administered by
the magistrates of Ayr, who were guilty of adultery could be deprived of
their landholding.[56] In contrast, but probably untypically for the rest of
Scotland, in early seventeenth century Shetland adulterers could escape
with a monetary fine.[57] Such a policy certainly would not have made
sense to the authorities in Dundee who in 1580 felt it to be necessary to
change the penalties imposed on adulterers between their conviction and
banishment in order to maximise their shameful public exposure. Before
these changes those guilty of adultery were to spend three hours in the
jougs at the market cross at the busiest time of day, and were then to
be ducked three times in the sea. The new regulations dispensed with the
salt water ducking, perhaps because of the costliness of erecting or maintaining the necessary gibbet, and specified eight days imprisonment on a
diet of bread and water, and three appearances at the market cross,
bound with a chain and wearing a crown of paper specifying that the
offence was adultery. The perpetual banishment that followed may not
have been strictly adhered to, but subsequent re-entry may have been
more difficult for adultery than for other offences for which banishment
could be prescribed. It was presumably also the gravity of the potential
punishment for adultery that prompted concern that individuals could
be wrongly accused by members of their household who bore a grudge
against them. In September 1619 the Dundee authorities ordered that
any servant who slandered their master or mistress with adultery should
be sentenced to 48 hours in the jougs and then be banished from the
burgh forever.[58]

The greater gravity of cases of adultery was also recognised by the Kirk,
which ruled that such cases should be settled by presbyteries rather than
at local level by the kirk session. The strength of Kirk discipline was

buttressed by the parliamentary statute of 1581 that prescribed capital punishment for notorious adulterers who refused to heed the admonitions of the Kirk and to perform satisfactory repentance. It was thus more reasonable than the Act of 1650 in England, which attempted to impose the death penalty simply for committing the offence, rather than for stubborn refusal to be reconciled afterwards.[59] In addition, the Kirk instituted a two-tier system of repentance designed to encourage offenders to make their peace with the Kirk and community as rapidly as possible. In 1569–70 the General Assembly laid down that those who had not stubbornly resisted the admonitions of the Kirk and had not been excommunicated for their offence should make public repentance at their kirk in sackcloth, barefooted and bareheaded on three preaching days and then be received into the congregation. Six days of such public repentance were prescribed for the more recalcitrant before they could be readmitted.[60] However, although the Kirk was usually able to secure compliance, the efficacy of such reconciliations can be questioned, perhaps especially when they involved members of the local elite. The kirk session of Monifieth, for example, made repeated efforts to deal with adulterous lairds in the parish and gained some success in eventually securing the performance of some acts of outward repentance. But, as Bargett concludes, 'Perhaps the only lasting result of these struggles was that Janet Braidy replaced Margaret Kinnaird as the concubine of the laird of Laws'.[61] More surprisingly, husbands could on occasion resist the Kirk's attempts to discipline their adulterous wives, although this may have been more an attempt to reduce their own shame as cuckolds than a merciful attitude towards their wives. The session of Aberdeen issued 'many exhortations' to William Davidson in 1574 to persuade him to allow his wife to do public repentance for her adultery, but 'he answered stubbornly, that in no way would he allow her to do any more than she had done'.[62]

However ineffective the discipline of the Kirk may have been in some cases, the Kirk's main concern in this period was not to strengthen such procedures, but to clarify its position on divorce for adultery and to resolve the problem of how to respond when an adulterous person married his or her paramour. The *First Book of Discipline*, picking up on the practice of some kirk sessions from 1559, stated that divorce was possible for adultery, and that the innocent spouse was able to remarry.[63] This position was codified in an Act of Parliament in 1563, but the problem of whether adulterers could remarry, and, in particular, whether they could marry their paramour, took almost 40 years to be completely resolved by statute. It was not until 1600 that parliament, urged to do so by the

General Assembly, prohibited marriage between an adulterer and paramour. The difficulty of this decision requires some explanation, especially since the eventual legal position does not seem to have been generally accepted in the seventeenth century. Mitchison and Leneman note that, after the passage of the Act, it became frequent practice not to name the paramour in divorce proceedings, presumably so that the couple could subsequently marry.[64]

From a religious point of view, the belief in the necessity of marriage for the avoidance of fornication could justify allowing the adulterer to marry. However, this view risked conceding that adultery was not a heinous sin, and sanctioning the exchange of marriage partners according to the dictates of sexual desire. For some, such new contracts were a defilement of marriage 'which is no punishment of sin, but a blessing of God ... which ought not to be granted and given to adulterers'.[65] A logical application of this second view was provided by the General Assembly in 1566. It noted that a subsequent marriage by men and women who had been separated from their spouses having committed adultery was 'contrary to the law of God' and produced 'great slander and inconvenience', and ordered that ministers who joined in marriage 'any party separated for adultery' should lose their positions. However, opposition to this stance within the Assembly, perhaps because its members included both clerics and laymen, was sufficient to ensure that the question would be reopened at the meeting the following year. On this occasion, the Assembly promised that further discussion would be held to resolve the matter and expressed its desire that in the interim no ministers should 'meddle with such marriages'. The same holding position was reiterated in 1574 and 1576, but a little more clarification was forthcoming when the Assembly met in 1595. This asserted that there were two types of unlawful marriage. The first occurred when someone married a person 'whom they have polluted by adultery'. The second reminds that divorce was not necessarily consequent upon adultery: if the innocent spouse was prepared to remain in the existing union, *any* new marriage contracted by the guilty party was invalid.[66]

Property considerations also played an important part in formulating policy concerning adulterers, especially women. The 1592 Act 'Against adulterers' was wholly concerned with the question of what should happen to the property of wives who were divorced from their husbands as adulteresses and entered into a 'pretended marriage' with the adulterer. It declared that such a woman was forbidden to give any of her goods to her unlawful husband or to the children of that union. Upon her death her heirs were to be the children of the lawful marriage or their heirs. It was only with the passage of the 1600 Act definitively outlawing such unions that the same property restrictions applied to fathers.[67]

Nevertheless, the economics of divorce reinforced the desire of an adulterous couple to cohabit. The legal rationale for divorce in the Reformation period depended on the guilty party, whether someone who committed adultery or someone who deserted his spouse for four years without reasonable cause (Act 1573 *c.*55), being considered legally dead. Only by this device could a full divorce, rather than the separation from bed and board of canon law, be conceived. When the wife was guilty of adultery the same arrangements came into force as if her husband had been made a widower and she was consequently worse off than if she had been left a widow. Her tocher remained with her husband and she lost all the moveable goods she had brought with her to the marriage. Unsurprisingly, she also lost her right to terce that she would have gained upon her husband's death. This essentially meant that the adulteress became dependent on her kin, her ability to gain her own livelihood, or the financial support of her lover. For both emotional and financial reasons, it is scarcely surprising that marriage between the adulterous parties was such a pressing concern.

The Reformation in England did not witness such a dramatic overhaul of marriage law as in Scotland. Despite the efforts of various reformers, canon law and the mediaeval system of church courts continued to prevail. This meant that, as in Scotland before the Reformation, a judicial separation, which allowed the couple to live apart but not to remarry, was available to the husband who could prove his wife's adultery, and to the wife who could prove her husband's excessive physical cruelty. But this legal distinction fitted quite awkwardly with protestant moral concerns, especially since adultery was defined as a sexual relationship with a married woman, and the married man who limited his promiscuity to single women and widows was merely guilty of fornication. These principles clearly contradicted the conclusions that could be drawn from ideas of the natural capacities of men and women for self-control. From this perspective, men who, unlike weak and emotional women, were assumed to possess superior judgement and self-control fell further from their natural abilities, sinned more grievously and set a more serious example of bad conduct. This resulted in a broadening of the definition of adultery to include sexual relationships involving a married person of either sex, a development that was more consistent with the idea that adultery was a serious undermining of marriage that had made the couple one flesh.

As these views gained ground, they encouraged calls for harsher penalties to be imposed on adulterers, and for adultery to entail the dissolution of the marriage bond. These attitudes featured strongly in the early years of the Reformation and should not be seen simply as a puritan concern. In fact, they were given great publicity by being included in the first official *Book of Homilies* (1547), a work that all parishes were ordered to purchase and from which ministers were to draw at least some of their sermons. Thomas Becon's 'homily of whoredom and uncleanness', which was part of this collection, was virulent in its condemnation of adultery, severe in its advocacy of Old Testament punishments, and clear that its warnings of damnation applied to 'unlawful conjunction' of a man with a woman who was not his wife and vice versa. Even the story of Christ telling the adulteress to go her way and sin no more was used as proof that adultery was sinful, rather than to extend mercy to the adulteress.[68] The homilist was not alone in his concern. Latimer bewailed the extent of whoredom in London, which, in his view, had not been reduced by the protestant closure of the Bankside stews. To avoid the fate of Ninevah, Sodom and Gomorrah, he advocated the death penalty for adultery, allowing the innocent party to plead for the reprieve of their spouse, but only for the first offence.[69] Such ideas were, however, unable to make significant legislative impact. The stillborn project to replace canon law with appropriate protestant legislation, the *Reformatio Legum Ecclesiasticarum* (1552), accepted that adultery of either party could dissolve marriage, but its specifications fell short of capital punishment. The adulterous husband, it was proposed, should restore his wife's dowry, forfeit half of his goods to her, and suffer either life imprisonment or perpetual banishment. Similar punishments were to be imposed on an adulteress. Efforts to strengthen punishments for adultery, including another failed attempt to institutionalise the *Reformatio*, were a recurring feature of Elizabethan and early Stuart parliaments, and there was probably significant sympathy for the complaint of a Norfolk parson that it was shameful that in so godly a country as England, there was no penalty for adultery but a white sheet.

However, when the death penalty for adultery was finally legislated for in 1650, the Act, despite being seen as the realisation of puritan aspirations, would have been considered highly inappropriate by the influential writers of puritan household advice literature of the early decades of the seventeenth century. Its provisions broke with the evolving protestant tradition by reinstating the double standard. It prescribed the death penalty for a husband who was twice convicted of adultery with a single woman, but sentenced an adulteress to death for the first offence. In contrast, as noted earlier, puritan authors, such as Gouge, argued for a reversal of the double standard, which would place the greatest responsibility for adultery upon the husband. These ideas did not, however, result in calls for draconian punishments for adultery but instead fostered the view that adultery by the husband or the wife should not necessarily result in the end of the marriage. Gouge recognised that there was scriptural warrant for divorce for adultery (Mat. 5:32 and Mat. 19:9), but, even though the adulterer became one flesh with his harlot, this did not automatically dissolve the marriage. Christ's words to the adulteress, and God's practice of retaining churches after they have committed spiritual adultery, were evidence that divorce should not follow if the innocent spouse was prepared to offer forgiveness to the repentant offender. The innocent spouse, whether the husband or the wife, should take on the role of Christ, which was normally associated with the husband, and determine the fate of the marriage. Following the model of Christ did, of course, carry with it a strong presumption in favour of mercy, but the heinousness of adultery meant that readmission was still envisaged as a real choice: it was 'not meet in this case to impose it as an inviolable law upon the innocent party'.[70]

Whately in his *A Bride-Bush* (1617) also argued that the wronged party could be readmitted to the marriage if repentant, since the love of a married couple should be fervent and abundant. However, he went further than Gouge in envisaging a situation in which receiving the penitent spouse would no longer be an option. In his view, if the sin was persistent, the injured party should separate 'for no man must make himself a member of a harlot, nor woman of a whore-master'.[71] Such arguments were controversial in implying that adultery dissolved marriage, and, under pressure, Whately in the preface to *A Care-Cloth* (1622) retracted them, together with his view that desertion dissolved a marriage. In England, at least amongst the godly, arguments for actual divorce were hard to sustain. Although in choosing a marriage partner individuals should look for parity in piety or godliness, the wife's duty of subjection to her husband, and the husband's duty of love for his wife, demanded that each spouse should bear with the faults of the other. The admission of the penitent spouse could not be openly stated as an inviolable law, but it was a strong presumption, which gave the innocent spouse little choice. Ideas of the nature of marriage also presented a fundamental religious objection to the idea that the innocent person was free to reject an adulterous partner. Marriage was based on the consent of the couple, but the covenant they formed was not with each other but with God and therefore the injunction that what God has joined together man should not put asunder applied. In such circumstances, it was hardly surprising that in England, despite the inappropriateness of protestants relying on the canon law of the Catholic church, the pre-Reformation situation of allowing marital separation, but not divorce, was widely considered to be appropriate, even if very different solutions prevailed in Scotland.

The lack of decisive change to the law of marriage in England in the period of the Reformation did, of course, apply equally to Wales. However, the nature of Welsh law may have meant that the experience of Welshwomen differed from that of their English sisters. Although the 'Act of Union' (1536) theoretically replaced Welsh law with English, it seems likely that this was incomplete. Some practices, particularly those concerning marriage, provisions for separation and *sarhaed* (insult) payments, which could be determined by family and kin rather than by law courts, are likely to have continued, even if such provisions as a *rhaith* of 50 male or female kin to deny adultery may have become less appropriate with the weakening of extended kinship structures by the early modern period. As mentioned in an earlier chapter, Welsh marriage practice prized the virginity of the bride whilst also providing for marital separation, which marriage contracts acknowledged as a distinct possibility. Separation could take place both in the first seven years of marriage, when a lesser payment was due to the bride, and also later when the wife was entitled to half of the moveable goods. The acceptance of marital separation and the frequency of concubinage arrangements in Welsh society meant that debates about the remarriage of separated or adulterous persons had little resonance. A subsequent marriage of a separated wife may not quite have carried the status of one involving a virgin bride, but it raised no problems of acceptability. Economically also, the wife probably did better out of a marital separation than was the case elsewhere in Britain. When the marriage had lasted more than seven years, it was described as *priodas*, a word that combined the senses of 'married' and 'one's own property', and if the couple separated, the wife was entitled to half the moveable goods even if she was at fault. In this case, moreover, to avoid unnecessary acrimony Welsh law laid down precisely which articles of household equipment and livestock should be given to the husband and which to the wife. For example, pigs, horses and cattle were the husband's, but the sheep and goats belonged to the wife. Curiously, given the normal association of women with care of poultry, all the hens and geese were to be given to the husband. If there was only one cat it belonged to the husband, but any other cats were to be given to the wife.[72] The first seven years of marriage were more probationary and here a distinction was maintained according to culpability. The guilty wife lost her right to *agweddi* (a payment calculated according to her father's status), but she did not leave the marriage empty-handed. She retained a right to *cowyll*, *gowyn* and *sarhaed*. Welsh law also prescribed the circumstances in which it was justified for a wife to leave her husband – if he was leprous, had foul breath, or was unable to have sex with her. Adultery by the husband was also grounds for separation. For the first two offences the husband was to pay his wife compensation (*gowyn* or *wynebwarth*), but at the third occasion the wife was expected to leave her husband or be disparaged as a wife lacking shame. A wife's adultery was equally serious, and was the greatest shame that a woman could bring upon herself and her kin.

Whatever the continuing strengths of these Welsh traditions, they also coexisted with other judicial systems. Sadly, with the exception of Welsh parts of the diocese of Hereford, church court records do not survive, although it can be assumed that similar disciplinary strategies were attempted in Welsh dioceses as in English ones, even if Penry was scathing of their efficacy. In his view, the punishment of adultery, fornication and illegitimacy was 'derided' by the Welsh: 'For what is it to them to pay a little money, or to run through the Church in a white sheet? They have made rhymes and songs of this vulgar penance'. As a consequence, he believed, both ministers and justices of the peace neglected their duties.[73] Although Penry's comments cannot be taken completely at face value, the weakness of the church courts helps explain the ease with which their jurisdiction was usurped by the Council of the Marches. This body, which was particularly active in the Welsh counties of Glamorgan, Monmouth, Brecon, Radnor, Montgomery and Denbigh, dealt principally with cases of adultery and fornication as well as riot and affray. In the early seventeenth century fines were fairly standardised but far from insignificant in wage-earning terms: adultery usually cost £3 6s 8d and fornication £2 13s 4d, a sum which could on occasion be reduced to £1. Particularly pernicious was the practice of the courts of relying on informers to bring cases of sexual misconduct, a phenomenon that rarely seems to have occurred in other branches of the court's business. Although precise statistics are not available, this practice may have been to the greater detriment of men than of women. As well as allegedly searching the registers of the church courts to produce offenders, informers were reputed to keep flocks of whores who would give evidence against their customers.[74]

Other aspects of relations within marriage were also regulated in traditional Welsh law by an elaborate system of compensation payments which could be paid by one spouse to the other. Again, as with customs concerning sexual fidelity, it is unclear how much of this detailed structure survived into the early modern period, but it provided a distinctive framework of ideas. For example, a *sarhaed*, or insult payment, was payable by the husband who unjustifiably beat his wife. Justifiable beatings included, perhaps unsurprisingly, those administered when the husband found his wife with another man. More restrictively from the wife's point of view, beatings were also considered appropriate if the wife gave away goods over which she had no right of disposition or if she used insulting language in speaking to her husband. It is perhaps not surprising that Gwerful Mechain, the only female poet whose work can confidently be dated to the second half of the fifteenth century, should write a poem expressing a wife's pain and anger at being beaten by her husband.[75] In England different concerns were expressed. The popular charivari shaming rituals singled out the wife who beat her husband for censure, and it was only in the eighteenth century that the tables were turned and these rituals focussed on the husband's physical chastisement of his wife.[76] There was a clear assumption that physical violence could be an acceptable tactic in the husband's governance of his wife, and, although the Elizabethan *Homilies* insisted that this should be moderate, popular proverbs suggested the opposite. If people took at face value the adage 'A spaniel, a woman and a walnut tree, the more they're beaten the better still they be', protestant views faced an uphill struggle.[77] Godly puritan authors argued that, since marriage made husband and wife one flesh, the husband who beat his wife was in the nonsensical position of inflicting corporal punishment upon himself. It was in part this lack of certainty about the acceptable level of chastisement that meant that in the London courts women seeking marital separation on the grounds of their husbands' violence towards them were almost half as likely to succeed as husbands who sought the same result because of their wives' adultery.[78] In Scotland the debate about domestic violence is less evident, perhaps partly because adultery could be adduced by both parties as grounds for divorce. Kirk sessions attempted to intervene in domestic disputes and may have had some success. The victims of domestic violence reported to them were usually women, but it was not always the case that this procedure improved their situation. When Richard Blyth was called before the session of North Leith in 1610 for striking his wife in

1610, he disdained its authority, saying that 'if the pastor had been present she should have got twice as much for his sake'. The session could also recognise that the wife could be partly at fault: it admonished Janet Porteous, a victim of her husband's blows, 'to behave herself dutifully to her husband'.[79]

Cases of domestic disputes suggest that women were most likely to respond to attacks from their husbands with words rather than blows, and it was as a scold rather than as a brawler that a woman was more likely to come to the attentions of the authorities. The association of women with words was strong, whether the loquaciousness of the gossip or the unruly tongue of the scold. The story of the devil Tutivullus, who struggled to keep pace writing down women's gossip, was frequently included in mediaeval sermons and imagery. In only one example, a piece of stained glass at Old (Northamptonshire), the artist chose to make the gossips male. Women's gossip was disparaged as idle tittle-tattle, which distracted wives from the proper performance of their household duties, but it was also feared as a source of power. Gossip could destroy reputation; identifying a neighbour as a witch, whore or cuckold, and a scolding tongue could prompt a crisis in which conflicting interpretations of that reputation had to be settled. In the form of a curse, the vituperative voice could be presumed to have an awesome power to conjure the intervention of God or the devil to damage its victim's fortune. That women throughout Britain were typically the scolders and cursers should not therefore only be seen in terms of the ignominious treatment of women being ducked in filthy ponds or brutally silenced and shamed by being forced to wear the branks, or scold's bridle. Such actions were not misogynistic, but they did respond to gendered assumptions about the power of each sex. In this perspective it makes perfect sense that the few men presented for scolding were described as 'barrators', a term of limited vernacular currency, and one which connected quarrelling with legal chicanery and the stirring up of unjust lawsuits, even if in practice male railing was not always so narrowly focussed. As always with gender assumptions, certain behaviour was particularly associated with each sex.[80] The differences, chronologically and regionally, did not concern the sex of scolds, but the extent to which they were seen as a problem and what strategies were considered appropriate to deal with them.

Underdown, in particular, has proposed, with reference to England, that the closing decades of the sixteenth century witnessed 'a crisis in gender relations' that was, at least partly, manifested in an upsurge of prosecutions for scolding.[81] The idea that the period 1560–1640 was one of increased concern about disorder, and also the general notion of a crisis in gender relations, has been criticised by a number of historians. Most notably, Ingram attempted to counter Underdown's thesis by gathering statistics of presentments for scolding from a wider range of jurisdictions than Underdown had used. Whilst admitting that changes in jurisdiction made comparison with the pre-1560 period difficult, he concluded that the meagre haul of cases from many places in the late sixteenth and early seventeenth centuries did not justify the use of a 'crisis' label. Rather than Underdown's 'epidemic' of presentments, Ingram suggested that it was more likely that many villages, and even some towns, went for years or decades without using the court to deal with a troublesome scold. In fact, the few 'hotspots' Ingram was able to identify were rapidly expanding urban areas, such as Manchester in the early seventeenth century, rather than rural parishes or stable market towns.[82] It seems, perhaps unsurprisingly, that the pattern of concern about scolding mirrored that of women using the church courts to bring actions of defamation. Gowing in her study of the London church courts noted that in the rural areas of this jurisdiction, which included Middlesex, 65 per cent of cases were brought by women, whilst in the more urban areas they were responsible for bringing nearly 80 per cent of cases. It seems very plausible that the litigiousness of women increased in proportion to their participation in marketing and urban trades.[83]

A similar pattern seems likely for Scotland, although here the evidence for the rural areas is much sparser than the documentation available for the burghs. On occasion urban authorities could specifically target groups of sharp-tongued female traders. In Edinburgh in 1594, for example, the provost and baillies ordained that any flesher wife found scolding, cursing or swearing in the landmarket was to be banned from the market.[84] In general, though, scolding seems to have elicited less concern than we might expect, at least from the minister and elders in kirk sessions. Graham's study of kirk session records from St Andrews, Edinburgh, Canongate, Aberdeen, Anstruther Wester, Dundonald, Monifieth and Rothiemay shows that cases of slander and backbiting always formed a very small proportion of business. At St Andrews, for example, only ten cases were dealt with by the session between 1559–72 and this represented less than 4 per cent of the total caseload. Even in the later decades of the sixteenth century, when Graham argues that sessions considered a wider range of disciplinary business, it was still possible for some sessions (Aberdeen, 1573–78 and Monifieth sample years between 1579 and 1606) to ignore this category of discipline completely. In all the other

sessions, with the exception of Canongate where the figure was 23 per
cent, slander and backbiting accounted for 2–4 per cent of the cases considered.[85] It is perhaps hardly surprising that the unruliness of
Canongate, indicated by the number of notorious harlots, should produce an increase in individuals endeavouring to use the session to protect
their reputation. This is also incidentally, a further reminder, if one is
needed, that the most sexually notorious cannot be hived off and be
assumed to have no impact on other women around them.

Stirling is the only Scottish burgh for which a detailed study of the
treatment of scolds is available. Harrison's analysis shows that, although
the burgh ordinances specified the use of the branks or scold's bridle for
both male and female offenders, in fact usually only women were
branked, even when men and women were involved in the same incident.[86] In December 1644, for example, John Smith, his wife and sons
were warned that if they offended John Turnbull again the men would be
fined ten pounds and the woman would be branked. This case also highlights two characteristics of prosecutions for scolding in Scotland. First,
unlike in England where individuals were usually presented for being a
common scold and disturber of their neighbours, most Scottish cases
were initiated by someone who had been insulted on a particular occasion. Secondly, and here Scottish procedure was closer to that in England,
where, for example, a lesser penalty than being ducked was to have the
ducking stool placed next to one's front door, there was a carefully grad-
uated system of penalties that could be tailored to the gravity of the
offence and encourage the offender to conform in future. The individu-
alised nature of the Scottish system did, however, go further than the
English one in allowing the offended party more say in the punishment
of the defamer. It was common practice for the slanderer to be sentenced
to several hours in the branks on market day after which they were
expected to go and ask their victim's forgiveness at the place where the
scolding had occurred. However, in some cases the court could go further. In Glasgow in July 1584 Janet Foirside was found guilty of slander-
ing Margaret, the wife of William Flemyng, in the following terms, 'that
she had taken Duncan Leiche to a chamber and had lain with him and
he had used her as he thought good'. As a penalty, the court ordered that
Janet should be placed in the gyves and the branks should be put in her
mouth 'during the said Margaret Flemyng's will'.[87] Giving this power to
the offended party was not often explicitly stated in the record, but it was
a natural part of a system in which what was important was not simply that
certain set penalties could be exacted for each offence, but that the

outcome of the process would be the reconciliation of the parties, the vindication of the victim's honour and the exposure of the assailant to a sufficient level of shame. On occasion, of course, the local courts could get this balance wrong and inadvertently encourage aggrieved parties to take the matter into their own hands. A well-documented example of this comes from Nettleton (Wiltshire). In 1614 Margaret and Agnes Davis, who do not seem to have been closely related, were presented as common scolds for their longstanding quarrels with each other. The court decided that of the two only Margaret should be ducked which prompted her friends to get even with Agnes. At Christmas they entered her house, ate two mince pies and urinated in the pottage pot before dragging Agnes off to the cucking stool and plunging her into the river seven times.[88] Such cases of extra-legal action were unusual, although perhaps more common in England where there were obvious links with charivari and skimmington traditions, than in Scotland where traditions of dispute resolution, conditioned by the culture of feud, may have accommodated the levels of grievance of each party more effectively.

Scottish authorities certainly developed the theatre of shame and reconciliation into a fine art. In a device designed to focus the minds of less hardened offenders, individuals were not always sentenced to actually wear the branks. In Stirling in 1618 Helen Glook was ordered to kneel in the session house holding the branks in her hand and to ask for the pardon of God, the session and the woman whom she had offended. A different version of this idea was imposed on Margaret Algoe in 1631. The branks were to be carried before her as she went through the streets of Stirling to apologise to the people she had offended at their house. In such sentences different routes were even specified to increase the severity, through the Tolbooth, round the cross, the length of the main market, to the complainer's house and back, or the whole length of the town. For a first offence individuals could expect to be fined, subsequent offences usually involved the branks in some form, and the ultimate sanction of banishment seems generally to have been kept in reserve.

This pattern, observed most clearly in Stirling, was, however, not followed in all Scottish burghs. In Dundee in 1580 the Scottish system of punishment followed by the offender asking for forgiveness was adhered to, but the punitive device used was not the branks. Instead, before asking forgiveness, scolds were given the option of remaining in ward until they paid 40s or of being put in the cucking stool for three hours at the busiest time of day when their shame would be sure of attracting maximum publicity. In England patterns of punishment were even more varied. There was a general trend away from small monetary fines to physical shaming punishments, which paralleled that already observed for sexual immorality. However, some manors, for example Acomb (Yorkshire), continued to deal with scolds by exacting small fines. Jurisdictions that moved to physical punishments were likely to proceed against fewer scolds, and thus to single out only those whose behaviour seemed more serious. For their discipline the cucking stool was the standard expectation, at least in the view of authors of legal manuals, but it is also clear that many communities, including large urban centres like Southampton, were negligent in the erection and maintenance of these structures. There were also occasional scruples about ducking women in the winter months: at Dorchester (Dorset) in 1631 Mary Tuxbery was ordered 'to be plounced [ducked] when the weather is warmer'. Other forms of discipline, such as the carting of scolds, were also possible and in the seventeenth century the Scottish branks began to spread to England, although it seems never to have been adopted in the southern counties. Its use can be attested in Bridgnorth, Chester, Preston, Manchester and Newcastle, but this migration probably did not involve the adoption of all the features of Scottish disciplinary ritual.[89]

The variety of disciplinary approaches, together with the strong association of particular methods with certain offences, initially appears puzzling. If ducking was associated with scolding, why was that penalty sometimes deemed an appropriate means of disciplining harlots, or, even more surprisingly, a group of female enclosure rioters in Northamptonshire? Similarly, although the branks was generally reserved for scolds and slanderers in Scotland, there are also examples of its use for cases of sexual incontinence. For contemporaries, these offences, though distinct, were related. Each was a manifestation of disorder, and of an inability of the actors to exercise self-control, whether of their tongue or their sexual desires. Specific offences needed publicising, either by the type of discipline exacted or by forcing the culprit to wear a piece of paper detailing the offence, but they were all seen as part of the interconnected problem of disorder. Moreover, since the hierarchy of sexual relations was considered the cornerstone of all order, they could all be discussed in sexual terms. It was thus perfectly natural that the scold could be 'a whore of her tongue', and that writers of godly advice literature considered every omission of the duty of subjection on the part of the wife to bring her a step closer to adultery. It is, however, less clear that such observations, and the evidence of the disciplinary strategies that has been discussed in this chapter, justify the argument that the status of women, but not that of men, depended on their reputation for sexual honesty.

Gowing, who argues strongly for this position primarily from the evidence of defamation suits, goes on to assert that 'there was no way of calling a man a whore or condemning his sexual promiscuity'. Men, in her view, could only be labelled as cuckolds, and thus criticised not for their own sexual promiscuity but for that of their wives. The net result, she concludes, was that 'women remained the focus of sexual guilt and responsibility'. This argument raises several problems. Between a quarter and a third of defamation cases in Gowing's London consistory court material were brought against men, and of these slanders at least a third were clearly sexual. Moreover, contrary to what we might expect from Gowing's argument men rarely brought cases to protect their reputations from the insinuation of cuckoldry. In the London consistory court imputation of cuckoldry only constituted 19 per cent of slanders of men in 1572–94, and 17 per cent in 1606–40, and Ingram's statistics for Wiltshire, York and Ely in the late sixteenth and early seventeenth centuries produce a figure of only 10 per cent.[90] Slanders against women may have accounted for the bulk of court business, but when male reputation needed to be defended it was similarly most likely to be in terms related to their own sexual activity. The words 'whoremaster' and 'whoremonger', which were used to disparage male reputation, are disregarded by Gowing as simply accusing the man of being a pimp, but contemporary references also make it clear that they often referred to a man's promiscuity. Of course, this does not mean that 'harlot' and 'whoremaster' were completely equivalent terms: they could not be applied to members of the opposite sex. It is also true that the male terms describe the offence in relation to women, and to women of dubious sexual morality, whilst the term 'whore' defines female nature. But this distinction disguises the underlying similarity. It may be more significant to focus on the continuity of mastery and its debasement in the role of the whoremaster. Real male mastery occurs in the successful performance of the role of the male household head and involves a wider range of responsibilities than the mere sexual and/or financial satisfaction of a woman. The whore-master opts out of adult manhood. He retains mastery, but does not perform effectively or prove himself as a wife-master or a husband. Dominated by passion, rather than a mature acceptance of duty and responsibility, the whoremaster in this sense, no less than the harlot, is defined by sexual urges which lead him to neglect what society views as his true, and more difficult, role.

This did not, as we have seen, mean that no double standard operated in practice, but such assumptions were not axiomatic. Sexual reputation affected the standing of both men and women, but the pervasiveness of the language of sex as the most powerful image of disorder actually contributed to the dilution of its significance. Those Scottish women who wore their gowns and petticoats round their heads knew that they were not wanton women, even if such habits made their marital status opaque. Actual fornication or adultery could diminish their reputation, but chastity, as Dorothy Leigh realised, did not relate only to the sexual act but also to the due performance of housewifely duties. The two, of course, overlapped, and both could generate substantial concerns, the first nourishing claims and counterclaims of sexual dishonesty, and the second underlying many of the stories told by women in identifying witches in their community. But, at the same time, the language of sex was understood as a metaphorical one. When Dame Elizabeth Maxwell was excommunicated for popery by the presbytery of Dumfries in 1629 she was sent to prison in Edinburgh but initially refused to enter its gates, saying that 'her sentence of imprisonment did not class her with harlots, and that she neither would nor ought to associate herself with women of infamous life by inhabiting the same prison'.[91] In fact, both catholics and protestants recognised the theory that heresy was spiritual adultery – the soul which should be the bride of Christ had abandoned its husband for another – but neither side felt that religious defection was actually primarily sexual. It was another manifestation of disorder, and another reminder that all such acts were potentially interconnected and were symptoms of the failure of control, which could cause the entire edifice of society to crumble. The responsibility for that failure lay with women, but it also, and more disquietingly, could be seen to lie with men, who ought to be innately more able to rule themselves, and upon whom God had placed the duty of governing their weaker wives.

Chapter 4: Witchcraft, the Devil and the Elfin Queen

The stereotype of the witch as an elderly woman with a black cat, a steeple hat and a habit of flying around on a broomstick was gradually formed in the closing decades of the seventeenth century in a period in which belief in witches, or at least the prosecution of them, was in decline. By then the characteristic black hat was no longer part of contemporary fashion, being worn only by the old-fashioned, elderly, poor woman who fitted the image of the marginalised witch. Beliefs in witches, no less than the assumptions made about their modes of dress and transport, were continuously evolving and could differ markedly in different areas of Britain. In England the antecedents of the black cat lay in the assumption that the witch would have an animal familiar, whether a cat, ferret, toad or bumble bee. In Scotland such ideas were absent, and the identification of teats on the witch's body where such animals had sucked was replaced by searches for the witch's mark made when she had been nipped by the devil. It was here alone that the full prosecution of a witch required confession of a pact with the devil. Legal requirements encouraged the spread of elite demonological ideas in Scotland, but the law was not always such an effective stimulus for the diffusion of witch beliefs. Most strikingly, Wales witnessed very little prosecution of witches in comparison to England, despite the fact that after the Acts of Union both areas shared the same legal system. However, this was not because the concept of a witch was unknown: the word 'wits' was adopted by the Welsh to describe a category for which the rich Welsh vocabulary of magical practitioners had no equivalent. In Scotland similarly Lowland Scots terminology was absorbed in Gaelic-speaking Highland areas. These patterns suggest that there is no single history of witchcraft in Britain, but rather a plurality of interacting histories, which relate as much to regional cultures as to the well-worn theme of a popular-elite divide. They suggest the possibility of cultural areas in which greater or lesser emphasis was placed on black and white witchcraft, and of areas in which beliefs in elves and fairies were more significant in shaping conceptions of contact with the supernatural than the teachings of the Church and beliefs in powers of the devil.

Taking these suggestions as the starting point, this chapter will seek to assess the extent to which the experience of witchcraft was regionally distinctive, and the degree to which processes of acculturation had lessened these differences by the end of the period. The central preoccupation in the course of this analysis will be to assess the place of women in this process. Although evidence provided by prosecutions will inevitably form the basis of this discussion, the aim is to go beyond the agenda set by Larner's question, 'Was witch-hunting woman-hunting?'.[1] This is not only because, as Larner herself concluded, witchcraft prosecution was sex-related rather than sex specific, but also because capturing the significance of women's experience of witchcraft and the supernatural requires more than this. It requires imagining a world in which such beliefs were not only concerned with explaining misfortune in terms of vengeful acts of maleficium carried out by witches.

Belief in fairies, witches and the precepts of the established Church created a potentially cohesive world of explanation not only of misfortune, but also of the powers of particular individuals to heal or to predict the future. Considering one aspect in isolation risks producing a misleading picture. These systems of belief, although distinct, were fluid and overlapping: the witch who harmed could also heal; the curse of the witch, or of the curate, could bring retribution; the holly stick given by the fairies and subsequently blessed by the curate could be used to find lost treasure. However, despite these supportive interactions, fairies, familiars and demonic pacts were not easily interchangeable means of expressing and explaining the acquisition of powers of healing, harming and divining. In practice cooperative ventures were easier to envisage than conceptual substitutions. The latter was possible but it was not as easy as the shared aim of explaining the same practical outcomes seems to suggest. This was so because each mode of thinking was not simply about explaining why butter did not churn, why a cow or a child sickened and died, or why certain individuals had the power to locate lost or stolen property. Purkiss may be going too far in reading some narratives of witchcraft as covert ways for women to articulate their experience of incest, but she is surely right to wish to situate witch and fairy beliefs in a wider framework of understanding which reinforced and explored the conventions of gender in society.[2]

The contrasting roles assigned to women in the two different patterns of belief in Scotland make this point particularly clear. Each developed aspects of gender assumptions within Scottish society, but, whilst retaining a focus on women, allotted them distinctly different roles. In the first, the liminality of women in structures of marriage and kinship gave them a special affinity with the supernatural world of the fairies and made them natural recipients of requests from the wandering dead. The later development of a culture of witchcraft based on the demonic pact similarly saw women as particularly suitable agents of the supernatural, but its underlying rationale was totally different. This identification depended on disruptive notions of female vulnerability to temptation, sexuality and cursing. In contrast, the role of a woman who encountered one of the fairies could be seen in the restorative mode of the marriage alliance. Both systems of belief explained access to supernatural power and its effects, but, despite the weight of the state, Church and legal system, the supporters of the demonic pact could not easily erase fairy beliefs. To a large extent this was because such beliefs also said something important about gender, and could convey more positive messages about the role of women in family and society.

The most influential interpretation of witchcraft beliefs and prosecutions, the one developed by Thomas and Macfarlane, was not developed from this standpoint.[3] They were, of course, aware of the need to explain the preponderance of women among accused witches, but viewed this primarily as linked to their economically marginal position. In their interpretation, based on English evidence, and, in the case of Macfarlane, on a detailed study of Essex, the typical situation leading to the identification of the witch is a symptom of neighbourly tensions in fairly small-scale face-to-face communities. Animosities between neighbours were given an extra sharpness in the later sixteenth and seventeenth centuries as the institutionalisation of the local poor rate encouraged people to refuse informal requests for charity made by their neighbours. The continuing co-existence of ideas of neighbourly assistance did, however, make it difficult for people to view their negative response with equanimity. As a result, it is argued, the classic scenario was to displace one's guilt onto the alms seeker. In itself, this did not need to result in an identification of this person as a witch. Classification as an undeserving member of the poor, or conversely as someone too prosperous to be seeking alms, were both possible strategies that fulfilled the same psychological need. What potentially changed the situation was the need to explain an unexpected misfortune that afflicted the refuser or members of the family. Given the power attributed to curses in early modern society, the disgruntled mumblings of the alms seeker who had been turned away from the door empty handed could be graced with the dignity of a curse. Moreover, even if no words were spoken, the possibility of identifying the alms seeker as a witch still existed. All that was needed was to produce evidence of a grudge that would explain why the witch had attacked her victim since the malice of witches was assumed to be carefully targeted rather than random.

Although Thomas and Macfarlane provide little statistical evidence for this being the dominant scenario leading to the identification of a witch, there is no doubt that similar sequences of events frequently occur in the court record. However, this may not indicate its predominance in the process by which individuals made their neighbour a witch. It is also possible that this reflects the desire of the court to prove a motive in order to secure a conviction for a crime that by its nature could not be witnessed. In the same way as legal awareness encouraged those prosecuting witches in the seventeenth century to adapt to the judges' concerns to convict only when the witch's intervention had led to loss of human life rather than harm to livestock, basing one's case on the witch's response to the refusal of charity may have seemed the most effective strategy. Other forms of identifying witches also appear in the court record but are much harder to transform into an acceptable motive in the male world of the courtroom. The woman who commented on a child's good looks, offered him an apple, or joined other female neighbours visiting a woman in childbed, could, if the child subsequently sickened, be accused as a witch. Such coincidences, as they may appear to us, may have been as, if not more, important in crystallising the reputation of a neighbour as a witch. Moreover, although advocates of the refusal of charity mechanism often fail to recognise it, they had the same underlying psychological rationale.

Purkiss, approaching this from an understanding of a woman's role as the maintainer of boundaries, offers an important insight here.[4] During a woman's lying in period the safety of the household was most vulnerable as the housewife was unable to carry out her duty of policing the boundaries of the house effectively. The tradition of hospitality encouraged female visitors to the birth room, and made the access of suspect neighbours who may normally not have been allowed to cross the threshold difficult to control. A lurking fear of danger complicated by conflicting codes of obligation created a situation in which the child who sickened was not the responsibility of the skills of the midwife or of domestic standards of infant care and nutrition, but could be displaced onto the wicked female outsider so familiar from the world of folk tale. Similarly, the apparently harmless act of offering an apple to a neighbour's child could be seen as an implicit criticism of the care offered by the mother. The natural mother's anxieties that her child might see a neighbour as more of a mother than herself could increase as domestic tasks, the proof of her status as a housewife and a mother, began to go awry. It did not matter whether the insecurity was intensified by butter not churning, or by the inability to brew a good batch of ale, or by failures more directly related to the health of her children, the effect could be the same. Failure to keep the expected standards and maintain the ideal of housewife and mother could involve a terrible responsibility and loss of status both in the eyes of the individual concerned and those of her neighbours. As with the householder who refused a neighbour charity, there were ways of rationalising this and of blaming misfortune on the workings of fate, but these were ultimately less satisfying forms of displacement than the personalised scapegoat offered by the identification of a witch.

Seeing the process of the crystallisation of an individual's reputation as a witch in these terms, rather than concentrating on the consequences of the refusal of charity in a society in which different notions of obligation still coexisted, helps to explain some of the awkwardnesses that Macfarlane encountered in his detailed analysis of the Essex evidence. The emphasis on charity suggested that patterns of witchcraft prosecution should correlate with economic pressures, but he found it hard to fit his Essex data into such patterns. The geography of witchcraft prosecutions did not correlate with areas of dense or increasing population, or with levels of agrarian poverty. In Boreham the poor relief accounts maintained a healthy surplus while there were a number of prosecutions for witchcraft whereas in Heydon, where agrarian poverty was acute, there were no prosecutions. Moreover, there was no upsurge in cases in the 1620s and 1630s, decades of crisis for the cloth industry.[5] In part, the reason for this is, as Macfarlane realised, that it typically took a long period of time, often as much as ten years, for the identification of a witch to result in an attempt to deal with the problem by prosecution in the law courts. Suspicions took a long time to crystallise and in the interim other measures of dealing with the suspect witch in the community could seem more appropriate. Protestants may have frowned upon counter magic, but, judging by the frequency with which cunning folk are mentioned in the records, it was resorted to even in strongly protestant counties like Essex.[6] The second approach, that of appeasing the witch so that she should have no motives to cause harm to one's family, could be adopted whatever the strength of one's religious scruples. Given these options, a legal remedy was not the obvious first choice. In both Knaresborough and Pendle Forests, where the inhabitants conciliated the local witch clans for years, it was only the intervention of members of the elite that brought the witches to trial.[7]

However, such observations only account for the difficulty of synchronising the persecution of witches with particular periods of dearth or recession, and not for the generally poor correlation with areas with a high level of social strain. In the three Essex communities that Macfarlane studied in detail there were no presentments for scolding in Hatfield Peveril, the community that produced fourteen of the twenty prosecutions for witchcraft in the sample.[8] In fact, it may be more plausible, as Larner suggested, to see the kinds of neighbourly tensions that provided the motives for the witch's malefice as omnipresent in small communities.[9] Within this, particular tensions related to charity should not be given such a central position, even if they may have provided the best evidence for the court. Suspicions that a neighbour was a witch crystallised in overlapping, but nevertheless gendered, spheres. As Holmes has noted, prosecutions for witches were usually brought by men, even if women accounted for around half of those called upon to testify against the witch. The court was still primarily a male sphere, and a significant part of the process of identifying the witch took place in the female sphere as part of women's subconscious protection of their reputations as housewives and mothers. But, even if the court was not likely to give such tales lacking in convincing motive much credence, it is unlikely that their men folk felt so able to ignore them. That both spheres of concern counted in the local making of a witch and in the, usually communal, decision to prosecute explains why economic mappings of prosecutions will not work. A society that respected women's domestic skills, attached importance to birth rituals and churching, and saw both as female preserves could not consider women's allegations of witchcraft as mere old wives' tales.

This interpretation strengthens arguments for rejecting the notion that witch-hunting was a manifestation of early modern misogyny. Not only were women frequently the witnesses and victims of witchcraft, but a large part of the process by which witches were identified sprang from female anxieties about living up to the ideals prescribed for them in a patriarchal society. A feminist might label such women accusers as victims, but such arguments would not have made sense to contemporaries who generally accepted the status quo and tried to live up to its ideals. Moreover, the harder such ideals were to achieve, the more important it was to align oneself publicly in their support. The role of the anxious housewife who suspected a witch was no different than that of women who participated in charivaris when a wife had beaten her husband, or of women who accorded the scold, or the whore, an evil reputation.

Broadening the sphere of concerns for which the identification of witches was a remedial response also helps to explain why the majority of witches accused were women. If charitable assistance was primarily at stake there seems little reason why the psychology outlined by Thomas and Macfarlane would not have operated equally in the male world of requests for seed corn or the loan of tools and draught animals. But this was not the case, despite the greater ease with which men were able to bring cases to court. However, the disparity of social status between witch and accuser suggests that there was some role for economic factors in the pattern of prosecutions. Essex witches typically came from families of labourer or husbandmen status whilst their accusers were from the ranks of yeomen.[10] Unfortunately, this evidence cannot be easily compared with similarly detailed analyses of social status for other parts of England, and it may be that Essex was unusual in this respect. Its commercial links with London, and strong involvement in cloth production, may have caused a higher level of social polarisation that explains why here, in contrast to the pattern found in Wales and in Scotland, witches and their accusers were not of similar social rank. Social conflicts may have encouraged cases to be brought to the courts, but did not necessarily underpin the identification of the witch.

Whatever the importance of concepts of charity and their practice, the distinctive feature of the English witch was her malice. It was the disproportionate acts of harm inflicted deliberately upon her neighbours when she felt that she had been treated badly, or when she envied their prosperity and good fortune, which were the hallmark of the witch. However, and rather surprisingly, it was this aspect of the definition of a witch that proved difficult to disseminate. Historians of Welsh witchcraft argue that the principal concern was the practice of white witchcraft, especially healing, divining and the use of charms, and that the notion of the maleficent female witch was an English import that did not strike deep roots.[11]

Thus, when Robert Holland, the only demonologist to write in Welsh, published his *Dialogue on Witchcraft* in *c*.1595, the question of the legitimacy of beneficent magic was his main topic. This was not because of his lack of awareness of the theory of maleficent witchcraft or his lack of Calvinist commitment. Having been born into a Conway gentry family, he had studied at Cambridge and in the 1580s had acted as a preacher and schoolmaster in East Anglia before returning to Wales in 1591 to become rector at Prendergast, near Haverfordwest. However, unlike his brother Henry who remained in England and was responsible for disseminating continental ideas of the demonic pact, Robert's text adopted the popular form of a dialogue between two characters, Tudor and Gronow, and was rooted in his Welsh experience and drew on Welsh proverbs and customs of propitiatory sacrifice of animals. Robert Holland's emphasis on the dangers of beneficent magic was not an isolated phenomenon in Wales. The popular verses written by vicar Rhys Pritchard share the same preoccupation, with titles like 'Warning to the sick to beware of seeking help from sorcerers and wizards' and 'Against conjurors'. However, the works of both of these men had no counterparts amongst those produced by authors responding to the situation in England.[12]

In view of this discrepancy the gradual assimilation of the English term 'wits' or 'witsh' into Welsh in the later sixteenth and seventeenth centuries takes on a new importance. It seems plausible, as Suggett argues, that this does not merely represent linguistic mixing but the incorporation of a new notion of witchcraft. Based on an analysis of the definitions of various types of magical practitioners given in Holland's *Dialogue*, and comparisons with the use of Welsh and English equivalents in dictionaries and Biblical translations, Suggett concludes that what was imported was the figure of the malevolent female witch. From the mid-sixteenth century, earlier notions of sorcery carried out by men were gradually displaced and the English notion of a witch gained ground, due in part to its compatibility with the importance of cursing in Welsh culture. If accepted, these arguments suggest that economic structures and tensions between neighbours were less important in shaping the development of witch beliefs than inherited assumptions about the nature of supernatural powers and the sex of magical practitioners. For our understanding of Wales, and of other parts of Britain, it is worth re-examining Suggett's evidence.

In Holland's *Dialogue* there were three main categories of magical practitioners. The first consisted of prophets, soothsayers and interpreters of prophecy who were highly revered by the local elite and gained knowledge through divine inspiration. In the second group the figure of the charmer predominated, although in earlier times wise men and enchanters had similarly been called upon for information and to heal. Unlike those in the first group, charmers were not assumed to be divinely inspired, but owed their effectiveness to prayer and to their knowledge of herbs and charms. The last group comes the closest in Holland's classification to the English notion of a witch. *Rheibiwyr* were destructive despoilers whose actions were associated with envy and the power of the evil eye. A striking feature of this categorisation is the prominence of male practitioners. All those who claimed divine inspiration and enjoyed the highest social esteem were male. However, the other two categories witnessed a gradual feminisation, which may already have been underway by the time of Suggett's mid-sixteenth century turning point. Of the three categories of charmers, it was the ascendant group of *swynwr* that was given a female equivalent (*swynwraig*). Similarly, although it is clear from fifteenth-century charms against *rhaib* that the danger was perceived to be male, by the time Holland wrote the destructive *rheibwr* had gained a female form (*rheibes*).

Suggett's dating of the transition during the second half of the six-teenth century depends on the inclusion of 'wits' in William Salesbury's 1547 Welsh–English dictionary. His translation of 'wits' as *dewin-wraig* is certainly, as Suggett notes, a surprising formulation, but less for its definition of a witch as female than for the fact that it accords to women the most exalted status of prophet (*dewin*). In rejecting the options of *swynwraig* or *rheibes*, Salesbury's definition is far from conveying a 'sly misogyny'. Instead, it picks up on an idea of the great power of a witch without any pejorative overtones of harm. Outside the world of dictionary definitions, Salesbury's formulation was less useful. The general Welsh reverence for prophets made it an impossible translation for all those biblical passages condemning witchcraft or sorcery, and it was similarly unavailable as a term to defame one's neighbour. For the latter purpose 'wits' became standard in the seventeenth century, whilst translators, although preferring to use words of Welsh origin rather than foreign imports, showed no clear stability. *Rheibes* was preferred for the translation of the 1588 Bible and by Holland as a Welsh synonym for witch. *Hudoles*, defined by Holland in the 1590s as almost obsolete and as carrying overtones of juggling and deceit, could replace the more predatory *rheibes* in the 1620 Welsh translation of the Bible. Moreover, that in these cases female forms of words were chosen simply reflected the language of the original Hebrew.

Salesbury's definition may not have succeeded in according women the highest status as supernatural practitioners in Welsh society, but its concern to disconnect the word 'wits' from negative acts of malefice may have lasted for almost four decades. Although there were some witchcraft trials in Wales before the 1590s, the first prosecution for maleficent witchcraft took place in 1595 when Gwen ferch Ellis was indicted at the Denbighshire Great Sessions, not long after *rheibes* had been chosen for the Bible translation, and at about the time that Holland was writing. The main thrust for acculturation of the idea of maleficent female witchcraft may have occurred in Wales not in the mid-sixteenth century, but in its closing decades. It thus matched the peak of English prosecutions and coincided with more strenuous attempts to diabolise the powers of the witch. But even in the 1590s such ideas seem to have been weakly developed in Wales.

Gwen ferch Ellis was a *swynwraig* who gained her 'chief maintenance' from making plasters, salves and charms. As such she gave a valued service to the community, and like many others may have continued to practise undisturbed. Her misfortune was the activist agenda of the local bailiff rather than widespread community discontent and fear of her powers. Setting out to test her, the bailiff and several others arrived at Gwen's house where they demanded ale. Discontented by her refusal 'they somewhat abused her' and thus provoked Gwen to pray 'to her God' for revenge upon them. Within a few days, some of Gwen's uninvited visitors claimed to be suffering from various unusual ailments, and accused her of witchcraft. The details of the evidence presented by Gwen's accusers clearly demonstrate the difficulty they had in making what they had witnessed fit into an English tradition. Unable to find any obvious evidence that Gwen kept an animal as her familiar, they claimed that the fly they had seen in her house was 'bigger and more ugly than any other fly' and must have been 'her devil by which she works mischief'. However, although such observations were enough to sentence Gwen to death for murder by witchcraft, the activities of such people were not sufficient to implant many of the characteristics of English witchcraft in Wales. With the exception of the confession of a Cambridge-born female traveller in the late seventeenth century, no Welsh case would make any mention of a witch's familiar, an aspect that was so characteristic of English trials. In general, what rendered victims like Gwen vulnerable was the widespread practice of cursing, and the belief in its power. In the minds of her accusers, when Gwen 'prayed to her god', she was seeking the assistance of some diabolical power. In her mind, convinced of the justice of her position, she was appealing for divine intervention to assist the weak rather than the socially powerful.

Formal cursing by both men and women was a noticeable feature of Welsh culture, most frighteningly perhaps in the borderlands where the actual content of the torrent of words delivered by a kneeling woman could be incomprehensible. The churchwarden of Westhide (Herefordshire) who knew no Welsh, was disturbed by his encounter with Joanna Powell in 1617 who cursed him 'in Welsh language, kneeling down upon her bare knees and holding up her hands'. In theory such maledictions were perfectly orthodox. Despite the insinuations of Gwen's accusers, it was the curse of God that was sought. Thus, in 1613 Elizabeth Harris, the wife of William Walter of Tre-frân (Pembrokeshire) prayed that the curse of God might fall on Jane Walter, and trusted to 'see the day that Jane should not be worth a cow or a calf'. The response of Marsli ferch Thomas, when asked by William Lewis to explain why she and her children had cursed him in Flintshire in 1584, shows the same understanding of the process; 'If you deserve it God sends it to you, other-wise you shall not need to care.' Moreover, female cursers who bared their breasts whilst seeking retribution for a wrong modelled themselves on the supplicant figure of the Virgin Mary, an iconographical variant of the Marian cult that continued longer in Wales than in other parts of Britain.[13]

For divines and writers on witchcraft the invocation of God, rather than of the devil, offered no protection to the curser. Kilby's *The Burthen of a Loaden Conscience* that had reached its sixth edition by 1616 asserted confidently 'cursers are murderers' and gave the explanation 'for if it please God to let their curse take effect, the party cursed is murdered by the devil'. Thomas Cooper, who published his *Mystery of Witchcraft* the following year maintained the same position, noting that when the witch resorted to 'invocating on her bare knees (for so the manner is) the vengeance of God', the resulting evil was the work not of God but of Satan.[14] However, not only were such texts probably largely unknown in Wales, but their message was bound to run into difficulties given the strength of the sanction given to ritualised cursing by the Church. As Tyndale observed in the early sixteenth century, 'In the Marches of Wales it is the manner, if any man have an ox or a cow stolen, he comes to the curate, and desires him to curse the stealer; and he commands the parish to give him, every man, God's curse and his.'[15] The arrival of protestantism did little to change this: the commination service in the 1549 Prayer Book included scriptural curses against, for example, those removing boundary markers in fields. In fact, what mattered was not a position on whether or not cursing was sinful, but rather whether the curse's victim, and his or her neighbours, saw the ensuing misfortune as likely to have been in accordance with God's judgement. If so, the curse was a granted petitionary prayer, but if not, a special relationship between the curser and evil forces could be suspected, and, as the option became available, the curser could gain the reputation of a witch. However, creating witches in such a way, although possible, was always going to be a minor phenomenon. The tradition of ritualised cursing, and the custom that allowed women to curse both sexes and men to curse only other men, were not new developments in the sixteenth century. Moreover, the cursing woman was not Robert Holland's *rheibes* who made sacrifices, and it was as a *swynwraig* that Gwen ferch Ellis first attracted the attention of the witch-hunting bailiff.

This is not to say that the tradition of cursing and belief in the power of the curse was insignificant in shaping the nature of Welsh witchcraft, but it was a background feature that helped to consolidate the dangers for women inherent in the feminisation of charmers. It was also a contributory factor not unique to Wales. Most obviously, cursing retained an important, even if weaker, place in English culture. An incident in Gilden Morden (Cambridgeshire) in the late fifteenth century illustrates this well. A certain Thomas Perne reported a theft to his vicar who announced it in church and threatened to curse the thieves if the goods were not immediately restored to their owner.[16] In the English equivalent to Tyndale's observation about the practices of Welsh curates, issuing the curse was not the automatic response but a threat held in reserve. Nevertheless, if the thief failed to take advantage of the period of grace offered, it was still a threat with full religious sanction. Moreover, although in most cases the disgruntled mumblings of the putative witch who left her neighbour's house empty-handed are not recorded, some examples suggest a culture of cursing similar to that of Wales. The Essex witch, Elizabeth Lowys was reported as saying in 1564, 'if you be a saviour come down and avenge me of my enemies, or else you shall not be a saviour'.[17] In making Christ's assistance of her the test of his role in christian history, Elizabeth was worryingly close to crossing the bounds of orthodoxy, but, like the Welsh cursers, could still be considered as not having sold out to the devil.

The association of women with words, and of witchcraft with the socially powerless, increased women's vulnerability to accusations of witchcraft in both England and Wales but does not in itself explain their incidence. Although it suited Reginald Scot's sceptical position to claim that 'the chief fault of witches is that they are scolds', it is clear that contemporaries differentiated clearly between the two. Only one in five of those accused as scolds in Macfarlane's three Essex villages were also accused of witchcraft. In Scotland, Harrison notes the absence of presentments for witchcraft in Stirling, and speculates that the scold was the 'Scots urban witch'. If so, this was a very different species. Bad and quarrelsome neighbours were not the same as those who had access to supernatural power. More interestingly, Goodare, commenting on Scottish witchcraft cases in general, observes that 'hardly any male witches' were charged with malevolent cursing and that for 'even fewer' was it a central feature of their reputation. In contrast, and by way of an explanation, he notes that a higher proportion of men than women accused of witchcraft enjoyed a reputation as healers or cunning folk.[18]

A correlation between the sex of cunning folk and the varying proportions of men and women accused of witchcraft has often seemed an attractive hypothesis, albeit one bedevilled by the difficulty of identifying whether cunning folk in a particular area were predominantly men or women. Contemporary authors could come to startlingly opposed conclusions. According to Thomas Cooper, cunning folk were female, but John Stearne maintained that while black witches were nearly all women, cunning folk 'almost generally they be men'. Macfarlane's evidence from the Essex records (1560–1640) suggests a more complex situation. Of the 54 names just over two thirds were men. However, within this sample Macfarlane notes a gender specialisation that makes the significance of this male dominance less clear: 'while men were more likely to be presented at court, since they predominated in finding lost goods, and possibly as healers, women were often consulted in the attempt to counter witchcraft'.[19] From this evidence, if there was a connection between cunning folk and witchcraft, it seems that this was due to the belief that those who could unwitch could also bewitch: it was as specialists in counter magic, rather than divination, that women could be considered vulnerable. However, few women accused of witchcraft actually had a reputation as cunning women or charmers. If the connection operated at all in England, it was as a latent gendered association between women and the possibility of magical bewitchment. In Wales it may have had a greater importance, but it operated here almost by default. In a culture that was resistant to the development of other distinguishing characteristics of a witch, it was more likely that those few witches who came before the courts would be *swynwragedd*. The paucity of prosecutions in Wales provides in fact possibly the most powerful evidence for the general weakness of the correlation.[20]

Cursing and charming are the two elements Suggett uses to explain the pattern of witch prosecution and belief in Wales, and that both explanations seem quite insubstantial might be sufficiently explained by the low level of persecution in the area. However, there is another important element of belief in supernatural powers that needs to be considered in this discussion: the belief in fairies. Murray's attempt to prove that witchcraft was an extremely organised fertility cult formed Thomas and Macfarlane's principal target in their reinterpretation of witchcraft belief in terms of its social function. Their work has resulted in fairies being largely neglected by historians, if not by literary scholars. This bias is unfortunate, particularly in the case of Wales, a region in which contemporary commentators were convinced that fairies were held in 'astonishing reverence', but also in other parts of Britain. Reginald Scot might claim that the fear of witches had replaced the fear of fairies in England, but this replacement was far from complete. Moreover, it seems plausible that the distinctively English feature of the witch's animal familiar was originally connected with fairy beliefs, and remained so until the concerted puritan attempts to diabolise it in the late Elizabethan period. In the Highlands and Islands of Scotland witchcraft beliefs remained largely impervious to other interpretations.

John Penry's *A treatise containing the aequity of an humble supplication* (1587) was mainly concerned with attributing the failure of protestantism in Wales to the ignorance, absenteeism and immorality of the clergy which resulted in the continuing strength of old magic and catholicism. As he explained,

> Hence flow our swarms of soothsayers, and enchanters, such as will not stick openly to profess that they walk on Tuesdays and Thursdays at night with the fairies of whom they brag themselves to have the knowledge. These sons of Belial, who should die the death, Levit. 20. 6, have struck such an astonishing reverence of the fairies into the hearts of our silly people, that they dare not name them without honour ...[21]

Such imaginings were not just the figment of Penry's imagination: Henry Lloyd appeared before the Caernarvon Quarter Sessions in 1632 for communing with friendly fairies and spirits every Tuesday and Thursday night in order to make his neighbours rich.[22] Robert Holland's soothsayers may have gained their inspiration not from the divine, as he has Tudy claim in the *Dialogue*, but from fairies. In his debate with Gronow/ the author, Tudy may have been tactically given a more orthodox voice.

Whatever the case, reinserting fairies into Welsh beliefs may affect explanations of witchcraft in Wales. In contrast to conclusions drawn from
Scottish material, communing with fairies in Wales appears to have been
a male preserve, strongly connected with the elite type of magical practitioner, and with obtaining knowledge to use beneficently – Henry Lloyd's
meetings made his neighbours rich. Furthermore, although it seems
somewhat surprising, it appears that Welsh beliefs included no cantan-
kerous or ill-intentioned fairies, and thus were less easily transformed
into a belief in maleficent witchcraft.[23]

Wales lacked the Germanic tradition of malevolent elves that could
inflict mysterious illnesses and wounds on humans, which was commonly
believed in Anglo-Saxon England.[24] Instead, aspects of Welsh religious
beliefs encouraged a beneficent outlook in which saints and magical
practitioners shared some common attributes and there was a reluctance
to accept that sin merited harsh divine punishment. Saints were also seers
and healers, and manifested their power in ways that were virtually indistinguishable from magic. The abundant cow that supplied unlimited milk
to the neighbourhood could be provided by the fairies or by a saint, and
only stopped giving milk when her human beneficiaries broke the rules
and attempted to collect it in a sieve. Moreover, when confronted with
evil forces in the form of serpents, Welsh saints did not adopt the violent
tactics of St George, but overcame the beast by their spiritual presence,
and in the case of Samson by drawing a (magic) circle round it.[25] Penry,
bemoaning the slow progress of protestantism in Wales, noted that there
was little understanding of religion in terms of a struggle between the
forces of good and evil. Rather, people believed that God was bound to
save all men because they were all his creatures, or that all those under
the mantle of the Virgin Mary would be saved by her intercession at the
Last Judgement. In this outlook, savage cruelty was not the prerogative of
the devil, but of God the Father who punished sins too severely, even to
the extent of allowing the crucifixion of his own son.[26]

These observations may explain the difficulty of grafting the English
concept of the witch onto Welsh beliefs. The lingering idea that one
could be elf-shot may underpin the development of the English belief in
the witch's familiar. The absence of such beliefs in Wales may also explain
the difficulty of transforming *rhaib* from its mediaeval association with the
power of the evil eye into a belief underlying the power of the maleficent
witch to enact revenge when she felt wronged. The male reputation for
communing with fairies, and the vestiges of a belief in the innate power
of *rhaib* as male, may account for Morgan and Clark's observation that

in the witchcraft cases in which evidence of deliberate *maleficium* was presented the accused was usually not a man but a woman.

The plausibility of these conclusions can be tested to some extent by comparison with the situations in both England and Scotland. In the English case, Reginald Scot was clearly exaggerating when he claimed that the fear of fairies had been replaced by the fear of witches. Belief in fairies was still quite strong in Elizabethan England, even in the supposedly more sophisticated metropolis. In 1595 Judith Philips, a London cunning woman, was whipped through the streets for receiving large sums of money from credulous people who had been eager to pay her for the privilege of meeting the Queen of the Fairies.[27] In general though, despite the suggestion that figures like Robin Goodfellow, who gave positive assistance rather than helping to wreak vengeance, declined in popularity, fairies were often seen as sources of helpful knowledge. Joan Tyrry, a Somerset woman presented to the court at Taunton in 1555, maintained that the fairies 'taught her such knowledge that she gets her living by it'. By the power of God, the fairies had taught her to heal both people and animals, and acting on information given to her by the fairies she was able to publicly identify local witches.[28] John Walsh, a cunning man from Netherbury (Dorset) questioned at Exeter in 1566, claimed that his ability to know whether individuals were bewitched came from his acquaintance with fairies.

Yet, not all English fairies were helpful spirits, and it seems likely that there was some overlap between fairies and the idea of the witch's familiar. As John Walsh explained to his interrogators,

> there are three kinds of fairies, white, green and black, which, when he is disposed to use, he speaks with them upon hills where there are great heaps of earth, as namely in Dorsetshire. And between the hours of twelve and one at noon, or at midnight, he uses them, whereof, he says, the black fairies are the worst.[29]

The traditional belief in elves or sprites taking up residence in houses and disrupting the ordinary running of the household also suggests that the little people were not always thought to be a benign presence, even if such commotion could also be seen as appropriate punishment for a badly run household. Conversation with elves was also perceived as dangerous: in 1499 a Suffolk woman explained that her head had suddenly become twisted backwards after she had talked with 'the elves'.[30]

Nevertheless, there were still significant differences between the idea of consulting with fairies and the relationship of a witch with her familiar.

The transition to a situation in which a familiar was a pet animal kept and nurtured by the witch and used to harm her enemies was facilitated, but not fully explained, by the possibility of defining the familiar as a spirit. When John Walsh wished to find out about lost or stolen goods, rather than know who was bewitched, he did not consult with the fairies in the barrows of Dorset. Instead, using his 'book of circles', he conjured up his 'familiar spirit', which provided him with the information he sought. Other witches lacking magical books could envisage their familiars in the same way. According to the pamphlet account, Joan Willimot confessed,

> That she has a Spirit which she calls *Pretty*, which was given to her by *William Berry* of *Langholme* in Rutlandshire, whom she served three years; and that her Master when he gave it to her, willed her to open her mouth; and that presently after this blowing, there came out of her mouth a Spirit, which stood upon the ground in the shape of a Woman, which Spirit asked her for her Soul, which she then promised to it, being willed to do so by her Master.

However, both John Walsh and Joan Willimott were adamant that they did not use their spirit familiars to cause harm. Walsh's familiar spirit, which appeared in diverse forms including a dark grey pigeon, a brindled dog and a man with cloven feet, gave him information about stolen goods and served 'for no other purpose at all'. Willimott's only gave her updates on the health of the individuals whom she was trying to cure. Moreover, Walsh explained that when any of the three kinds of fairies 'did hurt' they 'did it of their own malignity, and not provoked by any man'. In addition, their victims were not entirely innocent since the fairies 'have power over no man, except those who lack faith, which is the reason why they have more power over some people than others'. It was a long way from this position to one in which familiars caused harm and were directed in so doing by their human nurturers.[31]

That this distance was travelled was due, in large part, to the intervention of the elites. The inclusion of nurturing animal familiars in the terms of the 1603 witchcraft statute did not create the phenomenon, but it focussed attention upon it. The desire for legally sustainable proof encouraged the idea that familiars were identifiable creatures of flesh and blood, and that witches could be identified by the teats on their bodies where their familiars had sucked drops of their blood. Related to this was the concern of divines to diabolise the witch's familiars, but this was always an 'uneasy synthesis', which suggests that this was not entirely their own creation. As Gifford asked rhetorically, if Satan and his minions were 'so mighty terrible spirits, full of power, rage and cruelties' why were they masquerading as 'such paltry vermin, as cats, mice, toads and weasels'. His answer, that the devil uses such disguises so as not to terrify prospective witches, pandered to the assumptions that witches were weak, foolish women, even if not quite explaining why this should be the case.[32] Moreover, as Gibson points out, the concern to diabolise witch beliefs coincided with a change in the type of story told in witchcraft pamphlets which gradually shaped popular beliefs. From the 1590s, pamphlet accounts became less dependent on recycling legal records and, freed from the need to supply the witch with a motive, painted the witch's victim as entirely innocent. As witch's familiars became emanations of the devil, so witches were painted as blacker figures.[33]

In these circumstances the witch's familiar was no longer a fairy, not even a malevolent one. The animal familiars that arrived in Elizabeth Bennet's house behaved like malicious fairies disrupting the running of the household and drinking her milk, but they had been sent by another witch, a certain Mother Turner, after Bennet had refused her request for some milk. But nor were they quite servant-demons completely under the witch's control. If the witch did not nurture them satisfactorily, they might pine to death or wander away and leave her. Furthermore, they might take it into their heads to carry out some malicious errand that she had not authorised on the excuse that the victim was the witch's enemy and that the familiar had been trying to please her. Purkiss observes convincingly that the witch–familiar relationship is modelled on the mother–child one with all its attendant anxieties.[34]

The connection between the witch's familiar and the world of malevolent fairies was therefore a complex one. The absence of malevolent fairies may explain why the Welsh were not receptive to the idea of the witch's familiar. However, familiars were also not a feature of witchcraft beliefs in Scotland where fairy beliefs might seem to have facilitated it. In Scotland, as in England, popular understanding of the supernatural was underpinned by the same ambivalence about the potential for good or ill to be gained from encounters with fairies. Nevertheless, in Scotland fairy beliefs appear to have been more resilient, perhaps as a result of the strength of the clan system. Although this impression may, in part, be due to the greater importance of witch's confessions in Scottish trial procedures, it seems unlikely that this accounts for the discrepancy. Those accused of witchcraft in Scotland were also subject to a much more vigorous campaign to view witchcraft in fully demonological terms, and yet resisted this pressure.

The case of Isobell Watson, who appeared before the Stirling Presbytery in 1590 charged with witchcraft, provides a good example.[35] Isobell, a poor widow of about 30 years old living in the parish of Glendevon, confessed that she got 'the mark on her head', which her accusers interpreted as the devil's mark, when she was 18 and had fallen asleep whilst tending sheep near her native Perth. But Isobell's story was largely an account of her relations with the fairy folk. While asleep,

> she was taken away by the fairy folk and remained with them for twenty-four hours, in the which time she said she passed through a rocky place under the earth into a fair house where there were people great and small.

It was when she was offered meat to eat that 'the king of the court' had made the mark on her head with some kind of oil. Nevertheless, it is unclear that for Isobell this represented the selling of her soul. The elf queen told her to 'reject God and stay with them because she would fare better', but Isobell returned to her sheep 24 hours later. It was only some time afterwards that she finally promised to serve them. Her dire poverty had encouraged her to leave her two-year-old son to be cared for by the fairies so that she could look after her husband and 'so that she might get her child back again she made a promise to serve them'. In doing so, 'she received their mark upon her head by one Thomas Mcray who is with them and who once had sex with her', and since then she had ridden out with the fair folk on each new moon. Even when explaining what her interrogators were convinced was the devil's mark, a woman as vulnerable and emotionally disturbed as Isobell could not be persuaded to describe her experience in clearly demonic terms.

The same was true of women who were more self-confident in their dealings with the fairies than was the case for Isobell who only sought to have her child restored to her and needed the human finger bone given to her by her aunt to protect her 'from all the blows of the fairy folk'. In other examples, talking directly to fairies could have severe adverse consequences, and yet, at the same time, the mortal individual could resist the fairies' demands whilst still continuing to profit from the relationship. Fairies, especially those who inhabited middle earth as unquiet souls who had met untimely deaths, had access to power and knowledge, but in their dealings with mortals could appear somewhat forlorn and powerless figures.

The trial of Bessie Dunlop in 1576 for using sorcery to find lost property and to heal the sick illustrates this well.[36] Bessie claimed that her

powers derived from a certain Tom Reid who had died at the Battle of
Pinkie (1547), but it is also evident from her confession that Tom was not
fully in control. He had appeared to her for the first time when she was emotionally vulnerable, bewailing the death of her cows and full of fear that her
sick husband and child would not live long. Nevertheless, at this first meeting
Tom did little to press home his advantage. Unlike the stereotypical devil he
did not promise the health of her family if she agreed to serve him. Instead,
invoking the Virgin Mary, he offered her words of comfort and gave an
orthodox religious interpretation of her troubles,

> Bessie you have provoked God, and asked for something you should
> not have done; and therefore, I advise you to make amends with him:
> for I tell you that your child will die, and your sick cow, before you
> come home; your two sheep will die too: but your husband will recover
> and will be as well and strong as he was before.

The next time Tom appeared, there was no invocation of St Mary or
explanation in terms of God's displeasure. Instead, he offered her horses,
cattle and other goods if she would renounce her baptism. To this Bessie
replied firmly, declaring 'That if she were dragged at the horse's tail, she
would never do that', but also promised 'to be loyal and true to him in
any thing she could do'. Tom was 'somewhat angry' with her response,
but it did not mean the end of their relationship. He told her what herbs
to use to cure sick people, gave her a special beetroot from which she
could make a healing powder, and told her who had stolen people's property. This help seems to have continued even after Tom appeared to her
accompanied by eight women and four men who dwelled in the Court of
Elfame. These asked her to come with them, and, when she was dubious,
Tom added the extra enticement that just as he enjoyed better clothes,
food and life than he had previously so she would see her position much
improved. But Bessie was unconvinced, answering 'That she lived with
her own husband and children, and could not leave them'.

The strength of Bessie's position, and of those like her, in their
relations with the fairies lay in the fact that the fairy folk with whom they
communicated were seen as partly human. They were the wandering
dead who, like the ghosts in mediaeval catholic exempla, needed human
assistance. Although Bessie had never known Tom Reid during his life,
she was certain that it was he who appeared to her because

> He bade her go to Tom Reid, his son, now officiar in his place, to the
> Laird of Blair, and to certain other of his kinsmen and friends there,

whom he named; and bid them to restore certain goods, and to make amends for other offences that they had committed.

Conceptualising relations with fairies as being of a lasting reciprocity, in contrast to the assumptions that underpinned ideas of the power of the devil and the nature of the demonic pact, allowed mortal women to keep a significant degree of control. It also suggested that those to whom fairies would appear would, by and large, be women. As liminal figures and as kinship-maintainers women were obvious allies for the wandering dead. Moreover, the realm of the fairies was imagined as being presided over by the Elfin Queen and as a world of female power and influence in contrast to this world. The highest accolade that the fairies could bestow upon Bessie Dunlop was the appearance to her of the Elfin Queen while she lay in childbed.

These observations suggest that this system of belief was only tangentially related to the pattern of witchcraft prosecution. The world of fairies was a world of female power and provided a more effective fantasy of inversion than witchcraft beliefs fostered by demonologists. Despite Clark's insistence that contemporaries imagined witchcraft in terms of inversion,[37] the witches' sabbath and her relations with the devil in the demonic pact replicate more closely the real world of male authority than was the case in the fairy realm. Thus, although it might seem that beliefs in the female affinity with the fairy world may have encouraged ideas that women would be witches, from the perspective of women this option was far from as attractive. In the world of the demonic pact, the devil, not the witch, was in control. The witch could, it is true, usually determine who should become the victim of her maleficium, but in her relations with the supernatural she was under the control of the male devil. Goodare points out that in Scottish witchcraft confessions the devil appeared to female witches when he wanted, but some male witches were able to raise the devil themselves at will. Alexander Hamilton, for example, used his enchanted baton to summon the devil and could exchange blows with him. Similarly, the tradition of the witch's mark emphasised female inferiority. It was female witches, rather than male ones, who would confess that their mark was 'in their privy parts'.[38] In responding to their interrogators' suggestions, they were contributing to a much more sexualised understanding of female witchcraft. In doing so, they accentuated the inferiority of the female relationship with the devil. By contrast, although the logic of inversion identified by Clark as the organising principle of demonological thought would seem to demand it, male witches did not confess to sex with the devil. Instead, in the few cases in which in the male imagination the encounter with the devil was lightly sexualised, the devil took female form. In 1605 Patrick Lowrie described how 'the devil came as a woman named Helen McBrune. She gave him a belt with four claws like the devil's'.[39]

The awkward fit between the gender assumptions that underpinned relations with fairies and those of an intensely proselytised belief in a demonic version of witchcraft may also explain why more men were accused of witchcraft in Scotland than in England. The example of Finland shows that a tradition of male cunning men and male witch prosecution could be transformed into one of female witches with the arrival of demonological ideas.[40] For demonologists, women, as daughters of Eve, were the devil's natural targets. The competing strengths of these two traditions explain why it was the case both in Finland and Scotland that when accused witches were forced to name new suspects during witch-hunts the proportion of men accused was much lower than in the isolated trials arising from individual communities.[41] As Goodare notes, male witches in Scotland were either married to witches, or were folk healers or notorious criminals. Although women had a special affinity with fairies and the wandering dead, Alexander Hamilton's enchanted baton provides a reminder that much of the explanation for the high figure in British terms of 20 per cent of accused witches being men may be due to the Scottish equivalent of those Welsh male soothsayers who consorted with fairies on Tuesday and Thursday nights. That their Welsh counterparts did not attract the same degree of legal attention need not relate to the different basis of folk belief, but to the simple fact that, compared to Scotland and to a lesser extent England, the hand of government and of religious zeal was lighter there.

In the decades immediately following the passing of the 1563 witchcraft statute in Scotland very few cases were presented, leaving historians to speculate that the passing of the Act was motivated simply by a desire for legal 'tidying up'.[42] But, as Larner suggested, as kirk sessions and presbyteries became more established, the prosecutory potential of the Act could be more fully realised. In this process King James's intervention and the high profile North Berwick witch trials provided an influential stimulus and encouraged the dissemination of demonological ideas. However, as Wormald has argued, they did not trigger this process: in the North Berwick trials a demonological element was introduced by the bailie depute of Tranent, David Seaton, before James VI became involved.[43] The tradition in Aberdeenshire and elsewhere of dedicating a piece of fallow land to the devil also shows the extent to which belief in the devil's power was entrenched in popular culture.[44] A growing interest in witchcraft prosecution predates these cases and those wishing to advance a prosecution could take advantage of the wide terms of the witchcraft Act of 1563. This allowed for the possibility that not only witches but also those who consulted them could be sentenced to death, and, unlike in England, its terms embraced the use of witchcraft to heal and harm. Prosecutions of witchcraft may have been more the result of elite direction in Scotland than in other parts of Britain, but this was the responsibility of zealous Calvinists, both clerical and lay, as much as, if not more than, of the Crown. Under their leadership, the connection between sin, witchcraft and the devil was more tightly drawn than any-where else in the British Isles. Some leniency in this system was possible, but the example of Nicol Dalgleish, minister of Pittenweem who was accused in 1597 by his parishioners of being too slow to prosecute witches indicates the difficulties of adopting a more moderate approach.[45]

The victims of this intense Calvinist culture were not only peasant women who suddenly found themselves caught up in prosecutions of demonic witchcraft, but also members of the godly elite. In recounting the stages of her religious development, the Scottish puritan, Mistress Rutherford, explained how she had come to fear that she might be a witch. As a twelve-year-old suffering from measles, she had felt the first stirrings of religion within her. The experience was one not of joy, but of terror. Her sense of her personal worthlessness led her to fear that the devil would snatch her away and made the idea of suicide seem increas-ingly attractive and a fate that seemed only avoidable if she could contrive to die by a less sinful means, as an innocent victim of war. These feelings intensified, despite the support of friends and family, and her view of herself as evil and worthless crystallised in the self-perception that she was a witch. It was only, as she was ashamed to admit later, when a fortune-teller predicted that she would live to an old age that these fears began to recede.[46]

Mistress Rutherford's story is remarkable. The devil and witchcraft loom larger in her writing than is the case in other puritan autobiographies. Consciousness of human sinfulness was, of course, a common theme, but most, like Bessie Clarksone, were content simply to acknowledge them-selves as a 'wretched, sinful and wicked woman'. Nevertheless, Rutherford's narrative serves as a helpful reminder of the reality of witchcraft, and the ease with which, at least in Scotland, godly struggle against the devil could convince an individual that she was a witch. It also serves as a reminder of the intensity with which witchcraft beliefs could be experienced. Although she was presumably aware that a compact with the devil was the official cornerstone of the making of a witch, for Mistress Rutherford her ungodly obsession with thoughts of suicide seemed to provide sufficient proof. Unlike those who explained infanticide and other crimes as carried out by the instigation of the devil, she did not simply see herself as the target of the devil's onslaughts. The fusion of the recognition of her sinfulness, and her vulnerability to the devil, resulted in a belief not only in her own frailty, but an identification of herself as a personified figure of evil. In doing so, she created a version of witch self-belief that does not seem to be empowering. Turned inward and focussed on her attraction towards, and fear of, taking her own life, it was a metaphor for her own loss of control.

Yet, the relationship between witchcraft and fairy beliefs with ideas of female empowerment is a complex one. In believing that she was a witch, Mistress Rutherford also shed some of the responsibility for her own depression: she was in the grip of forces much larger than herself. The problem of determining the appropriate terms with which to describe Mistress Rutherford's experience bedevils all efforts to assess whether such beliefs should be seen as positive for women. They did, after all, give them social power that they would have otherwise been unable to attain. The idea of witchcraft validated female weapons of words rather than deeds and strengthened their significance. The witch who directed acts of maleficium towards her neighbours, however her supernatural powers were believed to have been obtained, had agency and power that suggested to her, and to others, that she was in control, and that appeasement could be the right response. Moreover, similar arguments of empowerment could operate for both the witch and her accuser. Identifying one's neighbour as a witch gave women a way of displacing the responsibility for their housewifely failings onto another woman. Paradoxically, by surrendering control in acknowledging the existence and action of witchcraft both the witch and her accuser were able to claim a degree of control over their situation. To a large extent fairy beliefs did the same thing, even if often in a more positive way, since the female characteristic they validated was not the power of words. Indeed, talking directly to fairies could be both dangerous and presumptuous. In validating the instrumental role of women in reconstructing social harmony, and in offering a positive model of an alternative world ruled by women, fairy beliefs can be seen as enhancing the position of women. However, both were worlds that had their dark sides. The devil's promises of support could often turn out to be hollow. Isobell Watson understood her infanticide trauma in the language of fairy beliefs, but this mode offered little comfort, despite the reputation of the fairies in caring for abandoned children.

However this balance sheet is drawn up, and much depended on the emotional and psychological state of the particular individuals involved, it seems clear that the period saw an increased vulnerability in all parts of Britain, albeit with different patterns and causes. Perhaps the greatest challenge occurred in Scotland where fairy beliefs had to coexist with a militant demonological interpretation. That this was so was due most obviously to the uncompromising characteristics of the Scottish Reformation. But fairy beliefs, cast in kinship terms, were also vulnerable to any kind of protestant change that would cast doubt on the idea of the wandering dead and the ability of the living to help them make amends. Beyond religion, the gradual transformation of the clan system would have helped to make fairy beliefs in Scotland as lacking in resilience as those in England. In Wales, the challenge, conceived in terms of imported maleficent witchcraft beliefs, found less fertile ground. This was due, in perhaps equal measure, to the strength of an almost exclusively beneficent magic tradition and to the weakness with which protestantism, and its attendant witchcraft message, were promulgated in Wales. But Wales also experienced a more subtle form of increasing vulnerability. From a world in which all practitioners of beneficent magic were male, women gradually gained an acknowledged place amongst the ranks of charmers. From this advance, it also became more possible for women to be categorised as *rheibes* and for innate *rhaib* to be confused with maleficent witchcraft. But the danger in numerical terms remained slight, and was strenuously policed by women more than men. Seventeenth-century cases for slander as 'wits' were brought only by women against other women. In England, by contrast, women and men appeared equally in such cases. It is in England too that the gender implications of witchcraft belief are most ambivalent. Prosecutions uniting both male and female concerns about the perceived workings of magic in local society nevertheless privileged a male agenda. The strength of the stereotype of the witch as a woman, whether deluded, vindictive or innately evil was not counterbalanced by strong views of women as healers and diviners. Their reputation as specialists in counter-magic, rather than divination, did little to salvage their reputation. Nevertheless, in the long term it was this same pitiable, feeble image of the female English witch that would encourage elite scepticism that such figures could really be the agents of the devil.

Chapter 5: Female Piety and Religious Change

It was a commonplace in early modern culture that women were 'to piety more prone'.[1] The stereotype of the godly woman was a natural part of the idea that the soul and the true church were brides of Christ. Conversely, of course, the false church of Antichrist was the Whore of Babylon. Following this model, protestants could describe the popish mass as Mistress Missa, whilst the reformed communion was a 'simple maid'.[2] However, as well as being a useful metaphor to convey the stark contrast between good and evil, the general association of women with piety was descriptive of actual practice and was rooted in the characteristics associated with gender. The nurturing, emotional female could be the ritual specialist in a catholic world, and was also particularly well suited to making the leap of faith required for true devotion in both confessions. However, although this means that the upheavals of the Reformation were particularly important for women, the impact of these changes, and the comparative attractiveness of different religious positions, is less clear. Even in broad terms the balance sheet of the effect of the Reformation on women is hard to draw up. In many ways, protestantism might be thought to have created a religious environment that was hostile to this style of female piety. In dispensing with the cult of the Virgin Mary and the saints, protestantism removed influential models that attested to the possibility of female sanctity. At the same time, its attack on intercession, whether for the salvation of souls or for curing a sick child, denied the legitimacy of the practical acts of devotion that had been most closely associated with the devotional sphere of the female. Furthermore, as a religion of the word in an age in which female literacy lagged significantly behind men's, the demands of protestantism left women poorly qualified. Against this list of 'losses' the attractions of protestantism might seem slight indeed. The assertion of spiritual equality and the priesthood of all believers could count as positive developments, but it was quite clear that they should not entail any notion of social equality. The patriarchal family was not a creation of protestants but their teachings did little to shake its foundations. The re-evaluation of the status of sacred virginity may have been more important. The closure of monasteries and nunneries was a highly visible statement, and since marriage was the fate of most women the raising of its status from a second best religious option supports the claim that the Reformation improved the lot of women.

But this balance sheet is inadequate in many ways, even if it does provide some insights that explain why it was possible for women to become tenacious adherents of either faith. Each item, when examined more closely, had a different value in the various parts of Britain. The 'loss' of the Virgin Mary presumably meant more in Wales, where, as well as being a nurturing mother, Mary was also the figure most relied upon to secure the salvation of the soul, than it did in England where the development of a particular form of Christocentric piety resulted in the displacement of Mary and the saints. Similarly the significance of the attack on nunneries must have appeared differently in Wales where there were only about 35 nuns on the eve of the Dissolution than it did in England where the population of female religious numbered between 1500–2000.[3] But it is also possible to suggest that focussing on nunneries is misleading. The significance of sacred virginity and of the idea of godly women as brides of Christ was more similar in England and Wales than it was in Scotland where the reputation of virgin saints was stronger, and consequently it was only in Scotland that leading protestants enthusiastically embraced imagery from the Song of Songs. As these examples suggest, to assess the impact of religious developments on women in Britain we need to define more closely the regional nature of later mediaeval and Reformation Britain. The different processes of institutionalisation of the Reformation in England and Scotland make the latter self-evident, but just as there was no single experience of the Reformation so there was no single brand of late mediaeval piety upon which protestantism could be superimposed.

Whatever the precise nature of the religious transition, it is clear that women could be enthusiastic and staunch supporters of catholicism, but could also be attracted in significant numbers to protestantism, and to its precursor lollardy. In discussing the Reformation in England, Brigden has drawn attention to the attraction of the early revolutionary phase of protestantism to young people for whom it provided opportunities to rebel against authority.[4] Similar considerations can also account for the participation of women, whose position was also defined in terms of subordination, whether to husband or parents. Thus, according to Henry Machyn, the sermon preached by Dr Bourne, the chaplain of Mary I, at Paul's Cross in 1553 was greeted with

> great uproar and shouting at his sermon, as if it were by mad people, what young people and women as ever was heard, as hurly-burly, and casting up of caps.[5]

Of course, such descriptions may be misleading. Young people and women were thought to be endowed with less reason than men and it therefore suited a chronicler with catholic sympathies to portray those disrupting Bourne's sermon in this way. It was a handy polemical device, and one which could be deployed by both catholic and protestant commentators alike.

However, that strong female commitment to both religions was not simply a handy myth in the service of polemic is suggested by the part women played in resisting aspects of religious policy. When the protestant Edward Underhill attempted to remove the pyx from the altar of the chapel of Stratford le Bow during Mary's reign, he was obstructed by the wife of Justice Tawe and other women of Stepney.[6] In Exeter in 1536, the resistance to the dismantling of the rood loft at St Nicholas Priory by two Breton carvers seems to have been carried out by women.[7] At Stoke by Nayland (Essex) although both the men and the women of the parish initially refused to receive catholic mass, all the men took advantage of the 16-day amnesty and conformed. The women were more steadfast in their resistance and managed to escape punishment when the bishop's officers arrived by going into hiding.[8] Perhaps most famously, even if the story of Jenny Geddes throwing the first stool in St Giles' Kirk is not documented in contemporary sources, women began the opposition to Charles I's imposition of the Prayer Book in Scotland in 1637, which led to the Covenanting movement and to the outbreak of the Civil War.

All these examples are, however, less straightforward than they first appear. In Exeter the authorities were reluctant to believe that a group of mere women had caused the undignified flight of the Breton carvers from the Priory church. In February the Mayor and Sir Thomas Denys reported to the Marquis of Exeter that they had examined 'a great number of women who were among others the chief doers of the said unlawful assembly and also diverse of their husbands', who denied that 'there were any men disguised or dressed in women's clothing amongst them' and that 'they were commanded, procured, advised or abetted by their husbands or by any other men'.[9] Whether or not the Mayor and Sir Thomas Denys were correctly convinced by the testimony they were given will, of course, never be known, but the nature of their enquiry draws attention to the legal loophole which meant that female rioters could be punished less severely than men if it could be demonstrated that they had acted without being incited to do so by any member of the opposite sex. One of the ironic advantages of women's reputation for emotional weakness was that they could not be held to be as responsible for their actions as men were. This raises the possibility that women's participation in incidents like that at Exeter was simply a useful legal tactic.

It is clear that this legal position was known and could be exploited in riots designed to advance economic causes. How else to explain the actions of male enclosure rioters at Ystrad Marchell (Montgomeryshire) in 1569 who carried out their action dressed in women's clothing?[10] However, it does not seem that this was a guiding principle in popular protest generally. Women, led by Ann Carter a butcher's wife, did take a key role in the grain riots at Maldon (Essex) in 1629, but, although the first disturbance of that year was apparently carried out entirely by women, the second, which took place a few months later when economic conditions had deteriorated further, was carried out by men and women despite keeping the same leader.[11] Lindley's study of Fenland riots in the early seventeenth century shows that examples such as that at Soham (Cambridgeshire) in 1629 in which a crowd of two or three hundred women threw stones at the drainage commissioners were not typical of Fenland protest generally. Instead, when women participated it was usually as part of a male plan and in association with them. The ostensibly independent female action at Soham was less typical than the action at Haxey on the Isle of Axholme the previous year when women took the lead in distracting the workmen with threats so that their menfolk could approach from the rear unnoticed and pelt them with stones. However, other female rioters thought, or at least were believed to have thought, that their sex gave them some immunity. Enclosure rioters in Dorset in 1619 thought that no legal sanction was possible since they were but women and boys, and female rioters in Rotherham (1606) considered 'themselves lawless because they were but women'.[12] However, the actions of a group of women who pulled down an enclosure in Northamptonshire show how far this could be from an instinctively deployed ruse. These women deliberately dressed themselves in male clothing to carry out their demonstration, and were punished in Star Chamber for 'putting off that shamefacedness which befits their sex'.[13] From this evidence, it seems unlikely, at least in England, that the prominence of women's participation in acts of disorder designed to impede unpopular religious practices was simply a cunning tactic to make a point whilst evading the full rigour of the law.

In Scotland, the context was different. There was no highly developed custom of popular protest. Enclosure was less of an issue, and, as Lynch argues, the intensity of price and trade regulation in Scottish burghs meant that discontent, if it occurred, was confined to producers and retailers whose livelihoods were threatened, rather than involving hungry and impoverished consumers.[14] In this situation religious protest was as likely to borrow from the practices of clan warfare as it was to be modelled on the demonstrative gestures of moral codes of protest. When, for example, the Sinclairs wished to ensure the performance of catholic marriage ceremonies for several of their number in 1561, their tactic was to seize control of the appropriate location in Birsay by force and install a priest to perform the necessary rites.[15] In such practices the participation of women was no advantage. But they did have a role in appealing for compensation as representatives of kin who were victims of feud. The procession of poor women from Nithsdale who reached Edinburgh in 1593 carrying the bloody shirts of their slain kinsmen were using a traditional mode of appeal.[16] It is not inconceivable that the association of women and piety could have encouraged women to participate in religious protest.

It seems likely, however, that the famous incident against the Prayer Book in July 1637, although carried out entirely by women ostensibly spontaneously, was part of a larger opposition plan. Henry Guthrie, an opponent of the new liturgy who signed the Covenant in 1639, described the events in his diary as follows,

> No sooner was the service begun, but a multitude of wives and serving women in the several churches, rose in a tumultuous way, and having prefaced awhile with despiteful exclamations, threw the stools they sat on at the preachers, and thereafter attacked them from closer range, and strove to pull them from their pulpits, whereby they had much ado to escape from their hands, and retire to their houses.

but went on to explain that,

> This tumult was taken to be but a rash emergent, without any prede-liberation; whereas the truth is, it was the result of a consultation at Edinburgh in April, at which time Mr Alexander Henderson came thither from his brethren in Fife, and Mr David Dickson from those in the west country; and those two having communicated to my lord Balmerino and Sir Thomas Hope the minds of those they came from, and gotten their approval thereto, did afterwards meet at the house of Nicholas Balfour in the Cowgate, with Nicholas, Eupham Henderson, Bethia and Elspa Craig, and several other matrons, and recommended to them that they and their adherents might give the first affront to the book, assuring them that men should afterwards take the business out of their hands.[17]

However, even if these events were orchestrated and were given encouragement and the promise of support from influential men, groups of women continued to be to the fore in disrupting ministers who were loyal to the King and to his liturgy. At the Synod held at Glasgow in August, William Annan, the minister of Ayr, aroused the wrath of the women of the town for his use of the Prayer Book, and in the evening when he was on his way to meet the Bishop 'some hundreds of enraged women, of all qualities are about him, with fists, staves and peats, but no stones: They beat him sore; his cloak, ruff and hat were torn: however because of his cries, and the candles lit in many windows, he escaped all bloody wounds; yet he was in great danger even of being killed.'[18] Other ministers also suffered at the hands of women during the following year. The Bishop of Galloway was harassed by women in Edinburgh, Stirling and Dalkeith, and the railing at him by the wives of Falkirk was interspersed with volleys of stones. At Lanerick the women's victims were Robert Hamilton and John Lindsay, at Kinghorn they set upon Monroe, who was thought to be a spy in the service of the bishops, and at Collingtone female members of the congregation showered blows upon their own minister because of his insistence that they should answer his examination before being admitted to communion 'on their knees, as the priests do in their shriving'.[19] In all these examples, although the women taking part may have been encouraged to do so by the knowledge that local male elites would be unwilling to prosecute, this was a result of sympathy with their cause rather than a specific idea of greater legal immunity.

Nevertheless in both England and Scotland, as also in Wales, women, especially those who were married, had a greater freedom to exercise their religious preferences than men. The story of the resistance of the women of Stoke by Nayland in the reign of Mary I points in this direction, even if the legal clarification was an Elizabethan development. The women may have been largely successful because they concealed themselves from the bishop's officers, but the ingrained notion that the family was the microcosm of the state also raised questions concerning the regime's right to discipline women in matters of conscience who were under the authority of their husbands who had now chosen to conform. Disciplining married women therefore infringed the husband's authority and property, even if it could also be argued that it was the duty of the male household head to ensure his family's religious conformity. Thus, although modern observers might view women being under couverture as an indignity, it could also, paradoxically, provide a greater freedom of action.

This process can be illustrated most clearly with reference to recusancy, or refusal to attend the services of the established Church. The underlying assumptions of male household authority can be seen most clearly in the Scottish evidence, whilst the regime's legal wrestling with the consequences of couverture is easily visible in the recusancy legislation passed by the English parliament in the late sixteenth and early seventeenth centuries. The early-seventeenth-century records of the attempts of the kirk session of Dumfries to chase up non-communicants are particularly revealing. The list of those presented in 1606 contains men only, and when their excuses for absence were examined the failure of wife and children to attend the kirk was taken as supporting evidence for the man's wilful recusancy. In May, for example, the session heard the case of Adam Kersan, a bailie who claimed that he had been out of town at the time of divine service. The session was unwilling to accept his excuse, believing that he, being but seven or eight miles away from Dumfries, could have made the effort to attend had he so desired. They concluded, 'And because his wife and family were also absent from the communion without the same excuse, not only was he found guilty of absenting himself wilfully but also as the author of the same fault in them'.[20]

In England from the time of Elizabeth's Act of Uniformity onwards, the law opposed the idea that church attendance was only incumbent upon the male household head. Nevertheless, during the first decades of Elizabeth's reign, courts like the Northern Court of High Commission, which attempted to force husbands to make their wives conform, or at least to pay their fines for them, faced an uphill struggle. The official position was strengthened by the 1581 'Act to retain the Queen's

Majesty's subjects in due obedience' which authorised JPs to indict recusant wives but not to fine them since in law a married woman had no property of her own. Only if she became a widow could her property (two-thirds of her dower or jointure) be seized. Otherwise, the only course of action available to the justices was imprisonment, but this was an option that was only really viable if recusants were able to pay for their keep whilst in gaol: in Cheshire in 1582 many recusants of both sexes were released on bond due to their poverty. Heightened fear of catholicism in the immediate aftermath of the Gunpowder Plot (1605) resulted in the introduction of the oath of allegiance and gave the authorities greater powers regarding married women. But, as Rowlands notes, this went against the grain of seventeenth-century sensibilities and by the 1620s the oath was rarely tendered to women.[21]

The difficulties faced by the authorities in securing the religious conformity of women by legal means must be borne in mind in any interpretation of recusancy statistics as indicators of the religious preferences of men and women. Lists of catholic recusants in both England and Wales routinely include significantly more women than men. In the 1615 visitation of Yorkshire, for example, only one-third of those presented were men. In some parishes, as at Drax (9) and Aughton (4), only women were listed. Even in parishes where recusants were numerous, women still predominated: at Easington 27 of the 32 recusants were female.[22] Similar statistics could be cited from other regions of England and also from Wales where the number of recusants presented was generally lower. In Pembrokeshire in 1624, for example, ten people were presented as recusants, all but one of them women.[23] However, although such figures were once seen as indicating a greater female attachment to catholicism, historians are now more inclined to see them as an effect of the legal position of women and the strong reluctance of officials to interpose their power between the male household head and his wife in matters of conscience. The resulting lighter treatment of female recusants meant that the presentment of a few women was an attractive option for local elites that needed to present some catholic recusants to show willing, but wished to minimise the consequences of this for their neighbours.

However, there is some evidence that suggests that women were more committed to catholicism than men were. The reports compiled by members of the Franciscan mission to the Western Isles of Scotland in the early seventeenth century may have exaggerated their success in securing conversions, but they had no reason to inflate the number of women returning to the faith. It also seems that women were principally involved in supporting the network of priests necessary for the maintenance of catholicism in officially protestant states, an activity more hazardous than simple recusancy. Cornelius Ward and his assistants in the Western Isles found lodging in the homes of widows.[24] Sir James Perrot's report in 1627 assuaged government fears that Milford Haven (Pembrokeshire) could be used as a base for a catholic landing, but noted that, although there were not many recusants in Pembrokeshire, a small group of widows maintained a catholic network in the county and had connections with recusants in Montgomeryshire.[25] In England the 'caretakers' of otherwise empty rest houses for missionary catholic priests were usually women, and the action of women like Lady Aboyne and the Countess of Atholl in Scotland who maintained priests in their houses was matched by many gentry wives in England, three of whom, Margaret Clitherow, Margaret Ward and Anne Line, were sentenced to death as a consequence of their activities. In some areas women could further the cause of catholicism more openly. Dorothy Lawson took advantage of her social status and widowhood to maintain an extensive catholic network in the North-east.[26] Women of a humbler social level also made a significant contribution. In Newcastle in 1615 William Southerne, a seminary priest, said mass in the house of a widow who kept a small shop selling 'Ropes, Red herrings and some salt fishes, and many small trifles'. Upstairs the authorities discovered a red painted chest containing hosts 'in great number' as well as books and rosary beads.[27] The importance of women as pedlars and hucksters meant that they could have a vital role in the distribution of catholic literature, whether concealed in baskets of fish, as in the area around Newcastle, or on sale semi-openly as part of a broadsheet stock. John Rhodes warned in 1602 that there were 'many such pamphlets, together with other like Romish wares that are sent abroad among the common people both Protestants and Papists in London and in the country, and that certain women brokers and pedlars (as of late in Staffordshire there was) who with baskets on their arms, shall come and offer you other wares under a colour, and so sell you these'.[28] Anne Apicer, one of the recusants harboured by Frances Wentworth at Woolley, near Doncaster, who was described as a 'roamer to and fro' may have been such a pedlar, but it is also likely that many sellers only had a vague idea of the content of the literature in their pack.[29]

The attachment of women to catholic practice was most evident in terms of ritual. John Bossy has pointed out how women's control of the kitchen enabled them to sustain catholic fasting practices.[30] Significantly, this was one of the points of difference with some of the continental missionary priests who advocated different Tridentine fasting rules and were surprised that the English customs were so deeply rooted in the beleaguered English catholic community. However, it would be mistaken to see the attractions of ritual observance as tying women to catholicism and making them reluctant protestants. Maltby's discussion of prayer book protestantism suggests that Elizabethan protestants could become attached to the precise detail of the Prayer Book ritual.[31] Women's concern with the rituals surrounding rites of passage could also be catered for in the practice of both faiths, as indicated by the continuing popularity of churching. The example of Rose Hickman, a merchant's wife who went into exile to Antwerp with her husband in the reign of Mary I, shows how strong protestant commitment was compatible with a talismanic belief in the efficacy of ritual and a lack of interest in protestant sermons. When Rose was forced to have her child baptised by a catholic priest, she squared her conscience by substituting sugar for the usual salt in the baptismal water.[32] The particular tenacity of the Stoke by Nayland women mentioned earlier may also have been prompted by a similarly strong aversion to ritual pollution.

Unsurprisingly, given the doctrinal importance of baptism and the association of women with the nurturing of children, many examples of women who continued to adhere to catholic traditions focus on the health and well-being of children. In May 1599, for example, Elizabeth Burn who had recently given birth to a child, confessed to the presbytery of Ellon that Margaret Wood, the sister of Lady Wood of Boniton, a family well known locally for its support of catholics, had 'directed her from the gate of Birness to the burn next to Borrowly ... where she met strangers whom she did not know, of whom one dressed in a black plaid baptised the child'.[33] Those visiting holy wells could also expect the authorities to disapprove strongly of their actions. Margret Davidson, wife of Andro Adam, was fined £5 at Aberdeen 'for directing her nurse with her child to Saint Fiack's well, and washing the child in the water there to recover its health' and was also censured 'for leaving an offering in the well'. Not content with exacting this sizeable penalty, the authorities ordered that from now on anyone discovered going superstitiously to Saint Fiack's well for the health of themselves or of their children would be 'censured in penalty and repentance in such degree as fornicators are after trial and conviction'.[34] Considering the apparent slackness of the punishment of fornicators in Wales, drawing such parallels probably had less force there. However, on occasion the authorities were able to crack down on what they saw as superstitious visits to holy wells. In seventeenth-century

Denbighshire a father was fined the substantial sum of £10 'for allowing his three daughters being young girls and his maidservant to go out of his house at night to Winifred's well in a superstitious manner'.[35] The nocturnal expedition of these young girls may have been connected with some form of love magic, but the proscription of other ritual activities may have been more emotionally difficult. By the 1590s the Chanonry Kirk in the presbytery of Elgin was no longer in liturgical use, but parishioners continue to go there, against the orders of the authorities, to pray for those buried there. In November 1601, for example, the presbytery ordered Isabel Umphrey not to go to the Chanonry Kirk or to pray on her child's grave.[36]

In these examples the emotional cost of the transition from catholicism to protestantism seems clear, but such observations are only part of the picture. To understand the meaning of this change more fully, we need to understand more about the nature of catholicism and of the protestantism that was supposed to replace it. In particular, to examine the significance of this transition for women we need to assess the ways in which each religion offered models of female achievement, highlighted particular female virtues and stressed the idea of the exemplary christian as a godly woman. Patterns of devotion within Britain were, of course, varied. Catholicism, like protestantism, left a certain scope to individuals to construct their own devotional priorities, and particular patrons or godly ministers could also be influential in shaping the religious preferences of their fellow parishioners. Nevertheless, it is broadly true that by the eve of the Reformation there were different trends of catholic development in England, Scotland and Wales respectively, the characteristics of which shaped the nature of women's experience of the Reformation.

Late mediaeval devotion in England was strongly Christocentric in character and focussed on the passion and suffering of the adult Christ. Depictions of the Nativity and tender images of the Virgin suckling the Christ Child that had been frequent in the fourteenth century were rarely chosen by patrons in the course of the fifteenth century. New devotions, such as the cult of Christ's wounds and of the Instruments of the Passion, migrated from the world of the mystic and the cloistered to the parish, where they could often be found emblazoned on bench ends or incorporated into compositions of other religious subjects. It was also, of course, behind the banner of the Five Wounds that the pilgrims gathered in the Pilgrimage of Grace (1536). For mystics the cult of Christ's wounds had fostered a fantasy of fusion with Christ himself by entering the bleeding apertures in Christ's body. In the parish context, the devotion took on another meaning and did not hold out the hope of ecstatic union. Instead, it tended to deepen ideas of the sinfulness of humanity and of the mercy of Christ.

The new emphasis was epitomised in the change that occurred in depictions of the Last Judgement. In those parish churches for which evidence of mediaeval mural painting survives, the depiction of the Last Judgement was transferred to the east wall of the nave above the chancel arch. It thus occupied the focal point for the congregation assembled in the nave and, more importantly, was now juxtaposed with the rood group, the crucified Christ flanked by the Virgin Mary and St John. The direct relevance of the Passion of Christ for the Last Judgement was further emphasised by iconographical changes that took place within the portrayal of the Last Judgement itself as Christ was depicted with bleeding wounds and surrounded by angels carrying the Instruments of the Passion. The whole conveyed the promise that God's mercy, manifest in the crucifixion of his only son, would be re-enacted by the Son at the Last Judgement. These ideas demanded compassion rather than complacency on the part of the onlooker, who was called upon to identify himself with the role of Mary in the Pietà, and was also spurred on to make greater efforts to behave in the appropriate christian manner. The stories of the Warnings to Swearers and the Warnings to Sabbath Breakers demonstrated in a graphic way that the Crucifixion was not neatly sealed off in the distant past. Each oath sworn, or inappropriate task undertaken on the Sabbath, re-enacted the Passion of Christ and inflicted a further wound upon his body. And yet, Christ still held out the promise that mercy could be offered to frail humanity.

These developments reduced the status of the Virgin Mary and the cult of saints, giving them a less direct role in the process of salvation. In earlier depictions of the Last Judgement, but not in the later ones, the Virgin Mary was often portrayed showing her breast as she interceded with her son for the salvation of mankind, thus making a direct link with her maternity. The scenes of the Weighing of Souls could still include Mary assisting the soul by placing her rosary in the balance in the fifteenth century, but these images no longer formed part of the Last Judgement and could be read as giving Mary influence only over souls in purgatory. In general, with the exception of Mary whose demotion could not be so severe, the saints were reduced to witnesses of the potential for sanctity, but were closer to the human than to the divine. It was this that made them so effective in assisting individuals with the mundane problems of this world, whether it was St Apollonia's compassion for toothache, or

St Sythe, the servant girl's, understanding of the need for housewives to find their lost keys. In all this their virginity, although nominally recognised, played little part. As the acceptance of married saints indicates, their power came from divine favour and martyrdom, and not intrinsically from their physical virginity. Consequently, there was little emphasis on saints as the brides of Christ. Even in the fairly numerous English versions of the story of St Katherine, a saint who enjoyed considerable popularity, there was no word of her mystic marriage to Christ.

In Wales, although the cult of the Five Wounds had some impact, being portrayed for example on the rood screen at Llanegan (Caernarvonshire) and on shields at Llanelidan and Gresford (Denbighshire), the characteristics of late mediaeval devotion were significantly different from those in England. Interesting insights are provided by John Penry's description in his *Aequity of an Humble Supplication* (1587), despite his slightly jaundiced viewpoint in an essay designed to spur the English government to greater efforts to make Wales a more thoroughly protestant country:

> concerning salvation they either think, that the Lord is bound to save all men, because they are his creatures, or that all shall be saved at the last day, at the entreaty of the virgin Mary, who shall desire her son, after judgement has been given, to save as many of the damned as may be sheltered under her mantle; this being granted all the damned souls shall be there shrouded and so saved from hell fire. This is the reason why our people only make a mockery of sin. They think that only the soul shall go to heaven and not the body also, whence it comes that they say that they care not what becomes of their bodies, if their souls may be saved. They ascribe savage cruelty unto God the father, because he punished man's sin so severely even in his son Christ, the Lord Jesus they commend. *Nû waeth genûf dhim am y tad y gwr craûlon hinnû onûd cydymmaith da ûwr mab*: I care not says one for the father that cruel man, but the son is a good fellow.[37]

Certainly, in comparison to England, religion in Wales retained a strong attachment to the idea of the maternal, nurturing and interceding Virgin Mary. At Wrexham, which has the only surviving late mediaeval wall painting of the Last Judgement, Mary is shown displaying her breast as she intercedes on behalf of the souls of the departed. The unusual illustration of the Nativity in Peniarth Ms 23, which was copied in the late fifteenth century, depicts Mary completely barebreasted.[38] Religious poetry addressed to Mary included details of her life known from the apocrypha and concentrated on her role as the virgin mother of the infant Christ. The idea of the burning bush prefiguring the virgin birth, and of light passing through a window as a metaphor for the immaculate conception have obvious poetic attractions, but they were also part of a poetic output that was full of praise for Mary's tender care of the Christ Child. In contrast, the poets were almost silent concerning Mary's appearances in the New Testament, and did not even dwell on her behaviour at the foot of the Cross. Instead, they moved directly from the infancy themes to the question of salvation. As Williams points out, poems addressed to Mary 'unfailingly' include the request that she will remember the narrator at the last day and ensure that he will go to heaven.[39] In contrast to Penry's assertion, this assistance was less often imagined by poets in terms of the Madonna of Mercy sheltering the souls she saved beneath her mantle, but in terms of Mary's intervention at the Soul Weighing. Breeze notes that the image of the Virgin Mary putting her rosary in the scales occurs frequently in Welsh poetry, but is rare in English devotional poetry, and was not often included in the fairly large corpus of surviving Soul Weighings in English parish churches.[40]

As we might expect, given this description of the nature of devotion to the Virgin Mary, devotion to Christ in Wales took on other characteristics from those in England. Although later mediaeval poetry became increasingly Christocentric in character, the consideration of Christ's Passion was less likely to be prompted by the poet's empathy with the grieving Mary of the Pietà, but to address one of the number of famous roods in Wales. There was nevertheless a poetical trope that connected Mary's tears with Christ's blood, which was made most explicit in a poem by Dafydd Eppynt: 'After his body gave its blood for slaves, blood flowed again in the eye of the woman'. However, in contrast to England, despite the presence there of the same trope and a shrine of the holy blood at Hailes (Gloucestershire), concern for Christ's blood did not focus on empathy for Christ's suffering but was more eucharistic in character and fascinated with the blood itself.[41] In the crucifixion at Llanwrin (Montgomeryshire), for example, angels holding chalices collect blood from Christ's wounds. The Welsh translation of John Mirk's sermon for Good Friday adds an extensive description of the blood flowing from Christ's wounds, and the late fifteenth-century Welsh translations of the 15 Oes of St Bridget made the eucharistic imagery more emphatic than it was in the Latin original.[42]

Despite the importance attached to Mary's chaste motherhood, the virginity of saints appears to have occasioned little respect. In Welsh hagiography of St Katherine, as in English, there was no mention of the mystic marriage of the saint.[43] More surprisingly, it was possible for the poet, Lewis Môn to change the story of St Winifred completely. Instead of praising her for her commitment to chaste virginity, Môn used the story of her death as a terrible warning to a girl of what might happen if she rejected her lover.[44] Moreover, as Cartwright and Fulton have shown, *cywyddau* to nuns and to virgin laywomen 'reflect only a desire to corrupt the brides of Christ'. In a fifteenth-century *cywydd* by Hywel Dafi the poet imagines that through a keyhole, he catches sight of a young girl, who is kneeling and reciting psalms in front of a statue of the Virgin Mary, but, instead of writing a poetic eulogy to the girl's beauty and piety, the poet subverts Marian veneration to another end,

> Between two fine bed-curtains if only I could have her in a summer month, and throw her between two walls to the ground with her arms outstretched; I'd offer, colour of euphrasy flowers, on my knees up close, and she'd let me willingly, and I'd leap between her and heaven; coming down between her legs I'd worship forever Mary's image.

Other *cywyddau* praise the chastity of nuns, but, as in the case of secular love songs in which the poet is confident that the pure maiden will consent to woodland trysts, the poets encourage women who have vowed themselves to God to forget the nunnery to come and enjoy free love in the woodland. This poetic culture, as it had evolved by the fifteenth century, was far from the instructions laid down in the bardic grammars in which nuns were to be praised for their holiness, pure way of life, chastity and heavenly love of God, and contrasted sharply with the tradition of popular songs about nuns elsewhere in Europe.[45]

The pattern of devotion in late mediaeval Scotland contrasts with that of both England and Wales, partly because of the strength of contact with Bruges, the Scottish staple in mainland Europe, and the connections with France, which influenced its devotional traditions. In the fourteenth century liturgical observances in Scotland broadly followed those in England, the Use of Sarum, being predominant in both areas, but during the fifteenth century, partly as a result of the Great Schism, the two began to diverge. Although James IV's edict outlawing the future import of liturgical books according to the Use of Sarum in 1507 was not completely effective, the accompanying recommendation that henceforth books of devotion in Scotland should be 'after our own Scottish use and with legends of Scottish saints' struck an already resonant chord.[46]

A feature of early-sixteenth-century missals in use in Scotland was the addition of large numbers of supplementary saints. A copy of the Sarum missal produced at Rouen in 1506, for example, was customised for use in St Nicholas church, Aberdeen by the addition of about 90 saints, many of whom were not of Scottish origin. The proliferation of saints at Aberdeen was not an isolated phenomenon. The reforms that seemed necessary in 1507 included the publication of directories to instruct clerics what to do on dates when the celebration of more than one saint was desired.

This vibrant interest in the cult of saints was accompanied by the introduction in the fifteenth century of devotion to the Holy Blood, the Five Wounds and the Holy Name of Jesus. As in Wales, these cults formed part of a strongly eucharistic devotion rather than being part of an empathetic experience of the sufferings of Christ's passion as was the case in England. However, it seems that it was Scotland alone of the three areas that embraced the idea of displaying the consecrated host in a monstrance or in a sacrament house, like the elaborate example at Foulis Easter (Perthshire) where the recess is surmounted by a carved figure of Christ flanked by angels carrying instruments of the passion. Of these devotions, that to the holy blood perhaps had the longest tradition: the earliest recorded religious play in Aberdeen was the 'Holyblood' play performed in 1440, and a catalogue of surviving images of the Arma Christi suggests that no examples can be dated earlier than the closing years of the fifteenth century and that half date from the second quarter of the sixteenth century. These cults gave Christ's blood a talismanic quality and were compatible with the idea of Christ as a knightly warrior. The example of the women of Nithsdale coming to Edinburgh to present the bloody shirts of their kinsfolk killed in a feud suggests that the emotive power of Robert Henryson's poem *The Bludy Serk* would have been clearly understood. In this poem a princess, a metaphor for the soul, was taken from her father's kingdom by a great lion and placed in darkness until her father sent a knight (Christ) to defeat the lion and release the princess. In the course of his successful struggle with the lion, the knight was fatally wounded, and he told the grief-stricken princess that she could prove her devotion to him by never marrying and by keeping his bloody tunic (serk) and thinking of him, and the great love he bore her, as she looked at it for the rest of her life.[47]

The place of the Virgin Mary in this scheme is far from clear, and it seems tempting to assume that she was considered largely in the context of the holy company of saints, even if some liturgies introduced further feasts in her honour such as the Presentation, the Visitation and St Mary of the Snows. Mary's claim to special status as the mother of Christ was also modified by the unusual adoption of the feast of St Joseph in the late fifteenth century. This feast, which appeared first in Scotland in the missal of James Sibbald, vicar of Arbuthnott (Mearns) in 1491, was never included in the Use of Sarum and was rare in Continental calendars before 1510. As the 'foster-father of the Lord', to use the phrase employed in Sibbald's missal, the cult of St Joseph necessarily diluted the matriarchal vision of Christ's family. Mary still had a close connection with Christ, as the practice of including the monograms of both Christ and Mary in representations of the Arma Christi shows, but an emphasis on shared parenting made a difference to the importance of her nurturing role.[48]

The relationship of these three patterns of late mediaeval devotion to the specific experience of women is a complex problem. Easy assumptions that women would identify more closely with female saints and strive to emulate the values they embody have to be questioned and perhaps discarded. In England, at least, it is clear that in their pious bequests women did not favour female saints more strongly than male ones, and indeed in acts of deathbed piety of both men and women female saints were not popular choices, with the exception of the Virgin Mary. However, this may be the result of the process of specialisation by which divine assistance in the matter of salvation was increasingly not thought to be in the hands of the saints who were more human than divine. It does not necessarily mean that female saints had lost their power as models of exemplary conduct. Nevertheless, to the extent that the idea of saints as the virgin brides of Christ had also lost its resonance, at least in England and Wales, the exemplary conduct saints offered was that of human devotion and christian commitment. In England the emphasis on human weakness and the mercy offered by Christ to the devout meant that the figure of the Magdalen, rather than a virgin martyr, could best encapsulate the aspirations of the christian. In Wales, unsurprisingly, this solution was less appropriate. As Penry commented with despair, dwelling on the connection between sin and salvation seemed to be alien to the Welsh mentality. The Welsh version of the life of St Mary Magdalen placed little emphasis on her sinful life and conversion, but expounded upon her achievements as a desert ascetic and as a missionary in southern Gaul. In Scotland the continuing proliferation of saints, as well as the knight's expectation that the devout princess would not marry for his sake, suggest that the idea of sacred virginity and of the saint as the bride of Christ remained strong in the late mediaeval period. It therefore comes as no surprise that it was only in Scotland that protestant piety produced outpourings of bride of Christ imagery drawn from the Song of Songs.

The significance of the contrast between the late mediaeval English emphasis on Mary's role in relation to the adult Christ of the Crucifixion and the Pietà, and the stress on Mary's nurturing maternal role that preceded it and that remained dominant in Wales up to the Reformation needs closer examination. It is easy to assume that the Welsh pattern represented an elevation and sanctification of motherhood, and thus appealed especially to women and provided them with a powerful and comforting role model of which women in England were deprived by the fifteenth century. However, this may be part, but certainly is not all, of the story. Bynum's work on the importance of the idea of nurturing, and on the interchangeability in religious terms of milk, blood and the eucharist as sustaining metaphors, reminds us that such images could be more complex than a straightforward transcription of domestic circumstance. Moreover, it is not even clear that Mary was, in fact, less central to male than to female religious experience. Simone Roisin, for example, concludes an analysis of thirteenth-century visions with the observation that the Virgin Mary appeared more often to men than to women.[49] Intuitively, this seems surprising, if we expect women to be more devoted to Mary as a model mother. However, the process of devotional identification has two further attributes: female saints were exemplars of the christian humility commended to both sexes, and the worshipper of Mary could identify himself as the son in relation to the mother.

The equation of christian virtues with ideal female characteristics and the christian emphasis on the renunciation of worldly things in the service of the spirit, meant that spiritual attainment would be seen in terms of renunciation. Consequently, in Bynum's view, the model for the religious man had to be a woman, especially the Virgin Mary, but following the Virgin could not entail a satisfactory renunciation for women.

The male writer who saw his soul as a bride of God or his religious role as womanly submission and humility was conscious of using an image of reversal. He sought reversal because reversal and renunciation were at the heart of a religion whose dominant symbol is the cross – life achieved through death. When a woman writer (often but not always a virgin) spoke of herself as either bride or knight, each image was in a sense a reversal. But neither was as highly charged as the

notion of the male as bride or woman, for neither expressed renunciation. Because women were women they could not embrace the female
as a symbol of renunciation. Because society was male-dominated, they
could not embrace the male as a symbol of renunciation. To become
male was elevation, not renunciation, and elevation was a less significant reversal given the values at the heart of medieval Christianity.[50]

This understanding goes a long way towards explaining the capacity of
the Virgin Mary to appeal to the opposite sex, but is less convincing in its
labelling of female devotion as unsatisfactory. Saying that women could
not embrace the female as a symbol of renunciation ignores the fact that
there were two facets to the female, as summarised by the attributes of
the humble, chaste and devout Virgin Mary and the weak, foolish Eve. In
following the model of Mary a woman did in fact experience a renunciation as profound as that experienced by the man who exchanged male
authority for female humility. Both rejected what contemporaries saw as
their innate capacities and re-created themselves in the image of the
saints and of a feminine definition of virtue.

However, these observations, although instructive in clarifying the
power of female models for christian men and women, are of little help
in clarifying the significance of different emphases in the representation
of the Virgin Mary in local devotion. To understand the contrast between
Wales and England we need to know whether an image of the Virgin suckling the Christ Child works in the same way as one of a Pietà. In the former, from the perspective of the child, or the human soul, Mary
represents a haven of security, a source of nurture that is both comforting and essential to development and well-being. It is, moreover, an
image that has the potential to awaken the child within, whilst possibly
carrying erotic overtones, and, although much of this may be unac-
knowledged, its influence cannot be completely discounted. In contrast,
the image of the Pietà is self-evidently a less comforting one. Powerless
maternal grief has replaced maternal succour. The attractive vulnerability of the child, made possible by the fact that its wants are cared for, is
now the suffering of a man who is an instrument of his father's will and
whom his mother cannot assist or comfort. In late mediaeval England
therefore Mary had become the witness, representative and tutor of
mankind, largely drained of her maternal attributes. The changes in the
way in which she was perceived to intervene on behalf of the christian,
the stress on the passion of Christ and on the sinfulness of mankind
meant that the cult of saints, including that of the Virgin Mary, could not

be strongly gendered. In Wales, by contrast, an area in which the idea of the importance of the mother's blessing retained its strength, the maternal bond explained both Mary's motivation and the influence she could exercise over her son. Consequently, although some poems could recognise that the possibility of salvation came from Christ's passion, the soul's petition was addressed to Mary, and Penry believed that the most descriptive image was that of the Virgin sheltering souls beneath her cloak.

The particular characteristics of late mediaeval devotion in England, with its strong Christocentric focus on the Passion of Christ, which displaced the cult of saints from the economy of salvation, and emphasised the frailty of mankind, offered the possibility of a relatively easy transition to protestantism. The idea of salvation by the merits of Christ's passion was equally accessible to a late mediaeval catholic as it was to an early protestant evangelical. The 'loss' of the saints made less impact when they had already been demoted from a key role in salvation and the idea of sacred virginity was no longer so powerful. The attributes of the Virgin Mary as the representative devout, but still human, christian were gradually transferred to the Magdalen in a process that accentuated, but did not significantly deviate from, trends within her cult in the late mediaeval period. Even the protestant martyrs were not immune to such influence. During the era of persecution, Anne Askew was portrayed in the guise of a catholic saint assertively trampling evil underfoot, but by the seventeenth century a ballad could commemorate the martyr as the Magdalen. Askew had been led astray by bad doctrine, but had become humbly devout in her faith. This model presented women as receptive vessels, or, to adopt the metaphor used in Askew's ballad, as gardens in which those with influence could plant fruits or weeds. But, although powerful, such ideas should not be seen as indicating that women, including the most pious, were relegated to a humble, subordinate position in which they were unable to exercise control or to assert a contribution. The experience of Mrs Jane Ratcliffe, who gained local renown as a godly woman, does not quite deserve Lake's description in terms of 'emancipation' since her achievements did not transcend contemporary assumptions concerning the nature of her sex.[51] However, the study usefully highlights the way in which the religious lives of the godly conferred value on the contributions of both sexes. Although protestantism was a religion of the Word, and specialist knowledge might be needed to determine the correct translation of a Biblical passage from the Hebrew, both ministers and laymen recognised that although male intellect and rationality might decipher true doctrine, they were useless without a living faith. Women, on the other hand, being both emotional

and irrational, were better able to experience a true faith but might get
some misguided notions into their heads if they were not carefully
directed. Ideally therefore, the process of spiritual edification was best
pursued by a partnership of man and wife, or minister and godly lay-
woman, in which both the complementarity and the essential nature of
the two contributions was recognised.

Pastorally, the example of the godly woman could be seen as more
instructive than that of men. The fashion for publishing funeral sermons
describing the spiritual achievements of the godly laity embraced both
sexes, but it was the accounts of godly women that found the most enthusiastic audience and were subsequently printed. Although it is possible
that this discrepancy reflects female reading habits, the lower level of
female literacy, even amongst the godly, suggests that this preference was
more widely shared. Certainly the preachers of such sermons thought
that not only women but also men should learn from the lives of godly
women. Lancelot Langhorne in his funeral sermon for Mrs Mary Swaine
(1611) appealed to his audience 'Let us all for our application learn of a
woman of the weaker sex: especially women imitate her'. However, the
strength of the female model did not mean that the spiritual achievement
of godly women was seen as superior or even entirely feminine in character. Thomas Gataker, writing in praise of the life of Rebecca Crisp in
1620, considered the presentation of female models of godliness as a
good tactic to spur both sexes to greater spiritual application:

> Examples of this Sex are in some respects the more needful of the
> two ... for that as they shame men if they come short of such, so they
> give women encouragement to contend and good hope to attain what
> they see others of their Sex have before them by the same contending
> attained.

and praised his subject 'for such graces as are not so ordinarily incident
to that sex, sharpness of apprehension, and soundness of judgement'.
Similarly in his funeral sermon for Joyce Featley, he noted that God 'had
endowed her with a greater measure than ordinary, in that Sex especially,
of wisdom, of discretion, of understanding, of knowledge'.[52] Ultimately,
the complementary spiritual partnership of male and female should be
realised within each individual believer, an aspiration that contributed
to the blurring of gender identities, whilst, of course, using sharp distinctions of gender to describe that process and emphasising the female contribution. English protestantism adopted the frail and naturally emotional

godly woman as the emblem of all christians struggling with faith and an innate propensity to sin.

This process was encouraged by the continuing Christocentric emphasis of English protestantism which meant that individuals saved by the merits of Christ's passion could also be the brides of Christ. This connection was less explicitly made in the first decades of the Reformation, reflecting the weakness of the bride of Christ theme in pre-Reformation piety. In the early Elizabethan years popular love songs could be transformed to make Christ the object. For example, the song 'Dainty come thou to me' was rendered as 'Jesus come thou to me'. But, despite its source, there was a clear reluctance to develop the romantic theme in relation to Christ. After the address in the first verse, the idea of the singer as the spouse of Christ was not very clearly developed.

> Jesus my loving spouse,
> eternall veritie
> Perfect guide of my soule,
> way to eternitie, –
> Strengthen me with thy grace,
> from thee Ile never flee,
> Let them say what they will,
> Jesu come thou to me.[53]

It was only as the emphasis on the gulf between God and man intensified, a process epitomised by the replacement of the figure of God as an old man with the Hebrew tetragrammaton, that the need to humanise the spirituality of the godly was recognised. A means of balancing these conflicting demands was a renewed emphasis on the role of Christ who could be seen as the merciful aspect of God. Thus, at the same time that unease with the mingling of sacred and profane led to a phasing out of popular tunes and made modelling the relationship of the sinner and Christ on a popular love song impossible, the idea of the bride of Christ enjoyed a limited, but significant, revival in funeral sermons. Protestant fears of ecstatic physical union, the negative view of the fleshly man, and debates about whether the erotic language of the Song of Songs showed that it was not really scriptural, meant that the idea of the christian as the bride of Christ could only be envisaged when the union took place after death and could be safely divorced from the lusts of the flesh. In funeral sermons its usage was clearly linked to the concept of the godly woman: eulogies of both sexes could contain references to the theory of the soul as the bride of Christ, but it was only sermons on women that could envisage the union of the soul of the commemorated individual with Christ.[54] This greater confidence in the fate of a woman's soul was part of a wider pattern of association. In Welsh poetic elegies, such as those written in the early sixteenth century by Lewis Môn, more attention was paid to the fate of the soul of a female patron.[55] Conversely, when the salvation of the soul was less assured, as in English repentant sinner ballads before 1640, the subject was always male.[56]

A similar pattern might be expected in Scotland. Scottish preachers, like those in England, reminded their audiences that the spiritual commitment of women could be of value. David Dickson, commenting on the example of Rahab (Hebrews 11, 31) preached that 'the Faith of Women is worthy to be observed, and imitated, even as well as Men's Faith'. Alexander Henderson made a similar, if more detailed, argument.

> Not only men may be confident in the power of God, but even women also, who are more frail and feeble. Not only may women mourn to God for wrongs done to them, and have repentance of sin, but they may be confident in God also. ... And therefore we must not judge of grace as we do of nature; for there may be Christian courage in women as well as in men, albeit courage be not so natural to them: and they may adhere to Christ even when men forsake him.[57]

It was in keeping with these notions of the value of female piety that protestant ministers in Scotland, as in England, embraced the idea of the mutually supportive spiritual partnership of a man and a woman. The extensive correspondence of John Knox with women like Lady Elizabeth Bowes or between Samuel Rutherford and Lady Kenmure and Marion McNaught were matched by many other similar relationships. The more strongly Calvinist character of the Scottish Reformation from the time of its establishment in 1560 suggests that the development of bride of Christ imagery as an antidote to the awesome distance between the believer and the Almighty would have been more immediate, but would essentially mirror the English pattern. In fact, of course, the Scottish experience was quite different. Here, bride of Christ imagery blossomed, and not only, as Mullan points out, in the effusive outpourings of Samuel Rutherford, but also in the writings of men like John Welsh who preceded him.[58] At the same time, a much more negative view of female nature prevailed. Whilst in England, commentators on the theme were prepared to cast the blame on David for desiring Bathsheba, Scottish divines followed Calvin more closely and exonerated the psalmist. According to Archibald Simson writing in 1638, Psalm 51 showed 'what evils come of the beauty of Women when joined with impudence and levity. For if she had not washed herself naked before the Palace, and consented so readily to the King, that he should come in to her ... there had not been such abominable crimes committed'.[59]

Bride of Christ imagery as used by divines like Rutherford was deployed in two main directions. It could be used to describe the state of the Church, and especially its deviation from the purity intended by Christ. Thus in 1637 Rutherford could write that the Lord in his judgement was sending the Kirk 'to Rome's brothel-house to seek a lover of her own, seeing that she has given up with Christ her Husband'. More frequently, it was used as a means of encouraging the believer to set less store by human concerns. This was especially evident in letters written to console mothers on the deaths of their children. In 1629 Lady Kenmure was assured that although she had lost a daughter, the child was found to Christ, and reminded that 'What you love besides Christ is an adulterous lover'. Instead of mourning for her child, she should be grateful to God that by her daughter's death he has thickened the thorny hedge (Hosea 2: 6–7) that keeps her from worldly love and away from her first husband Christ. Similarly on the death of her husband five years later, she was told to welcome the opportunity that widowhood had brought her to concentrate all her love upon Christ: 'God has dried up one channel of your love by the removal of your husband. Let now that spate run upon Christ'. Such words provided some comfort by asserting that such bereavements were part of God's design, but they set up a ghastly conflict between loving Christ and loving one's children or one's husband.[60] In the writing of English ministers, by contrast, the idea of the christian as the bride of Christ was more closely modelled on the relationship between the wife and her husband which meant that correct performance of domestic duties could be seen as an apprenticeship and a preparation for the relationship with Christ.[61] The reward in Scottish piety for raising the stakes to this level of hard choice was the immediate promise of the consolations of the imagery of the Song of Songs. It is hard to think of an English minister writing to a new widow that God allowed her husband to die so that she could be 'a free woman for Christ, who is now suiting for marriage-love of you. And therefore since you lie alone in your bed, let Christ be as a bundle of myrrh, to sleep and lie all the night between your breasts (Canticles 1: 13), and then your bed is better filled than before.' Similarly, although such ministers might share the view that individuals came into contact with God by prayer and by hearing the word, they would probably consider Rutherford's description of this encounter to be over the top.

> For this is the house of wine, where you meet with your Well-Beloved. Here it is where he kisses you with the kisses of His mouth, and where you feel the smell of His garments; and they have indeed a most fragrant and glorious smell. You must, I say, wait upon Him, and be oft communing with Him, whose lips are as lilies, dropping sweet-smelling myrrh, and by the moving thereof he will assuage your grief.[62]

It seems likely that these characteristics of Scottish piety owed much to the strength of the cult of saints in pre-Reformation catholicism. The sharpness of the demand to renounce worldly things and receive the spiritual compensations offered by the heavenly Bridegroom to the christian during life recalls the spiritual struggles typical of cloistered lives. The continuity of this into a Calvinist Reformation sprang partly from the need for 'heart religion' to compensate for religious austerity. It was also compatible with a religious outlook in which the christian, who was painfully aware of the frailty of his own flesh, was constantly besieged by the devil and his minions. In this system the most fragile component was the Song of Songs compensatory vocabulary of myrrh and kisses. Elizabeth Melville, the author of *Ane Godlie Dreame* (1603), which was frequently reprinted throughout the seventeenth century and has the soul's yearning for Christ as its main theme, eschewed Song of Songs imagery whilst recognising Christ as the soul's spouse and postponing fulfilment of this relationship until death. But this reticence did not dilute the sense that worldly attachments were incompatible with love of Christ. Melville's lyric 'Away vaine world bewitcher of my heart' that was appended to the early editions of *Ane Godlie Dreame* contains the lines,

> Let the world be gone, I'll love Christ alone,
> Let the world be gone, I care not
> Christ is my love allone, I feare not. (lines 28–30)[63]

The consequence of this flexibility in the vocabulary acceptable in Scottish piety was to give respectability amongst the godly to a wide range of female expression. The prophetess, Margaret Mitchelson, who at the time of the National Covenant 'was transported in heavenly raptures and spoke strange things for the happy success of God's cause and Christ's crown in this kingdom which was already enacted in heaven', gained the approval of men such as Wariston, but may not have been so fortunate amongst English puritans. Of course, presbyterian acceptance of her was partly because her revelations supported the same cause, but they also chimed with a spirit of religious enthusiasm. The impressive sacramental communions developed by the presbyterians in the early seventeenth century and culminating in the celebration at Shotts in 1630 fostered a spiritual awakening, which, whilst focussed on the communion, was also compatible with the enthusiastic expression of individuals as apparently diverse as Margaret Mitchelson and Samuel Rutherford.[64] But this was only one side of the coin. For those of a different psychology the stark opposition between world and spirit could intensify the depressive dangers inherent in the Calvinist demand for a minute examination of one's conscience. It could lead to the morbid introspection and sense of low self-worth, which in the case of the early spiritual development of Mistress Rutherford could even be expressed in fears of committing suicide and of being a witch.[65] Moreover, in contrast to England, where the limited use of the imagery of the soul as the bride of Christ lent religious value to the effective performance of the role of a dutiful housewife, Scottish religiosity of this type did nothing to validate female activity, despite the more effusive use of a feminine language to express it. The English emphasis on the godly woman gave more support to the female sex than did the Scottish enthusiasm for the idea of the soul as the bride of Christ.

Part of this deficit in Scotland may have been made up by the opportunity provided by the Reformation for ministers to take wives. Despite the notion of the priesthood of all believers, clerics retained a special status, part of which could reflect upon their wives, and their marriage could serve as an example of godly matrimony and an embodiment of the protestant rejection of the spiritual value of celibacy. However, the position of clergy wives was often difficult, and this may have been especially the case in Scotland where there was no specific enactment authorising clerical marriage. Pre-Reformation habits of satirising the lustfulness of supposedly celibate priests who kept concubines or ravished the daughters of the parish could now be directed against protestant ministers who presumed to marry their mistresses and in doing so defiled the sacrament of marriage. The words of the catholic propagandist, Miles Huggarde, in his *The Displaying of the Protestantes* (1556) directed to an English audience summarise this viewpoint well. He wished that 'a just plague of God' might fall upon such clergy who

> cared not what women they married, common or other, if they might get themselves wives. For true are St Paul's words: they enter into houses bringing into bondage women laden with sin. The women of these

married priests were such for the most part that either they were kept by others before, or else as common as the cartway and so bound them to incestuous lechery.[66]

Clearly many priests did take the opportunity to regularise the status of their mistresses by offering them marriage, and in Scotland this policy could even be forced upon them by the kirk session to avoid further charges of fornication. For example, John Anderson, the vicar of Cleish, was persuaded by the kirk session of St Andrews to marry Eufame Pattoun in 1564.[67] On a local level such case histories probably had a similar impact to the more widely circulated stories involving the higher clergy elsewhere, such as Bishop Ponet of Winchester's 'divorce' in 1551 from his wife who was allegedly already married to a Nottingham butcher.[68] Not all opposition to clerical marriage was purely morally grounded. The economic costs of running a married household, providing dowries for daughters and inheritances for sons created severe economic problems for the Church, and fuelled accusations about clerical extravagance and social presumption, which was assumed to be prompted by the demands of their wives for excessive luxuries. The marriages of daughters of the clergy also aroused concern about inappropriate clerical social climbing and its consequences for lay families of good status. The marriage of Alexander Oliphant of Kellie to Jane Forman, an archbishop's daughter, prompted the complaint of Temporalitie in Lindsay's *Satire* that the marriages of prelates' daughters put intolerable pressure on the nobility to increase the dowries they offered with their daughters.[69]

Curiously, it appears that clerical marriage was no more popular generally in Wales than it was in Scotland and England, despite the fact that in this region the tradition of concubinage was more entrenched, and regular unions might have been thought to reduce the incidence of clerical fornication which was assumed to be high.[70] From the fourteenth century Welsh clerics paid fines for keeping concubines and 'cradle crowns' for each child born to them. According to the poet Gruffudd ap Tudor ap Hywel, such discipline did little to limit clerical fornication. In one of his poems a boat carrying a large number of priests and their women urges the waves to carry it to Bangor where the priests will be disciplined by their bishop, but has little hope that this will deter them in future. Moreover, although the image is contrived, its conclusion should not simply be dismissed as poetic licence. In 1503 it was reported to the Caernarvonshire sessions that the large number of priests and clerks in holy orders who were guilty of 'ravishing' the daughters of tenants of

Crown manors in North Wales was causing a financial crisis since their fathers were responsible for the payment of *amobr* fines and speculators, who had acquired the lease of the fines, were ruthlessly distraining their goods and property. That there was some truth in these allegations is suggested by the fact that the court took the complaint seriously and overturned the usual principle of payment of *amobr* fines by determining that guilty priests should henceforth pay a 'marriage fee' or suffer imprisonment. In 1536, as part of their petition to Thomas Cromwell that they might be allowed to continue their traditional practice of keeping 'hearth companions' (*focariae*), the clergy of the diocese of Bangor added in support of their case that 'No gentleman nor honest substantial man will lodge us in their houses, for fear of inconvenience and knowing our frailty'.[71]

Yet, in all areas as the Reformation became more established the marriage of clergy was gradually more accepted, and could even be necessary to safeguard a minister's protestant credentials: Hugh Tunckes of Winchester explained in 1571 that he had taken a wife because 'I am called a papist and so hooted at'.[72] If the funerary monuments of ministers and their wives are to be believed, such marriages gained a greater respectability in Scotland than was the case in England where monuments to parish clergy seldom made reference to their wives, perhaps because they often came from lower status families. In contrast, between 1560 and 1599, 54 per cent of clergy wives in Scotland were the daughters of lairds.[73] The memorial to John Hamilton, minister of Dunlop (Ayrshire) from 1567–1606 and his wife Jane Denham, the daughter of the laird of West Shields, is probably the earliest surviving monument to a clerical couple in Scotland. The inscription that accompanies the portrayal of husband and wife kneeling either side of a prayer desk begins conventionally outlining their parentage, their 45 years of marriage, and the names of their seven children. Only the verse that follows and the accompanying scriptural text distinguish this from a lay monument.

> The dust of two lyes in the arte-full frame,
> Whose birth them honor'd from an honoured name,
> A painefull pastor, and his spotles wife,
> Whose devout statues embleme here there (sic) life.

> Those that turn many to righteousness shall shine as the starrs for ever and ever. (David 12: 3)

As Sanderson notes, the memorial suggests that 'respectable lineage as well as exemplary life contributed to the reputation of the minister and his wife', but whilst the minister was 'praised for his labours', his wife was praised for her spotless character. Even if both were envisaged as stars that would shine forever, it was female chastity that complemented diligent protestant ministry.[74] Clerical wives in Scotland, far from being in the vanguard of a protestant inspired improvement in the status of the married woman, refocussed female reputation back onto the narrow question of sexual reputation.

The position of clerical wives in England is more obscure. It seems possible that the degree of opprobrium to which they were subjected may have been exaggerated by hostile commentators, although the presence in episcopal injunctions of exhortations to midwives not to withhold their services from the wives of the clergy suggests that it cannot be dismissed. The reluctance to commemorate these exemplary partnerships, in theory at least, in funeral monuments is puzzling, especially since wives of ministers could be celebrated in funeral sermons. Elizabeth Gouge, for example, was described as 'a pious, prudent, provident, painful, careful, faithful, helpful, grave, modest, sober, tender, loving wife, mother, mistress, and neighbour'.[75] Such commemoration may, of course, have had the advantage of placing the emphasis on the wife as a godly individual rather as a minister's wife. Certainly, the broader range of attributes expressed make such eulogies indistinguishable from those of other pious laywomen. The 'spotless' wife of the 'painful' pastor was largely confined to Scotland and was part of the enhanced emphasis there on the idea of the bride of Christ.

In all areas there was an essential continuity in the praise of women in which clerical wives took part, but could not shape significantly. Although the number of memorials surviving in Scotland in this period is relatively small, it is notable that the idea of the spotless wife was also applied to married laywomen, such as Bessie Adam, the wife of James Hamilton, who died in 1616 and is commemorated in Glasgow Cathedral.[76] In England, inscriptions on funerary monuments to laywomen mirrored the sentiments expressed in funeral sermons in detailing a wide range of pious attributes and in stressing the particular religiosity of the female sex. In Wales similarly the funerary praise of laywomen embraced a wide definition of female achievement, and one that underwent little change with the introduction of protestantism. The content of the guides to poets specifying how particular categories of patrons should be praised changed little, and poets considered charity and loving kindness to be the stock virtues of women. Tudur Aled's poem to Margret, the daughter of Gruffudd ap Rhys, for example, praised her in the following terms,

She heard the poor and gained praise for her generosity in response to beggars. Some in whom vanity sprouted, were bent on promising without giving. But she was as steadfast as the one moon, promising and giving silver from her hand. Was ever a maid born with nobler and more generous heart than this, the soul of Anglesey?[77]

And Harri Hywel's description of Margaret, the wife of Lewis Owain of Hafoddywyll (Merioneth), expressed similar ideas,

It was a cold day for the impoverished. She was a chaste and very sober housewife; warmhearted, pure, pious and virtuous. Her lineage, my Lord, shall prosper her, the wise, merciful and good lady.

It was the values of practical piety that defined the virtuous woman amongst her neighbours and made her worthy of praise. Such virtues were not especially protestant. The sentiments expressed in Siôn Phylip's praise of Catrin, the wife of Gruffudd ap Siôn of Penyberth and a prominent recusant, were indistinguishable from those addressed to protestant gentlewomen. Having praised her hospitality and generosity, the poet concluded, 'God sends a chaste lady, a devout moral lady; a lady who deserves exalted praise: good to the poor and the weak'.[78]

From this perspective it is tempting to conclude that women did not experience a Reformation. The values that defined their conduct and reputation appear to be unchanged. But this would be to overstate the case. The vocabulary of praise was always likely to be conservative and to repeat notions derived from the Seven Works of Mercy and the mediaeval personification of Charity as female, but this does not remove its significance. The femininity of these virtues shaped how women experienced the Reformation. They underpinned the continuing currency of the idea of the godly woman, and this, together with the idea that the stereotypical struggling christian was the weak emotional woman, ensured that the Reformation would not be such a hostile environment for women as is often assumed. For the same reasons that the austerities of an image-restricted culture presided over by the tetragrammaton needed to be tempered by a Christocentric emphasis in the piety of the godly, the style of protestant piety was consistently feminised. All this means that the transition for women from a catholic to a protestant culture was not primarily shaped by many of those entries on the balance sheet with which we began. The possibility of clerical marriage, the closure of nunneries, hostility to images and practices of intercession were important features defining the new religious landscape, but they did not determine the way in which ideas of the godly woman would be integrated in religious developments in England, Scotland and Wales. What remained decisive in defining regional variation were the particular devotional priorities that had developed in pre-Reformation catholicism.

In gender terms, the Reformation did not systematically erase existing assumptions, but took over much of the existing content and prevailing language. This was most obvious in the continued Scottish use of spotless bride of Christ imagery that was rooted in the thriving later mediaeval cult of saints, and had connections with the way in which kirk sessions were to exercise sexual discipline. Of course, this translation was not always so clear, especially when, as in the case of England, the prevailing religious principles were not so sharply gendered. The Passion centred Christocentric piety of late mediaeval England reduced Mary to a representative human witness, and, in emphasising the naturally weak and sinful nature of all christians in relation to God, rendered the difference in male and female capacities largely irrelevant. Yet the persistence of gender stereotypes, such as the idea of women as scolds or as sexual temptresses, meant that discipline would not be gender neutral, even if the largest imbalances were driven by economic, rather than religious, motivations. But it did also mean that if women were to be the brides of Christ it would be in a mode that related more closely to the domestic hearth than one that demanded stark choices characteristic of the cloister between things of the world and faith. In contrast, the benevolent outlook of the Welsh, who, if contemporary comment is to be believed, had little time for notions of sin and maleficium and saw the Passion as evidence of God's cruelty, could only be translated into a protestant framework with difficulty. But as this process made headway under pressure from English influences, Welsh disregard for the special value of virginity encountered the English unconcern, which, despite its different origins, also devalued this state.

Inevitably, such comparisons are vulnerable to the charge of being rather too broad brush. Religious commitment and understanding was essentially personal, and even more so in an era in which the introduction of protestantism opened up the possibility of a wider range of religious choice, of bricolage and of outright rejection of aspects of doctrine. We should not forget the women of Bromfield (Denbighshire) who routinely hired pipers to play for them during the time of divine service every Sunday to the displeasure of local protestants, or the response of the vagrant, Margaret Underwood, who told the kirk session of Dundonald that 'Christ would not have been so daft as to have died for her'.[79] But alongside such women we need to place not only the martyrs and the godly women eulogised in funeral sermons, but also women like Grace Coates of Basford (Nottinghamshire) who resisted the attempts of the authorities to prevent her from teaching local children to read without a licence, maintaining staunchly that she was obliged to teach them to read or else they would be damned.[80] However we turn the kaleidoscope to highlight individual pieces, there are patterns into which they fall. At the same time, such fragments also remind us of the oversimplification inherent in such shibboleths as the requirement of literacy being a barrier impeding women's adoption of protestantism.

Notes

Introduction

1. J.G.A. Pocock, 'British history: A plea for a new subject', *Jnl. Modern Hist.* 47/4 (1975), pp. 601–28; A recent example of this approach is K. Wrightson, *Earthly Necessities: Economic Lives in Early Modern Britain* (New Haven & London, 2000).

2. R.R. Davies, 'The status of women and the practice of marriage in late medieval Wales', in D. Jenkins and M.E. Owen (eds), *The Welsh Law of Women* (Cardiff, 1980), p. 101; F.J. Shaw, *The Northern and Western Islands of Scotland: Their Economy and Society in the Sixteenth Century* (Edinburgh, 1980), pp. 35–37.

3. T.M.Y. Mason, 'Shetland in the sixteenth century', in I.B. Cowan and D. Shaw (eds), *The Renaissance and Reformation in Scotland: Essays in honour of Gordon Donaldson* (Edinburgh, 1983), p. 213.

4. A. Clark, *Working Life of Women in the Seventeenth Century* (repr. London, 1982), p. 103.

5. P. Sharpe, 'Literally spinsters: A new interpretation of local economy and demography in Colyton in the eighteenth and nineteenth centuries', *Econ. Hist. Rev.* 44/1 (1991), pp. 52–53.

6. H. Owen, 'The mat-weaving industry in Newborough', *Transactions of the Anglesey Antiquarian Society and Field Club* (1923), pp. 62–64; M. Hughes, 'The marram grass industry of Newborough, Anglesey', *Transactions of the Anglesey Antiquarian Society and Field Club* (1956), pp. 22–28.

7. J.M. Bennett, *Ale, Beer and Brewsters in England: Women's Work in a Changing World*, 1300–1600 (Oxford, 1996); E. Ewan, ' "For whatever ales ye": Women as consumers and producers in late medieval Scottish

towns', in E. Ewan and M. Meikle (eds), *Women in Scotland c.1100–1750* (East Linton, 1999), pp. 125–35.

8. R.A. Dodgshon, *From Chiefs to Landlords: Social and Economic Change in the Western Highlands and Islands, c.1493–1820* (Edinburgh, 1988); A.I. Macinnes, *Clanship, Commerce and the House of Stuart, 1603–1788* (East Linton, 1996).

9. C.W.J. Withers, 'Conceptions of cultural landscape change in upland North Wales: A case study of Llanbedr-y-Cennin and Caerhun parishes, *c.*1560–*c.*1891', *Landscape History* 17 (1995), pp. 35–47; A. Ward, 'Transhumance and settlement on the Welsh Uplands: A view from the Black Mountain', in N. Edwards (ed.), *Landscape and Settlement in Medieval Wales* (Oxbow Monograph 81, 1977), pp. 97–111.

10. I. Whyte, *Agriculture and Society in Seventeenth Century Scotland* (Edinburgh, 1979), pp. 83–86; Shaw, *Northern and Western Islands in the Seventeenth Century*, p. 91.

11. J. Galbraith, 'The Middle Ages' in D. Forrester and D. Murray (eds), *Studies in the History of Worship in Scotland* (Edinburgh, 1984), pp. 17–32.

12. C. Peters, *Patterns of Piety: Women, Gender and Religion in Late Mediaeval and Reformation England* (Cambridge, 2003); G. Williams, *The Welsh Church from Conquest to Reformation* (1962, repr. 1993); M. Gray, *Images of Piety: The Iconography of Traditional Religion in Late Medieval Wales*, B.A.R. British series 316 (2000).

13. C. Larner, *Witchcraft and Religion: The Politics of Popular Belief* (Oxford, 1984), pp. 84–88; C. Larner, *Enemies of God: The Witch Hunt in Scotland* (London, 1981).

14. R. Suggett, 'Witchcraft dynamics in early modern Wales', in M. Roberts and S. Clark (eds), *Women and Gender in Early Modern Wales* (Cardiff, 2000), pp. 75–103; S. Clark and P.T.J. Morgan, 'Religion and magic in Elizabethan Wales: Robert Holland's Dialogue on witchcraft', *Jnl. Eccl. Hist.* 27 (1976), pp. 31–46.

15. C. Lloyd-Morgan, 'Women and their poetry in medieval Wales', in C.M. Meale (ed.), *Women and Literature in Britain 1150–1500* (Cambridge Studies in Medieval Literature, 17, 1993), pp. 183–201; N. Powell, 'Women and strict metre poetry in Wales' in M. Roberts and S. Clarke (eds), *Women and Gender in Early Modern Wales* (Cardiff, 2000), pp. 129–58; J. Bannerman, 'Literacy in the Highlands', in I.B. Cowan and D. Shaw (eds), *The Renaissance and Reformation in Scotland: Essays in Honour of Gordon Donaldson* (Edinburgh, 1983), pp. 214–35.

16. W. Matthews, 'The Egyptians in Scotland: The political history of a myth', *Viator* 1 (1970), pp. 289–306; M. Lynch, 'A nation born again? Scottish identity in the sixteenth and seventeenth centuries', in D. Broun, R.J. Finlay and M. Lynch (eds), *Image and Identity: The Making and Re-making of Scotland Through the Ages* (Edinburgh, 1998), pp. 82–104.

Chapter 1   Marriage, Kinship and Inheritance

1. A.E. Anton, 'Handfasting in Scotland', *Scottish Hist. Review* 37 (1958), pp. 89–102; W.D.H. Sellar, 'Marriage, divorce and concubinage in Gaelic Scotland', *Transactions of the Gaelic Society of Inverness* 51 (1979–80), pp. 464–93.
2. Sellar, 'Marriage, divorce and concubinage', p. 464.
3. G. Donaldson (ed.), *Scottish Historical Documents* (Edinburgh & London, 1970), p. 173.
4. A.I. Macinnes, *Clanship, Commerce and the House of Stuart, 1603–1788* (East Linton, 1996), p. 59.
5. Sellar, 'Marriage, divorce and concubinage', p. 484.
6. C. Giblin (ed.), *Irish Franciscan Mission to Scotland, 1619–46* (Dublin, 1964), p. 57.
7. Anton, 'Handfasting', p. 98.
8. D.B. Walters, 'The European context of the Welsh law of matrimonial property', in D. Jenkins and M.E. Owen (eds), *The Welsh Law of Women* (Cardiff, 1980), p. 118.
9. R.R. Davies, 'The status of women and the practice of marriage in late medieval Wales', in D. Jenkins and M.E. Owen (eds), *The Welsh Law of Women* (Cardiff, 1980), p. 113.
10. K. Nicholls, 'Irishwomen and property in the sixteenth century', in M. MacCurtain and M. O'Dowd (eds), *Women in Early Modern Ireland* (Edinburgh, 1991), pp. 17–31.
11. G. Morgan, 'Women's wills in West Wales, 1600–1750', *Trans. Hon. Soc. of Cymmrodorion* (1992), pp. 101–02.
12. E.J.L. Cole, 'Clandestine marriages: The awful evidence from a consistory court', *Transactions of the Radnorshire Society* 56 (1976), p. 69.
13. G. Dyfnallt Owen, *Elizabethan Wales: The Social Scene* (Cardiff, 1962), pp. 50–51; G. Dyfnallt Owen, *Wales in the Reign of James I* (Woodbridge, 1988), pp. 89–90.

14. R. Suggett, 'Slander in early modern Wales', *The Bulletin of the Board of Celtic Studies* 39 (1992), pp. 119–53.

15. M.H.B. Sanderson, *Scotland in the Sixteenth Century* (Edinburgh, 1982), pp. 58–60.

16. Sanderson, *Scotland in the Sixteenth Century*, pp. 136–37.

17. E. MacGillivray (ed.), *Richard James, 1592–1638: Description of Shetland, Orkney and the Highlands of Scotland*, Orkney Miscellany vol. 1 (1953), p. 53.

18. Anton, 'Handfasting', p. 99; J. Stuart (ed.), *Selections from the Records of the Kirk Session, Presbytery and Synod of Aberdeen* (Aberdeen, 1846), p. 11.

19. Anton, 'Handfasting', p. 96.

20. T.C. Smout, 'Scottish marriage, regular and irregular, 1500–1940', in R.B. Outhwaite (ed.), *Marriage and Society: Studies in the Social History of Marriage* (London, 1981), pp. 212–13.

21. A. Hudson, *The Premature Reformation: Wycliffite Texts and Lollard History* (Oxford, 1988), pp. 290–94; M. Aston, 'William White's Lollard followers' in her *Lollards and Reformers: Images and Literacy in Late Medieval Religion* (London, 1984); N.P. Tanner (ed.), *Heresy Trials in the Diocese of Norwich, 1428–31* (Camden Soc., 4th ser., xx, London, 1977), pp. 71, 111; S. McSheffrey, *Gender and Heresy: Women and Men in Lollard Communities, 1420–1530* (Philadelphia, 1995), pp. 83–85.

22. G. McN. Rushforth, 'Seven sacraments compositions in English medieval art', *Antiq. Jnl.* 9 (1929); A. Eljenholm Nichols, *Seeable Signs: The Iconography of the Seven Sacraments, 1350–1544* (Woodbridge, 1994); M. Gray, *Images of Piety: The Iconography of Traditional Religion in Late Medieval Wales*, B.A.R. British series 316 (2000), p. 51.

23. E.J. Carlson, *Marriage and the English Reformation* (Oxford, 1994), p. 42.

24. The interpretation of spousals that follows summarises arguments advanced in C. Peters, 'Gender, sacrament and ritual: The making and meaning of marriage in late medieval and early modern England', *P&P* 169 (2000), pp. 82–93.

25. R. Adair, *Courtship, Illegitimacy and Marriage in Early Modern England* (Manchester, 1996).

26. R.M. Smith, 'Some reflections on the evidence for the origins of the "European marriage pattern" in England' in C. Harris (ed.), *The Sociology of the Family: New Directions for Britain* (Sociol. Rev., Monograph 28, Keele, 1979), p. 88. This estimate is based on fourteenth-century data from the diocese of Ely.

27. J. Habbakuk, 'The rise and fall of English landed families, 1600–1800', *T.R.H.S.* 29 (1979), pp. 189–94.
28. A.G. Macpherson, 'An old Highland genealogy', *Scottish Studies* 10/1 (1966), pp. 1–43; J. Wormald, *Lords and Men in Scotland: Bonds of Manrent, 1442–1603* (Edinburgh, 1985); K.M. Brown, *Bloodfeud in Scotland, 1573–1625: Violence, Justice and Politics in an Early Modern Society* (Edinburgh, 1986).
29. Macinnes, *Clanship, Commerce and the House of Stuart*, p. 9.
30. M. Gluckman, 'Peace in the Feud', in his *Custom and Conflict in Africa* (Oxford, 1970), pp. 1–26; I. Whitaker, 'Tribal structure and national politics in Albania, 1910–50', in I.M. Lewis (ed.), *History and Social Anthropology* (London, 1968), pp. 253–93.
31. J.D. Marwick and R. Renwick (eds), *Extracts from the Records of the Burgh of Glasgow*, 6 vols (Glasgow, 1876–1916), vol. 1, 1573–1642 (Glasgow, 1876), p. 49.
32. E. Ewan, 'A realm of one's own? The place of medieval and early modern women in Scottish history', in T. Brotherstone, D. Simonton and O. Walsh (eds), *Gendering Scottish History: An International Perspective* (Glasgow, 1999), p. 26.
33. Wormald, *Lords and Men*, p. 79.
34. P. Williams, 'The Welsh Borderland under Queen Elizabeth', *Welsh History Review* 1 (1960), p. 20.
35. Wormald, *Lords and Men*, p. 79.
36. Wormald, *Lords and Men*, p. 79.
37. Anton, 'Handfasting', p. 98.
38. Wormald, *Lords and Men*, p. 61.
39. Wormald, *Lords and Men*, p. 161.
40. R.A. Dodgshon, *From Chiefs to Landlords: Social and Economic Change in the Western Highlands and Islands, c.1493–1820* (Edinburgh, 1988); A.I. Macinnes, *Clanship, Commerce and the House of Stuart, 1603–1788* (East Linton, 1996).
41. I. Carter, 'Marriage patterns and social sectors in Scotland before the eighteenth century', *Scottish Studies* 17 (1973), pp. 51–60.
42. J. Gwynfor Jones, *The Wynn Family of Gwydir: Origins, Growth and Development c.1490–1674* (Aberystwyth, 1995), pp. 124–26.
43. K.W. Swett, 'Widowhood, custom and property in early modern North Wales', *Welsh History Review* 18/2 (1996), p. 226.
44. A.D. Carr, 'The Mostyns of Mostyn, 1540–1642, part II', *Jnl. of the Flintshire Hist. Soc.* 30 (1981–2), pp. 140–41.

45. J. Gwynfor Jones, 'The gentry of East Glamorgan, 1540–1640', *Morgannwg* 37 (1993), pp. 11–12.

46. K.M. Brown, 'The Scottish aristocracy, anglicization and the court, 1603–38', *Hist. Jnl.* 36/3 (1993), pp. 543–76.

47. Smout, 'Scottish marriage, regular and irregular, pp. 213–14.

48. S. Hindle, 'The problem of pauper marriage in seventeenth century England', *T.R.H.S.* 6th ser. 8 (1998), pp. 71–89.

49. F.M. Heal, *Hospitality in Early Modern England* (Oxford, 1990), pp. 369–70; M. Wood (ed.), *Extracts from the Records of the Burgh of Edinburgh*, vol. 3 (Edinburgh, 1936), p. 171; In Glasgow in 1583 those who authorised bridals above a certain amount were to be fined 8s. Marwick and Renwick (eds), *Extracts from the Records of the Burgh of Glasgow*, vol. 1 1573–1642 (Glasgow, 1876), p. 106.

50. Hindle does not note that the couple married two months later, and that at least some of Alice's neighbours thought that her stead-fast loyalty to her husband reconciled her to God and the world. D. O'Hara, 'Ruled by my friends: Aspects of marriage in the diocese of Canterbury, *c.*1540–1570', *Continuity & Change* 6/1 (1991), pp. 9–41; D. O'Hara, *Courtship and Constraint: Rethinking the Making of Marriage in Tudor England* (Manchester, 2000), pp. 44–45.

51. Hindle, 'Problem of pauper marriage', pp. 78–79, 86.

52. K. Wrightson and D. Levine, *Poverty and Piety in an English Village: Terling, 1525–1700* (1979, repr. Oxford, 1995), p. 126.

53. J.O. Halliwell, (ed.), *A Minute Account of the Social Condition of the People of Anglesea in the Reign of James I* (London, 1860), p. 17.

54. T.C. Smout, N.C. Landsman and T.M. Devine, 'Scottish emigration in the seventeenth and eighteenth centuries', in N. Canny (ed.), *Europeans on the Move: Studies on European Migration, 1500–1800* (Oxford, 1994), pp. 78–85; M. Perceval-Maxwell, *The Scottish Migration to Ulster in the Reign of James I* (London, 1973), p. 126.

55. Sanderson, *Scotland in the Sixteenth Century*, p. 181.

56. C. Peters, 'Single women in early modern England', *Continuity and Change* 12/3 (1997), pp. 325–45.

57. S. Mendelson and P. Crawford, *Women in Early Modern England* (Oxford, 1998), p. 172; J.D. Marwick (ed.), *Extracts from the Records of the Burgh of Edinburgh* (Edinburgh, 1871), p. 27; N. Mayhew, 'Women in Aberdeen at the end of the Middle Ages', in T. Brotherstone et al. (eds), *Gendering Scottish History: An International Perspective* (Glasgow, 1999), p. 155, n. 39.

58. Peters, 'Single women', p. 329; M.D. Harris (ed.), *The Coventry Leet Book*, Early English Text Society, orig. ser. 135 (Oxford, 1908), pp. 545, 552, 568.
59. Peters, 'Single women', p. 331.
60. P. Redwood, 'Life in Elizabethan Breconshire as portrayed in contemporary wills', *Brycheiniog* 24 (1990–92), p. 44.
61. J. Woodfall Ebsworth (ed.), *The Roxburghe Ballads*, vol. 8, pt. 2 (Hertford, 1897), pp. 676–77.
62. P. Sharpe, 'Literally spinsters: a new interpretation of local economy and demography in Colyton', *Econ. Hist. Rev.* 44/1 (1991), pp. 52–53.
63. G. Dyfnallt Owen, *Elizabethan Wales: The Social Scene* (Cardiff, 1962), p. 45.
64. J. Woodfall Ebsworth (ed.), *The Roxburghe Ballads*, vol. 7 (Hertford, 1890), pp. 155–56.
65. G. Morgan, 'Women's wills in West Wales, 1600–1750', *Trans. of the Hon. Soc. of Cymmrodorion* (1992), pp. 103–05.
66. R.K. Marshall, *Virgins and Viragos: A History of Women in Scotland from 1080–1980* (1983), pp. 29–30, citing *The Practicks* of Sir James Balfour of Pittendreich, Stair Soc. 1962, vol. 1, pp. 99–100, 105–07.
67. F. Jones, 'Customs of the manor and lordship of Castlemartin (1592)', *Bull. of the Board of Celtic Studies* 34 (1987), p. 202.
68. R.H. Hilton, *The English Peasantry in the later Middle Ages* (Oxford, 1975), p. 99.
69. Sanderson, *Scotland in the Sixteenth Century*, pp. 53–54.
70. Davies, 'The status of women and the practice of marriage', pp. 101–02.
71. L. Beverley Smith, 'The gage and the land market in late medieval Wales', *Econ. Hist. Rev.* 29/4 (1976), pp. 537–50.
72. B. Howells (ed.), *Elizabethan Pembrokeshire: The Evidence of George Owen*, Pembrokeshire Record Series 2 (1972), p. 7.
73. Swett, 'Widowhood, custom and property', p. 212.
74. Marshall, *Virgins and Viragos*, pp. 75–76.
75. Swett, 'Widowhood, custom and property', pp. 201–07.
76. Swett, 'Widowhood, custom and property', pp. 214–17.
77. Howells (ed.), *Elizabethan Pembrokeshire*, p. 7.
78. P.G.B. McNeill (ed.), *The Practicks of James Balfour of Pittendreich*, Stair Society, 2 vols (1962–63), vol. 1, p. 216.
79. M. Prior, 'Wives and wills 1558–1700', in J. Chartres and D. Hey (eds), *English Rural Society 1500–1800: Essays in honour of Joan Thirsk* (Cambridge, 1990), pp. 201–25.
80. A.L. Erickson, *Women and Property in Early Modern England* (London, 1995), pp. 143–7, 182–85.

81. A.D.M. Forte, 'Some aspects of the law of marriage in Scotland, 1500–1700', in E.M. Craike (ed.), *Marriage and Property* (Aberdeen, 1984), pp. 110–11.
82. Erickson, *Women and Property*, p. 123.
83. W. Gouge, *Of Domesticall Duties* (London, 1622), p. 294.
84. Erickson, *Women and Property*, p. 125.
85. W. Cramond (ed.), *The Records of Elgin, 1234–1800*, (Spalding Club, Aberdeen 1903), pp. 67–68, 79.

Chapter 2   Work and the Household Economy

1. M. Roberts, 'Gender, work and socialisation in Wales *c.*1450–*c.*1850', in S. Betts (ed.), *Our Daughters' Land Past and Present* (Cardiff, 1996), p. 35.
2. 'Historical MSS. Commission', *Archaeologia Cambrensis* 4th ser. 9 (1878), pp. 70–71.
3. 'Historical MSS. Commission', pp. 304–05.
4. A.L. Erickson, *Women and Property in Early Modern England* (London, 1993), pp. 164–65.
5. Worcs. R.O.C.C.W. 165 p. 145.
6. M. Roberts, 'Sickles and scythes: women's work and men's work at harvest time', *History Workshop Jnl.* 7 (1979), pp. 3–29.
7. A.J.S. Gibson and T.C. Smout, *Prices, Food and Wages in Scotland, 1550–1780* (Cambridge, 1995), p. 265.
8. D. Woodward, 'The background of the Statute of Artificers: The genesis of labour policy, 1558–63', *Econ. Hist. Rev.* 33 (1980), p. 42.
9. S. Mendelson and P. Crawford, *Women in Early Modern England* (Oxford, 1998), p. 266.
10. B. Howells (ed.), *Elizabethan Pembrokeshire: The Evidence of George Owen*, Pembrokeshire Record Series 2 (1973), pp. 34–37.
11. Woodward, 'The background of the Statute of Artificers', *Econ. Hist. Rev.* 33 (1980), p. 43.
12. A. Laurence, *Women in England, 1500–1760: A Social History* (London, 1994), p. 118.
13. L. Beverley Smith, 'Towards a history of women in late medieval Wales', in M. Roberts and S. Clark, (eds), *Women and Gender in Early Modern Wales* (Cardiff, 2000), p. 35.
14. A. Clark, *Working Life of Women in the Seventeenth Century* (repr. London, 1982), p. 103; In Wales female weavers seem to have been predominant in the fourteenth century but thereafter the craft

became increasingly masculinised. L. Beverley Smith, 'Towards a history of women in late medieval Wales', in M. Roberts and S. Clark, (eds), *Women and Gender in Early Modern Wales* (Cardiff, 2000), p. 34.

15. Cited in S. Wright, 'Churmaids, huswyfes and hucksters': The employment of women in Tudor and Stuart Salisbury', in L. Charles and L. Duffin (eds), *Women and Work in Pre-industrial England* (London, 1985), p. 107.

16. Clark, *Working Life of Women in the Seventeenth Century*, p. 103.

17. J.D. Marwick (ed.), *Extracts from the Records of the Burgh of Edinburgh* 4 vols. (Edinburgh, 1869–82), vol. 4, p. 161.

18. Beverley Smith, 'Towards a history of women in late medieval Wales', pp. 32–33.

19. J.E. Ashby, 'English medieval murals of the Doom' (York University M.Phil. thesis, 1980), p. 177.

20. J.M. Bennett, *Ale, Beer and Brewsters in England: Women's Work in a Changing World, 1300–1600* (Oxford, 1996), p. 140.

21. Bennett, *Ale, Beer and Brewsters*, p. 73; S. Cahn, *Industry of Devotion: The transformation of women's work in England, 1500–1660* (New York, 1987), p. 48 (reference to dairying)

22. S. Wright, 'Churmaids, huswyfes and hucksters': The employment of women in Tudor and Stuart Salisbury', in L. Charles and L. Duffin (eds), *Women and Work in Pre-industrial England* (London, 1985), p. 106.

23. Bennett, *Ale, Beer and Brewsters*, pp. 106–21; P. Clark, *The English Alehouse: A Social History, 1200–1830* (Longman, 1983), pp. 79, 102, 169–76.

24. Bennett, *Ale, Beer and Brewsters*, pp. 77–97.

25. M. Lynch, 'Continuity and change in urban society: 1500–1700', in R.A. Houston and I.D. Whyte (eds), *Scottish Society 1500–1800* (Cambridge, 1989), p. 109. The formation of the Society of Brewers in Edinburgh 'probably did more than any other single act to undermine the economic status of women'.

26. Bennett, *Ale, Beer and Brewsters*, p. 81.

27. M. Wack, 'Women, work and plays in an English medieval town', in S. Frye and K. Robertson (eds), *Maids and Mistresses, Cousins and Queens: Women's Alliances in Early Modern England* (New York & Oxford, 1999), pp. 34–42; R.K. Morris (ed.), *Chester in the Plantagenet and Tudor Reigns* (Chester, 1894), p. 425.

28. Marwick (ed.), *Extracts*, vol 3, p. 86.

29. Marwick (ed.), *Extracts* vol. 4, p. 154.

30. Marwick (ed.), *Extracts*, vol 3, p.186.

31. M. Wood (ed.), *Extracts from the Records of the Burgh of Edinburgh* (Edinburgh, 1931), vol. 2, p. 38.

32. J.M. Bennett, 'History that stands still: Women's work in the European past', *Feminist Studies* 14/2 (1988), pp. 269–83; Bennett, *Ale, Beer and Brewsters*, pp. 145–47.

33. Bennett, *Ale, Beer and Brewsters*, pp. 140–41.

34. E. Ewan. ' "For whatever ales ye": Women as consumers and producers in late medieval Scottish towns' in E. Ewan and M. Meikle (eds), *Women in Scotland c.1100–c.1750* (East Linton, 1999), pp. 126–29.

35. Wood (ed.), *Extracts*, vol. 1, p. 274.

36. J.P. Earwaker (ed.), *The Court Leet Records of the Manor of Manchester vol. 1, 1552–86* (Manchester, 1884), p. 241.

37. Marwick (ed.), *Extracts*, vol. 2, p. 27.

38. Marwick (ed.), *Extracts*, vol. 2, p. 124; M. Lynch, 'Social and economic structures of the larger towns, 1450–1600', in M. Lynch, M. Spearman and G. Stell, *The Scottish Medieval Town* (Edinburgh, 1988), pp. 277–78.

39. Wood (ed.), *Extracts*, vol. 1, p. 274.

40. M. Bateson (ed.), *Records of the Borough of Leicester, being a Series of Extracts from the Archives of the Corporation of Leicester, 1509–1603*, vol. 3 (Cambridge, 1905), p. 147.

41. J.D. Marwick (ed.), *Extracts from the Burgh of Edinburgh vol. 1 1403–1528* (Edinburgh, 1869), pp. 198–201.

42. E. Ewan, 'Mons Meg and Merchant Meg: Women in later medieval Edinburgh', in T. Brotherstone and D. Ditchburn (eds), *Freedom and Authority: Scotland c.1050–1650, Historical and Historiographical Essays Presented to Grant G. Simpson* (East Linton, 2000), p. 137.

43. Laurence, *Women in England*, p. 126.

44. Bennett, *Ale, Beer and Brewsters*, pp. 60–72.

45. Gibson and Smout, *Prices, Food and Wages*, p. 45.

46. P. Hume Brown (ed.), *Scotland before 1700 from Contemporary Documents* (Edinburgh, 1893), p. 197.

47. J.D. Marwick and R. Renwick (eds) *Extracts from the Records of the Burgh of Glasgow*, 6 vols (Glasgow, 1876–1916), vol. 1, p. 66.

48. E. Gemmill and N. Mayhew, *Changing values in Medieval Scotland: A Study of Prices, Money and Weights and Measures* (Cambridge, 1995), p. 55.

49. Mendelson and Crawford, *Women in Early Modern England*, pp. 291–92.

50. Earwaker (ed.), *Court Leet Records of Manchester*, p. 237.

51. Gemmill and Mayhew, *Changing Values in Medieval Scotland*, p. 60.

52. Bateson (ed.), *Records of the Borough of Leicester*, p. 243; Roberts, 'Gender, work and socialisation in Wales', p. 31.
53. Gemmill and Mayhew, *Changing Values in Medieval Scotland*, p. 63. The council also ordered that no huckster should be in the burgh unless she was the wife of a free burgess.
54. E.P.D. Torrie (ed.), *The Gild Court Book of Dunfermline, 1433–1597* (Edinburgh, 1986), p. 154.
55. Clark, *Working Life of Women*, p. 173.
56. Mendelson and Crawford, *Women in Early Modern England*, p. 264; P. Sharpe, 'Literally spinsters: A new interpretation of local economy and demography in Colyton in the eighteenth and nineteenth centuries', *Econ. Hist. Rev.* 44/1 (1991), pp. 52–53.
57. V. Fildes (ed.), *Women as Mothers in Pre-industrial England* (London, 1990); Marwick (ed.), *Extracts*, vol. 4, p. 517; M.F. Graham, *The Uses of Reform: 'Godly Discipline' and Popular Behaviour in Scotland and Beyond, 1560–1610* (Leiden, 1996), p. 228; G. Desbrisay, 'Wetnurses and unwed mothers in seventeenth-century Aberdeen', in E. Ewan and M. Meikle (eds), *Women in Scotland, c.1100–c.1750* (East Linton, 1999), pp. 210–20.

Chapter 3   Disorderly Women

1. P. Clark, *The English Alehouse: A Social History, 1200–1830* (Longman, 1983), p. 158.
2. C. Levin, *The Heart and Stomach of a King: Elizabeth I and the Politics of Sex and Power* (Philadelphia, 1994), pp. 83–84.
3. L. Gowing, *Domestic Dangers: Women, Words and Sex in Early Modern London* (Oxford, 1996).
4. J.D. Marwick (ed.), *Extracts from the Records of the Burgh of Edinburgh* 4 vols (Edinburgh 1869–82), vol. 2, pp. 248–49.
5. M. Wood (ed.) *Extracts from the Records of the Burgh of Edinburgh*, 3 vols. (Edinburgh, 1927–36), vol. 1, p. 295, vol. 3, pp. 47, 91, 196.
6. R.H. Morris (ed.), *Chester in the Plantagenet and Tudor Reigns* (Chester, 1894), pp. 375–76.
7. B.A. Hanawalt, 'Separation anxieties in late medieval London: Gender in "The Wright's Chaste Wife"', in her *'Of Good and Ill Repute': Gender and Social Control in Medieval England* (Oxford, 1998), pp. 88–103.
8. P.H. Barnum (ed.), *Dives and Pauper*, vol. 1, part 2, E.E.T.S. orig. ser. 280 (1980), pp. 67, 110–11, 70–72, 80–81, 84–88.

9. J.E. Ashby, 'English medieval murals of the Doom', M.Phil. thesis, University of York, 1980, pp. 180, 237, 240.

10. T. Erbe (ed.), *Mirk's Festial: A Collection of Sermons by Johannes Mirkus*, E.E.T.S. extra ser. 96 (1905), p. 287.

11. Erbe (ed.), *Mirk's Festial*, pp. 288–89.

12. Erbe (ed.), *Mirk's Festial*, p. 292.

13. Gouge, *Of Domesticall Duties* (London, 1622), p. 221.

14. For the adoption of these ideas by Scottish divines see, D.G. Mullan, *Scottish Puritanism, 1590–1638* (Oxford, 2000), pp. 140–70.

15. D. Leigh, *The Mother's Blessing* (1616) Chapter 9, reprinted in S. Brown (ed.), *Women's Writing in Stuart England* (Stroud, 1999), pp. 27–30.

16. *The Acts of the Parliament in Scotland*, vol. 3, 1567–92 (1814), pp. 25–26.

17. A. Maxwell, *The History of Old Dundee, Narrated out of the Town Council Register* (Edinburgh & Dundee, 1884), pp. 82–83.

18. M. Spufford, 'Puritanism and social control?', in A.J. Fletcher and J. Stevenson (eds), *Order and Disorder in Early Modern England* (Cambridge, 1985), pp. 41–57.

19. B. Lenman, 'The limits of godly discipline in the early modern period with particular reference to England and Scotland', in K. von Greyerz (ed.), *Religion and Society in Early Modern Europe, 1500–1800* (London, 1984), pp. 128–29.

20. G. Parker, 'The "kirk by law established" and the origins of "The Taming of Scotland": St. Andrews, 1559–1600', in L. Leneman (ed.), *Perspectives in Scottish Social History: Essays in Honour of Rosalind Mitchison* (Aberdeen, 1988), p. 13.

21. E. MacGillivray, *Richard James, 1592–1638: Description of Shetland, Orkney and the Highlands of Scotland*, (Orkney Miscellany 1, 1953), p. 53.

22. M.F. Graham, *Uses of Reform: 'Godly Discipline' and Popular Behavior in Scotland and Beyond, 1560–1610*, (Leiden, 1996), pp. 88, 281–89, 345–46.

23. M. Ingram, *Church Courts, Sex and Marriage in England, 1570–1640* (Cambridge, 1987), p. 261.

24. M. Ingram, 'Religion, communities and social discipline in late sixteenth and early seventeenth century England: Case studies', in K. von Greyerz (ed.), *Religion and Society in Early Modern Europe* (London, 1984), pp. 177–93.

25. R. von Friedeburg, 'Reformation of manners and the social - composition of offenders in an East Anglian cloth village: Earls Colne, Essex, 1531–1642', *Jnl. British Studies* 29/4 (1990), pp. 362–65.

26. Ingram, *Church Courts*, pp. 220–33.

27. D. Underdown, 'The taming of the scold: The enforcement of patriarchal authority in early modern England', in A. Fletcher and J. Stevenson (eds), *Order and Disorder in Early Modern England* (Cambridge, 1985), pp. 125–27, 134–35; D. Underdown, *Revel, Riot and Rebellion: Popular Politics and Culture in England 1603–1660* (Oxford, 1987), pp. 73–105.
28. K. Wrightson and D. Levine, *Poverty and Piety in an English Village, Terling, 1525–1700* (1979, repr. Oxford, 1995 with a postscript by Wrightson), pp. 28, 215.
29. R. Adair, *Courtship, Illegitimacy and Marriage in Early Modern England* (Manchester, 1996), p. 92.
30. Wrightson and Levine, *Poverty and Piety*, p. 126; Ingram, *Church Courts*, p. 233 taking the percentage of pregnant brides in the total known.
31. von Friedeburg, 'Reformation of manners', p. 367.
32. C. B. Herrup, 'Law and morality in seventeenth century England', *P&P*106 (1985), pp. 102–23.
33. Ingram, *Church Courts*, pp. 236–37.
34. S. Mendelson and P. Crawford, *Women in Early Modern England* (Oxford, 1998), p. 148.
35. Adair, *Courtship, Illegitimacy and Marriage*, pp. 37–39.
36. Ingram, *Church Courts*, p. 262.
37. W.P.M. Kennedy (ed.), *Elizabethan Episcopal Administration* (Alcuin Club Coll. 25–7, 1924), pp. 148, 151.
38. D. Cressy, *Birth, Marriage and Death: Ritual, Religion, and the Life-cycle in Tudor and Stuart England* (Oxford, 1997), p. 210.
39. Cressy, *Birth, Marriage and Death*, p. 215.
40. S. Hindle, *The State and Social Change in Early Modern England, 1550–1640* (Basingstoke, 2000), p. 161.
41. E.J. Burford and S. Shulman, *Of Bridles and Burnings: The Punishment of Women* (London, 1992), p. 71.
42. Ingram, *Church Courts*, pp. 338–39.
43. W.J. King, 'Punishment for bastardy in early seventeenth century England', *Albion* 10 (1978), pp. 130–51.
44. Ingram, *Church Courts*, pp. 338–40.
45. M. Wood (ed.), *Extracts from the Records of the Burgh of Edinburgh*, vol. 2 (Edinburgh 1931), p. 38.
46. J. Stuart (ed.), *Selections from the Records of the Kirk Session, Presbytery and Synod of Aberdeen* (Aberdeen, 1846), p. 11.
47. A.B. Calderwood (ed.), *The Buik of the Kirk of the Canagait, 1564–67*, (Scottish Record Society, Edinburgh, 1961), pp. 8–9, 74–75.

48. Parker, 'Kirk by law established', p. 13.

49. RNLKS 14/11/1605, p. 44, 9/10/1606, p. 108.

50. RNLKS 21/6/1610, pp. 313–14.

51. J. Stuart (ed.), *Selections from the Records of Aberdeen*, p. 8.

52. J.K. Cameron (ed.), *The First Book of Discipline* (Edinburgh, 1972), pp. 193–94, 196–98.

53. J.D. Marwick (ed.), *Extracts from the Records of the Burgh of Edinburgh*, 4 vols. (Edinburgh, 1869–82), vol. 4, p. 490.

54. Wood (ed.), *Extracts from the Records of the Burgh of Edinburgh*, vol. 1 (Edinburgh, 1927), p. 11.

55. Marwick (ed.), *Extracts from the Records of the Burgh of Edinburgh*, vol. 4, pp. 72, 195.

56. J. Strawhorn, *The History of Ayr: Royal Burgh and County Town* (Edinburgh, 1989), p. 47.

57. G. Donaldson, *Shetland Life under Earl Patrick* (Edinburgh, 1958), p. 122.

58. Maxwell, *History of Old Dundee*, pp. 84–85.

59. K. Thomas, 'The Puritans and adultery: The Act of 1650 reconsidered', in D. Pennington and K. Thomas (eds), *Puritans and Revolutionaries: Essays in Seventeenth Century History Presented to Christopher Hill* (Oxford, 1978), pp. 257–82.

60. A. Peterkin (ed.), *The Booke of the Universall Kirk of Scotland* (Edinburgh, 1839), p. 118.

61. F.D. Bargett, 'The Monifieth Kirk Register', *Records of the Scottish Church History Society* 23/2 (1998), pp. 186–89.

62. Graham, *Uses of Reform*, p. 121.

63. Cameron, *The First Book of Discipline*, p. 196.

64. R. Mitchison and L. Leneman, *Sexuality and Social Control: Scotland 1660–1780* (Oxford, 1989), p. 86.

65. *Introduction to Scottish Legal History*, Stair Society 20 (1958), p. 94.

66. Peterkin, *The Booke of the Universall Kirk*, pp. 54, 144, 160, 421.

67. *The Acts of the Parliament in Scotland*, vol. 3, p. 543, vol. 4, p. 233.

68. R.B. Bond, ' "Dark deeds darkly answered": Thomas Becon's *Homily against Whoredom and Adultery*, its contexts, and its affiliations with three Shakespeare plays', *Sixteenth Century Jnl.* 16/2 (1985), pp. 191–205. *Certain Sermons or Homilies, appointed by the King's Majesty to be declared and read by all parsons, vicars, or curates every Sunday in their churches, where they have cure* (London, 1547), Piii.r, Piv. v.

69. Rev. G.E. Corrie (ed.), *Sermons by Hugh Latimer, sometime Bishop of Worcester, Martyr 1555*, Parker Society (Cambridge, 1844), pp. 196, 244.

70. Gouge, *Of Domesticall Duties*, p. 220.

71. W. Whately, *A Bride-Bush, or a Wedding Sermon* (London, 1617), p. 2.

72. D. Jenkins and M.E. Owen (eds), *The Welsh Law of Women* (Cardiff, 1980), pp. 151–53.

73. D. Williams (ed.), *Three Treatises Concerning Wales* (Cardiff, 1960), pp. 35–36.

74. P. Williams, 'The activity of the Council of the Marches under the early Stuarts', *Welsh History Review* (1961/2), pp. 133–45.

75. C. Lloyd-Morgan, 'Women and their poetry in medieval Wales', in C.M. Meale (ed.), *Women and Literature in Britain, 1150–1500* (Cambridge Studies in Medieval Literature, 17, 1993), pp. 183–201.

76. E.P. Thompson, ' "Rough music": Le charivari anglais', *Annales E.S.C.* 27 (1972), pp. 294–95.

77. Mendelson and Crawford, *Women in Early Modern England*, p. 128.

78. L. Gowing, *Domestic Dangers: Women, Words and Sex in Early Modern London* (Oxford, 1996), p. 181.

79. RNLKS 11/1/1610, p. 295, 10/3/1608, p. 202.

80. M. Ingram, ' "Scolding women cucked or washed": A crisis in gender relations in early modern England?', in J. Kermode and G. Walker (eds), *Women, Crime and the Courts in Early Modern England* (London, 1994), pp. 51–52.

81. Underdown, 'The taming of the scold', pp. 116–36; S.D. Amussen, 'Gender, family and the social order, 1560–1725', in A. Fletcher and J. Stevenson (eds), *Order and Disorder in Early Modern England* (Cambridge, 1985), pp. 196–217.

82. Ingram, 'Scolding women', pp. 55–57.

83. L. Gowing, 'Gender and the language of insult in early modern London', *History Workshop Jnl.* 35 (1993) p. 3.

84. Wood (ed.), *Records of the Burgh of Edinburgh*, vol. 1, p. 119.

85. Graham, *Uses of Reform*, pp. 86, 100, 110, 120, 211, 225, 239, 247, 254.

86. J.G. Harrison, 'Women and the branks in Stirling, *c.*1600–1730', *Scottish Economic and Social History* 18/2 (1998), pp. 114–31.

87. *Extracts from the Records of the Burgh of Glasgow*, vol. 1 (1876), p. 109.

88. Ingram, 'Scolding women', pp. 61–62.

89. D. Underdown, *Fire from Heaven: Life in an English Town in the Seventeenth Century* (London, 1993), p. 98; Ingram, 'Scolding women', pp. 57, 62.

90. Gowing, *Domestic Dangers*, pp. 63–64; Ingram, *Church Courts*, p. 301.

91. W. Forbes Leith (ed.), *Memoirs of Scottish Catholics During the Seventeenth and Eighteenth Centuries*, vol. 1, 1627–49 (London, 1909), p. 64.

Chapter 4   Witchcraft, the Devil and the Elfin Queen

1. C. Larner, *Witchcraft and Religion: The Politics of Popular Belief* (Oxford, 1984), pp. 84–88.
2. D. Purkiss, 'Sounds of silence: Fairies and incest in Scottish witchcraft stories', in S. Clark (ed.), *Languages of Witchcraft: Narrative, Ideology and Meaning in Early Modern Culture* (Basingstoke, 2001), pp. 81–98.
3. K. Thomas, *Religion and the Decline of Magic: Studies in Popular Beliefs in Sixteenth- and Seventeenth-Century England* (London, 1971); A. Macfarlane, *Witchcraft in Tudor and Stuart England* (London, 1970).
4. D. Purkiss, 'The house, the body, the child', in her *The Witch in History: Early Modern and Twentieth Century Representations* (London, 1996), pp. 93–98.
5. Macfarlane, *Witchcraft in Tudor and Stuart England*, pp. 147–49, 156.
6. Macfarlane, *Witchcraft in Tudor and Stuart England*, pp. 115–34.
7. C. Holmes, 'Women: Witnesses and Witches', *P&P* 140 (1993), p. 52.
8. Macfarlane, *Witchcraft in Tudor and Stuart England*, pp. 95, 98.
9. C. Larner, *Enemies of God: The Witch Hunt in Scotland* (London, 1981), p. 22.
10. Macfarlane, *Witchcraft in Tudor and Stuart England*, pp. 150–51.
11. S. Clark and P.T.J. Morgan, 'Religion and magic in Elizabethan Wales: Robert Holland's Dialogue on Witchcraft', *Jnl. Eccl. Hist.* 27 (1976), pp. 31–46; R. Suggett, 'Witchcraft dynamics in early modern Wales', in M. Roberts and S. Clark (eds), *Women and Gender in Early Modern Wales* (Cardiff, 2000), pp. 75–103.
12. Clark and Morgan, 'Religion and magic', pp. 31–37, 43.
13. Suggett, 'Witchcraft dynamics', pp. 89–91.
14. Thomas, *Religion and Decline*, pp. 610–11.
15. Suggett, 'Witchcraft dynamics', p. 89.
16. Thomas, *Religion and Decline*, p. 599.
17. Thomas, *Religion and Decline*, p. 145.
18. Thomas, *Religion and Decline*, p. 632; Macfarlane, *Witchcraft in Tudor and Stuart England*, p. 160; J.G. Harrison, 'Women and the branks in Stirling from 1600 to 1730', *Scottish Econ. and Soc. Hist.* 18 (1998), p. 126; J. Goodare, 'Women and the witch-hunt in Scotland', *Social History* 23/3 (1998), pp. 297, 303.
19. Macfarlane, *Witchcraft in Tudor and Stuart England*, p. 127.
20. The strength of this correlation in Scotland is unclear due to the fact that both witchcraft and charming could be prosecuted, but

the latter accusation carried a lighter sentence and did not involve the death penalty. Different jurisdictions could have contrasting concerns. Miller shows that in the seventeenth century Stirling presbytery primarily accused charmers and Haddington presbytery witches. Goodare adduces evidence that a witchcraft accusation could be tactically downgraded to one of charming if the evidence appeared weak. J. Goodare (ed.), *The Scottish Witch-Hunt in Context* (Manchester, 2002), pp. 91–92, 131.

21. D. Williams (ed.), *Three Treatises Concerning Wales* (Cardiff, 1960), p. 33.

22. Clark and Morgan, 'Religion and magic', p. 43.

23. Fear of witchcraft should not be assumed to be always present in traditional societies. Hutton lists anthropological studies of societies that do not believe in maleficent witchcraft despite being adjacent to, and otherwise sharing strong similarities with, other tribes that were obsessed with the danger of witchcraft. R. Hutton, 'The global context of Scottish witch hunt', in J. Goodare (ed.), *The Scottish Witch-Hunt in Context* (Manchester, 2002), p. 20.

24. K.L. Jolly, *Popular Religion in Late Saxon England: Elf Charms in Context* (Chapel Hill & London, 1996), p. 134.

25. E.R. Henken, *The Welsh Saints: A Study in Patterned Lives* (Woodbridge, 1991), pp. 91–2, 95.

26. Williams (ed.), *Three Treatises Concerning Wales*, pp. 33–4.

27. Thomas, *Religion and Decline*, pp. 732–33.

28. Thomas, *Religion and Decline*, pp. 220, 296, 317.

29. M. Gibson, *Early Modern Witches: Witchcraft Cases in Contemporary Writing* (London & New York, 2000), p. 29.

30. Thomas, *Religion and Decline*, p. 303n.

31. Gibson, *Early Modern Witches*, pp. 29–30, 291.

32. Holmes, 'Women: Witnesses and witches', pp. 67–68.

33. M. Gibson, 'Understanding witchcraft? Accusers' stories in print in early modern England', in S. Clark (ed.), *Languages of Witchcraft: Narrative, Ideology and Meaning in Early Modern Culture* (Basingstoke, 2001), pp. 41–54.

34. D. Purkiss, 'The body of the witch', in her *The Witch in History: Early Modern and Twentieth Century Representations* (London, 1996), p. 135; Gibson, *Early Modern Witches*, pp. 89–93.

35. M.F. Graham, *The Uses of Reform: 'Godly Discipline' and Popular Behaviour in Scotland and Beyond* (Leiden, 1996), pp. 299–301.

36. P. Hume Brown (ed.), *Scotland Before 1700 from Contemporary Documents* (Edinburgh, 1893), pp. 208–17.

37. S. Clark, 'Inversion, misrule and the meaning of witchcraft', *P&P* (1980), pp. 98–127.

38. Goodare, 'Women and the witch-hunt', pp. 302, 304–05.

39. Larner, *Enemies of God*, p. 149.

40. A. Heikkinen and T. Kervinen, 'Finland: The male domination', in B. Ankarloo and G. Henningsen (eds), *Early Modern European Witchcraft: Centres and Peripheries* (Oxford, 1993), pp. 321–22.

41. Larner, *Enemies of God*, pp. 91–92.

42. C. Larner, 'James VI and I and witchcraft', in A.G.R. Smith (ed.), *The Reign of James VI and I* (Basingstoke 1973, repr. 1979), p. 76.

43. J. Wormald, 'The witches, the devil and the king', in T. Brotherstone and D. Ditchburn (eds), *Freedom and Authority: Scotland c.1050– c.1650: Historical and Historiographical Essays Presented to Grant G. Simpson* (East Linton, 2000), pp. 165–80.

44. Graham, *Uses of Reform*, p. 146.

45. Graham, *Uses of Reform*, p. 305.

46. D.G. Mullan, 'Mistress Rutherford's narrative: A Scottish puritan autobiography', *Bunyan Studies* 7 (1997), pp. 13–37.

Chapter 5   Female Piety and Religious Change

1. For a more detailed discussion of the material relating to England in this chapter, see C. Peters, *Patterns of Piety: Women, Gender and Religion in Late Medieval and Reformation England* (Cambridge, 2003).

2. H.L. Parish, *Clerical Marriage and the English Reformation: Precedent, Policy and Practice* (Aldershot, 2000), p. 174.

3. J. Cartwright, 'The desire to corrupt: Convent and community in medieval Wales', in D. Watt (ed.), *Medieval Women in their Communities* (Cardiff, 1997), pp. 21–24.

4. S. Brigden, 'Youth and the English Reformation', *P&P* 95 (1982), pp. 37–67.

5. Brigden, 'Youth and the English Reformation', p. 62; J.G. Nichols (ed.), *Diary of Henry Machyn*, Camden Soc. orig. ser. 42 (1847–48), p. 41.

6. J.G. Nichols (ed.), *Narratives of the Days of the Reformation* (Autobiography of Edward Underhill), Camden Soc. orig. ser. 77 (1859), p. 160.

7. R.A. Houlbrooke, 'Women's social life and common action in England from the fifteenth century to the eve of the Civil War', *Continuity and Change* 1/2 (1986), pp. 171–89.

8. Rev. J. Pratt (ed.), *Acts and Monuments*, 8 vols (London, 1877), vol. 8, pp. 556–57.

9. *L & P* x. 296, P.R.O. SP1/102.

10. G. Dyfnallt Owen, *Elizabethan Wales: The Social Scene* (Cardiff, 1962), pp. 89–90.

11. J. Walter, 'Grain riots and popular attitudes to the law: Maldon and the crisis of 1629', in J. Brewer and J. Styles (eds), *An Ungovernable People: The English and their Law in the Seventeenth and Eighteenth Centuries* (London, 1980), pp. 47–84.

12. K. Lindley, *Fenland Riots and the English Revolution* (London, 1982), pp. 40–1, 63, 72, 254.

13. S. Mendelson and P. Crawford, *Women in Early Modern England* (Oxford, 1998), p. 44.

14. M. Lynch, 'Scottish towns 1500–1700', in M. Lynch (ed.), *The Early Modern Town in Scotland* (London, 1987), p. 26.

15. M.H.B. Sanderson, 'Catholic recusancy in Scotland in the sixteenth century', *Innes Review* 21/2 (1970) p. 97.

16. K.M. Brown, *Bloodfeud in Scotland, 1573–1625: Violence, Justice and Politics in an Early Modern Society* (Edinburgh, 1986), p. 29.

17. J.G. Fyfe (ed.), *Scottish Diaries and Memoirs, 1550–1746* (Stirling, 1928), pp. 136–38. John Spalding gives a similar, though less detailed, interpretation of these events. J. Spalding, *The History of the Troubles and Memorable Transactions in Scotland and England, 1624–45* vol. 1 (Edinburgh, 1828), pp. 47–48.

18. Fyfe (ed.), *Scottish Diaries and Memoirs*, p. 155; D. Laing (ed.), *The Letters and Journals of Robert Baillie A.M. Principal of the University of Glasgow 1637–1662*, 3 vols (Edinburgh, 1841), vol. 1, p. 20.

19. Laing (ed.), *The Letters and Journals of Robert Baillie*, vol. 1, pp. 23, 51, 65, 76, 93–94.

20. R.C. Reid, 'Papists and non-communicants in Dumfries', *Transactions of the Dumfriesshire and Galloway Natural History and Antiq. Soc.*, 32 (1955), pp. 188–90.

21. M.B. Rowlands, 'Recusant women 1560–1640', in M. Prior (ed.) *Women in English Society, 1500–1800* (London, 1985), pp. 150–56.

22. B. Shiels, 'Household, age and gender amongst Jacobean Yorkshire recusants', in M.B. Rowlands (ed.), *English Catholics of Parish and Town, 1558–1778*, Catholic Record Society Publications Monograph Series (London, 1999), pp. 147–80.

23. H.A. Lloyd, *The Gentry of South-West Wales, 1540–1640* (Cardiff, 1968), p. 189.

24. C. Giblin (ed.), *Irish Franciscan Mission to Scotland, 1619–46* (Dublin, 1964).

25. Lloyd, *The Gentry of South-West Wales*, p. 192.

26. W. Palmes (ed.), *Life of Mrs Dorothy Lawson of St Antonys near New Castle on Tyne* (Newcastle upon Tyne, 1851); A.F.B. Roberts, 'The role of women in Scottish catholic survival', *The Scottish Historical Review* 70 (1991), pp. 129–50.

27. P. Crawford, *Women and Religion in England, 1500–1720* (1993), p. 60.

28. M. Spufford, *Small Books and Pleasant Histories: Popular Fiction and its Readership in Seventeenth Century England* (London, 1981), p. 11.

29. Shiels, 'Household, age and gender', p. 140.

30. J. Bossy, *The English Catholic Community 1570–1850* (London, 1975), p. 158.

31. J. Maltby, *Prayer Book and People in Elizabethan and Early Stuart England* (Cambridge, 1998).

32. M. Dowling and J. Shakespeare (eds), 'Religion and politics in mid Tudor England through the eyes of an English protestant woman: The recollections of Rose Hickman', *B.I.H.R.* 55 (1982), p. 100.

33. Sanderson, 'Catholic recusancy', pp. 96–97.

34. J. Stuart (ed.), *Selections from the Records of the Kirk Session, Presbytery and Synod of Aberdeen* (1846), pp. 110–11.

35. M. Roberts, Gender, work and socialisation in Wales, *c.*1450–*c.*1850, in S. Betts (ed.), *Our Daughters' Land Past and Present* (Cardiff, 1996), p. 28.

36. Sanderson, 'Catholic recusancy', p. 104.

37. D. Williams (ed.), *Three Treatises Concerning Wales* (Cardiff 1960), pp. 33–4.

38. C. Lloyd-Morgan, 'More written about than writing? Welsh women and the written word', in H. Pryce (ed.) *Literacy in Medieval Celtic Societies* (Cambridge, 1998), p. 152.

39. G. Williams, *The Welsh Church from Conquest to Reformation* (1962; repr. University of Arkansas Press, 1993), pp. 481–86.

40. A. Breeze, 'The Virgin's rosary and St. Michael's scales', *Studia Celtica* 24 (1989–90), pp. 91–98.

41. A. Breeze, 'The Virgin's tears of blood', *Celtica* 20 (1988), pp. 110–23.

42. M. Gray, *Images of Piety: The Iconography of Traditional Religion in Late Medieval Wales*, B.A.R. British Series 316 (2000), pp. 7, 51, 21–22.

43. Gray, *Images of Piety*, p. 29.

44. Williams, *The Welsh Church*, p. 501.

45. H. Fulton, 'Medieval Welsh poems to nuns', *Cambridge Medieval Celtic Studies* 21 (1991), pp. 87–112; J. Cartwright, 'The desire to

corrupt: Convent and community in medieval Wales', in D. Watt (ed.), *Medieval Women in their Communities* (Cardiff, 1997), pp. 20–48 (quotes pp. 29, 33).

46. I.B. Cowan, *The Scottish Reformation: Church and Society in Sixteenth-Century Scotland* (London, 1982), p. 2.

47. A.B Fitch, 'Power through purity: The virgin martyrs and women's salvation in pre-Reformation Scotland', in E. Ewan and M.M. Meikle (eds), *Women in Scotland c.1100–1750* (East Linton, 1999), pp. 21–22.

48. J. Galbraith, 'The Middle Ages', in D. Forrester and E. Murray (eds), *Studies in the History of Worship in Scotland* (Edinburgh, 1984), pp. 17–32; C. Carter, 'The Arma Christi in Scotland', *Proc. Soc. Antiq. of Scotland* 90 (1959), pp. 116–29.

49. C.W. Bynum, *Fragmentation and Redemption: Essays on Gender and the Human Body in Medieval Religion* (New York, 1991), p. 153.

50. Bynum, *Fragmentation and Redemption*, p. 171.

51. P. Lake, 'Feminine piety and personal potency: The 'emancipation' of Mrs Jane Ratcliffe', *The Seventeenth Century* 2/2 (1987), pp. 143–65.

52. J.L. McIntosh, 'English funeral sermons, 1560–1640: The relationship between gender and death, dying and the afterlife', M.Litt. thesis, University of Oxford, 1990, pp. 10, 16 64–65.

53. T. Watt, *Cheap Print and Popular Piety, 1550–1640* (Cambridge, 1991), pp. 104–05.

54. McIntosh, 'English funeral sermons', pp. 181–86.

55. Williams, *The Welsh Church*, p. 468.

56. Watt, *Cheap Print and Popular Piety*, p. 108.

57. D.G. Mullan, *Scottish Puritanism, 1590–1638* (Oxford, 2000), pp. 140, 165.

58. Mullan, *Scottish Puritanism*, p. 161.

59. Mullan, *Scottish Puritanism*, pp. 145–46.

60. Rev. A.A. Bonar (ed.), *Letters of Samuel Rutherford* (London, 1894), pp. 41, 100, 198.

61. S. Hardman Moore, 'Sexing the soul: Gender and the rhetoric of puritan piety', in R. Swanson (ed.), *Gender and Christian Religion*, Studies in Church History 34 (Woodbridge, 1998), pp. 175–86.

62. Bonar (ed.), *Letters of Samuel Rutherford*, pp. 100, 46–47.

63. S.M. Dunnigan, 'Scottish women writers, c.1560–c.1650', in D. Gifford and D. McMillan (eds), *A History of Scottish Women's Writing* (Edinburgh, 1997), pp. 31–33. A.A. MacDonald notes the popularity among presbyterians of Granada's *Spiritual and Heavenly Exercises*, which emphasises the sinfulness of mankind, the vanity of the glory

and magnificence of the world, and an ever-present fear of death. A.A. MacDonald, 'Early modern Scottish literature and the parameters of culture', in S. Mapstone and J. Wood (eds), *The Rose and the Thistle: Essays in the Culture of Late Medieval and Renaissance Scotland* (East Linton, 1998), p. 90.

64. For the development of festal communions see L.E. Schmidt, *Holy Fairs: Scottish Communions and American Revivals in the Early Modern Period* (Princeton, 1989).

65. D.G. Mullan, 'Mistress Rutherford's narrative: A Scottish puritan autobiography', *Bunyan Studies* 7 (1997), pp. 13–37.

66. Cited in Parish, *Clerical Marriage*, pp. 183–84.

67. G. Donaldson, 'The parish clergy and the Reformation', *Innes Review* 10 (1959), p. 19.

68. M. Prior, 'Reviled and crucified marriages: the position of Tudor bishops' wives', in M. Prior (ed.), *Women in English Society, 1500–1800* (London, 1985), p. 125.

69. M. Mahoney, 'The Scottish hierarchy, 1513–65', *Innes Review* 10 (1959), p. 43.

70. G. Williams, 'Wales and the reign of Queen Mary I', *Welsh History Review* 10 (1980), pp. 340–45, suggests clerical acceptance and public hostility. *Cwndidau* in the diocese of Llandaff expressed hostility to married priests and their behaviour, but the high ratio of deprivations for clerical marriage as a result of the policy of Mary I (1554–55) indicates that a large number of priests had seized the opportunity to legitimise their unions.

71. Williams, *The Welsh Church*, pp. 340–42.

72. Parish, *Clerical Marriage*, p. 232.

73. The representation of wives on monuments to English bishops is discussed in Prior, 'Reviled and crucified marriages', pp. 140–41; I.D. Whyte and K.A. Whyte, 'Wed to the manse: The wives of Scottish ministers, *c.*1560–1800', in E. Ewan and M.M. Meikle (eds), *Women in Scotland c.1100–c.1750* (East Linton, 1999), p. 224.

74. M.H.B. Sanderson, *Ayrshire and the Reformation: People and Change, 1490–1600* (East Linton, 1997), p. 133.

75. J. Eales, 'Gender construction in early modern England and the conduct books of William Whateley (1583–1639)', in R.N. Swanson (ed.), *Gender and Christian Religion*, Studies in Church History 34 (Woodbridge, 1998), p. 173.

76. Rev. C. Rogers, *Monuments and Monumental Inscriptions in Scotland* 2 vols (London, 1871–72), vol. 1, p. 461.

77. Williams, *The Welsh Church*, pp. 384–85.
78. J. Gwynfor Jones, 'Welsh gentlewomen: Piety and christian conduct, *c.*1560–1700', *Jnl. of Welsh Religious History* 7 (1999), pp. 1–37.
79. G. Dyfnallt Owen, *Elizabethan Wales: The Social Scene* (Cardiff, 1962), p. 58; Graham, *Uses of Reform*, p. 256.
80. A. Fox, *Oral and Literate Culture in England, 1500–1700* (Oxford, 2000), p. 46.

Further Reading

The historiography of women in this period is much less developed for Scotland and Wales than it is for England, although substantial advances have been made in both areas in recent years. The suggestions for further reading below are necessarily more selective in relation to England and are limited to the specific themes considered in this book.

England

General Works

A. Fletcher, *Gender, Sex and Subordination in England, 1500–1800* (London, 1995).

E.A. Foyster, *Manhood in Early Modern England: Honour, Sex and Marriage* (Longman, 1999).

R.A. Houlbrooke, *The English Family, 1450–1700* (London, 1984).

A. Laurence, *Women in England, 1500–1760: A Social History* (London, 1994).

S. Mendelson and P. Crawford, *Women in Early Modern England* (Oxford, 1998).

M. Prior (ed.), *Women in English Society, 1500–1800* (London,1985).

M.R. Somerville, *Sex and Subjection: Attitudes to Women in Early Modern Society* (London, 1995).

Marriage, Family and Society

R. Adair, *Courtship, Illegitimacy and Marriage in Early Modern England* (Manchester, 1996).

S.D. Amussen, *An Ordered Society: Gender and Class in Early Modern England* (Oxford, 1998).

——, 'Gender, family and the social order, 1560–1725', in A. Fletcher and J. Stevenson (eds), *Order and Disorder in Early Modern England* (Cambridge, 1985), pp. 196–217.

D. Cressy, *Birth, Marriage and Death: Ritual, Religion and the Life-cycle in Tudor and Stuart England* (Oxford, 1997).

K.M. Davies, 'Continuity and change in literary advice on marriage', in R.B. Outhwaite (ed.), *Marriage and Society* (London, 1981), pp. 58–80.

J. Eales, 'Gender construction in early modern England and the conduct books of William Whateley (1583–1639)', in R.N. Swanson (ed.), *Gender and Christian Religion*, Studies in Church History 34 (1998), pp. 163–74.

A.E. Erickson, *Women and Property in Early Modern England* (London, 1993).

A. Fletcher, 'The protestant idea of marriage in early modern England', in A. Fletcher and P. Roberts (eds), *Religion, Culture and Society in Early Modern Britain: Essays in Honour of Patrick Collinson* (Cambridge, 1994), pp. 161–81.

C. Peters, 'Single women in early modern England: Attitudes and expectations', *Continuity and Change* 12/3 (1997), pp. 325–45.

——, 'Gender, sacrament and ritual: The making and meaning of marriage in late medieval and early modern England', *P&P* 169 (2000), pp. 63–96.

Economic Activities

J.M. Bennett, *Ale, Beer and Brewsters: Women's Work in a Changing World, 1300–1600* (Oxford, 1996).

S. Cahn, *Industry of Devotion: The Transformation of Women's Work in England, 1500–1660* (New York, 1987).

L. Charles and L. Duffin (eds), *Women and Work in Pre-industrial England* (London, 1985).

P.J.P. Goldberg, *Women, Work and Lifecycle in a Medieval Economy: Women in York and Yorkshire, c.1300–1520* (Oxford, 1992).

M. Roberts, 'Sickles and scythes: women's work and men's work at harvest time', *History Workshop Jnl.* 7 (1979), pp. 3–29.

——, 'Women and work in sixteenth-century English towns', in P. J. Corfield and D. Keene (eds), *Work in Towns, 850–1850* (Leicester, 1990).

Religion

K. Ashley and P. Sheingorn (eds), *Interpreting Cultural Symbols: Saint Anne in Late Medieval Society* (Athens, Georgia and London, 1990).

C.W. Atkinson, *Mystic and Pilgrim: The Book and the World of Margery Kempe* (Cornell, 1983).

——, 'Precious balsam in a fragile glass: The ideology of virginity in the later Middle Ages', *Jnl. Family Hist.* 8/2 (1983), pp. 131–43.

S. Beckwith, *Christ's Body: Identity, Culture and Society in Late Medieval Writings* (London and New York, 1993).

J. Bossy, *The English Catholic Community, 1570–1850* (London, 1970).

S. Brigden, 'Youth and the English Reformation', *P & P* 95 (1982), pp. 37–67.

C.W. Bynum, *Fragmentation and Redemption: Essays on Gender and the Human Body in Christian Religion* (New York, 1991).

P. Crawford, *Women and Religion in England, 1500–1720* (London and New York, 1993).

E. Duffy, 'Holy maidens, holy wyfes': The cult of women saints in fifteenth and sixteenth century England', in W.J. Shiels and D. Wood (eds), *Women in the Church*, Studies in Church History 27 (1990), pp. 175–96.

J.N. King, 'The godly woman in Elizabethan iconography', *Renaissance Quarterly* 38 (1985), pp. 41–84.

P. Lake, 'Feminine piety and personal potency: The emancipation of Mrs Jane Ratcliffe', *The Seventeenth Century* 2/2 (1987), pp. 143–65.

S. McSheffrey, *Gender and Heresy: Women and Men in Lollard Communities, 1420–1530* (Philadelphia, 1995).

H.L. Parish, *Clerical Marriage and the English Reformation: Precedent, Policy and Practice* (Aldershot, 2000).

C. Peters, *Patterns of Piety: Women, Gender and Religion in Late Medieval and Reformation England* (Cambridge, 2003).

M.B. Rowlands, 'Recusant women, 1560–1640', in M. Prior (ed.), *Women in English Society, 1500–1800* (London, 1985), pp. 149–80.

D. Willen, 'Godly women in early modern England: Puritanism and gender', *Jnl. Eccl. Hist.* 43/4 (1992), pp. 561–80.

K.A. Winstead, *Virgin Martyrs: Legends of Sainthood in Late Medieval England* (Ithaca and London, 1992).

Disorderly Women

F.E. Dolan, *Dangerous Familiars: Representations of Domestic Crime in England, 1550–1700* (Ithaca and London, 1994).

L. Gowing, *Domestic Dangers: Women, Words and Sex in Early Modern London* (Oxford, 1996).

R.A. Houlbrooke, 'Women's social life and common action in England from the fifteenth century to the eve of the Civil War', *Continuity and Change* 1/2 (1986), pp. 171–89.

M. Ingram, 'Ridings, rough music and the reform of popular culture in early modern England', *P&P* (1984).

——, 'Scolding women cucked or washed': A crisis in gender relations in early modern England', in G. Walker and J. Kermode (eds), *Women, Crime and the Courts in Early Modern England* (London, 1994), pp. 48–80.

R.M. Karras, 'Two models, two standards: moral teaching and sexual mores', in B. Hanawalt and D. Wallace (eds), *Bodies and Disciplines: Intersections of Literature and History in Fifteenth Century England* (Minneapolis & London, 1996), pp. 123–38.

W.J. King, 'Punishment for bastardy in early seventeenth century England', *Albion* 10 (1978), pp. 130–51.

D. Underdown, 'The taming of the scold: The enforcement of patriarchal authority in early modern England', in A. Fletcher and J. Stevenson (eds), *Order and Disorder in Early Modern England* (Cambridge, 1985), pp. 116–36.

J. Wiltenburg, *Disorderly Women and Female Power in the Street Literature of Early Modern England and Germany* (Charlottesville & London, 1992).

Witchcraft and Magic

S. Clark, 'Inversion, misrule and the meaning of witchcraft', *P & P* (1980), pp. 98–127.

S. Clark (ed.), *Languages of Witchcraft: Narrative, Ideology and Meaning in Early Modern Culture* (Basingstoke, 2001).

M. Gibson (ed.), *Early Modern Witches: Witchcraft Cases in Contemporary Writing* (London & New York, 2000).

C. Holmes, 'Women: witnesses and witches', *P&P* 140 (1993), pp. 45–78.

A. Macfarlane, *Witchcraft in Tudor and Stuart England* (London, 1970).

D. Purkiss, *The Witch in History: Early Modern and Twentieth Century Representations* (London, 1996).

J.A. Sharpe, 'Witchcraft and women in seventeenth-century England: Some northern evidence' *Continuity and Change* 6 (1991), pp. 179–99.

——, *Instruments of Darkness: Witchcraft in England, 1550–1750* (London, 1996).

K. Thomas, *Religion and the Decline of Magic: Studies in Popular Beliefs in Sixteenth- and Seventeenth-century England* (London, 1971).

D. Willis, *Malevolent Nurture: Witch Hunting and Maternal Power in Early Modern England* (Cornell, 1995).

Scotland

General Works

E. Ewan and M.M. Meikle (eds), *Women in Scotland c.1100–c.1750* (East Linton, 1999).

R.K. Marshall, *Virgins and Viragos: A History of Women in Scotland from 1080–1980* (1983).

Marriage, Family and Society

A.E. Anton, "Handfasting" in Scotland', *Scottish History Review* 37 (1958), pp. 89–102.

K.M. Brown, *Bloodfeud in Scotland, 1573–1625: Violence, Justice and Politics in an Early Modern Society* (Edinburgh, 1986).

G. Desbrisay, 'Wet nurses and unwed mothers in seventeenth century Aberdeen', in E. Ewan and M.M. Meikle (eds), *Women in Scotland c.1100–c.1750* (East Linton, 1999), pp. 210–20.

A.D.M. Forte, 'Some aspects of the law of marriage in Scotland, 1500–1700', in E.M. Craik (ed.), *Marriage and Property* (Aberdeen, 1984), pp. 104–18.

W.D.H. Sellar, 'Marriage, divorce and concubinage in Gaelic Scotland', *Transactions of the Gaelic Society of Inverness* 51 (1979–80), pp. 464–93.

T.C. Smout, 'Scottish marriage, regular and irregular, 1500–1940', in R.B. Outhwaite (ed.), *Marriage and Society* (London, 1981), pp. 204–36.

J. Wormald, *Lords and Men in Scotland: Bonds of Manrent, 1442–1603* (Edinburgh, 1985).

Economic Activities

E. Ewan, 'Mons Meg and Merchant Meg: Women in later medieval Edinburgh', in T. Brotherstone and D. Ditchburn (eds), *Freedom and*

Authority: Scotland c.1050–1650: Historical and Historiographical Essays Presented to Grant G. Simpson (East Linton, 2000).

——, ' "For whatever ales ye": Women as consumers and producers in late medieval Scottish towns', in E. Ewan and M.M. Meikle (eds), *Women in Scotland c.1100–c.1750* (East Linton, 1999), pp. 125–35.

E. Gemmill and N. Mayhew, *Changing Values in Medieval Scotland: A Study of Prices, Money and Weights and Measures* (Cambridge, 1995).

A.J.S. Gibson and T.C. Smout, *Prices, Food and Wages in Scotland, 1550–1780* (Cambridge, 1995).

R.A. Houston, 'Women in the economy and society of Scotland, 1500–1800', in R.A. Houston and I. Whyte (eds), *Scottish Society, 1500–1800* (Cambridge, 1989), pp. 118–47.

Religion

B. Lenman, 'The limits of godly discipline in the early modern period with particular reference to England and Scotland', in K. von Greyerz (ed.), *Religion and Society in Early Modern Europe, 1500–1800* (London, 1984), pp. 124–45.

D.G. Mullan, *Scottish Puritanism, 1590–1638* (Oxford, 2000) Chapter 8, 'The ambiguity of the feminine', pp. 140–70.

——, 'Mistress Rutherford's narrative: A Scottish puritan autobiography', *Bunyan Studies* 7 (1997), pp. 13–37.

R.C. Reid, 'Papists and non-communicants in Dumfries', *Trans. Dumfriesshire and Galloway Natural Hist. and Antiq. Soc.* 32 (1955), pp. 186–90.

A.F.B. Roberts, 'The role of women in Scottish catholic survival', *The Scottish Historical Review* 70 (1991), pp. 129–50.

M.H.B. Sanderson, 'Catholic recusancy in Scotland in the sixteenth century', *Innes Review* 21/2 (1970), pp. 87–107.

——, *Ayrshire and the Reformation: People and Change, 1490–1600* (East Linton, 1997).

Disorderly Women

F.D. Bargett, 'The Monifieth kirk register', *Records of the Scottish Church History Society* 23/2 (1988), pp. 175–95.

M. Graham, *The Uses of Reform: 'Godly Discipline' and Popular Behaviour in Scotland and Beyond, 1560–1610* (Leiden, 1996).

J.G. Harrison, 'Women and the branks in Stirling *c*.1600–1730', *Scottish Economic and Social History* 18 (1998), pp. 114–31.

G. Parker, 'The 'kirk by law established' and the origins of 'The Taming of Scotland': St Andrews, 1559–1600', in L. Leneman (ed.), *Perspectives in Social History: Essays in Honour of Rosalind Mitchison* (Aberdeen, 1988), pp. 1–32.

Witchcraft

J. Goodare, 'Women and the witch-hunt in Scotland', *Social History* 23/3 (1998), pp. 288–308.

J. Goodare (ed.), *The Scottish Witch-Hunt in Context* (Manchester, 2002).

C. Larner, *Enemies of God: The Witch Hunt in Scotland* (London, 1981).

——, *Witchcraft and Religion: The Politics of Popular Belief* (Oxford, 1984).

D. Purkiss, 'Sounds of silence: Fairies and incest in Scottish witchcraft stories', in S. Clark (ed.), *Languages of Witchcraft: Narrative, Ideology and Meaning in Early Modern Culture* (Basingstoke, 2001), pp. 81–98.

J. Wormald, 'The witches, the devil and the king', in T. Brotherstone and D. Ditchburn (eds), *Freedom and Authority: Scotland c.1050–1650: Historical and Historiographical Essays Presented to Grant G. Simpson* (East Linton, 2000).

Wales

General Works

G. Dyfnallt Owen, *Elizabethan Wales: The Social Scene* (Cardiff, 1962).

——, *Wales in the Reign of James I* (Woodbridge, 1988).

M. Roberts and S. Clark (eds), *Women and Gender in Early Modern Wales* (Cardiff, 2000).

Marriage, Family and Society

E.J.L. Cole, 'Clandestine marriages: The awful evidence from a consistory court', *Transactions of the Radnorshire Society* 56 (1976), pp. 68–72.

R.R. Davies, 'The twilight of Welsh law, 1284–1536', *History* 51 (1966), pp. 143–64.

———, 'The survival of the bloodfeud in medieval Wales', *History* 54 (1969), pp. 338–57.

D. Jenkins and M.E. Owen (eds), *The Welsh Law of Women* (Cardiff, 1980).

J. Gwynfor Jones, *The Wynn Family of Gwydir: Origins, Growth and Development, c.1490–1674* (Aberystwyth, 1995).

———, *The Welsh Gentry, 1536–1640: Images of Status, Honour and Authority* (Cardiff, 1998).

G. Morgan, 'Women's wills in West Wales, 1600–1750', *Trans. Hon. Soc. of Cymmrodorion* (1992), pp. 95–114.

———, 'Dowries for daughters in West Wales, 1500–1700', *The Welsh History Review* 17/4 (1995), pp. 534–49.

P. Redwood, 'Life in Elizabethan Breconshire as portrayed in contemporary wills', *Brycheiniog* 24 (1990–92), pp. 43–66.

K.W. Swett, 'Widowhood, custom and property in early modern North Wales', *Welsh History Review* 18/2 (1996), pp. 189–227.

Economic Activities

M. Roberts, 'Gender, work and socialisation in Wales *c.*1450–1850', in S. Betts (ed.), *Our Daughters' Land Past and Present* (Cardiff, 1996), pp. 15–54.

Religion

J. Cartwright, 'The desire to corrupt: convent and community in medieval Wales', in D. Watt (ed.), *Medieval Women in their Communities* (Cardiff, 1997), pp. 20–48.

H. Fulton, 'Medieval Welsh poems to nuns', *Cambridge Medieval Celtic Studies* 21 (1991), pp. 87–112.

M. Gray, *Images of Piety: The Iconography of Traditional Religion in Late Medieval Wales*, B.A.R. British series 316 (2000).

J. Gwynfor Jones, 'Welsh gentlewomen: Piety and christian conduct, *c.*1560–1700', *Jnl. of Welsh Religious History* 7 (1999), pp. 1–37.

G. Williams, *The Welsh Church from Conquest to Reformation* (1962, repr. Arkansas, 1993).

Witchcraft and Disorderly Women

S. Clark and P.T.J. Morgan, 'Religion and magic in Elizabethan Wales: Robert Holland's Dialogue on Witchcraft', *Jnl. Eccl. Hist.* 27 (1976), pp. 31–46.

R. Suggett, 'Witchcraft dynamics in early modern Wales', in M. Roberts and S. Clark (eds), *Women and Gender in Early Modern Wales* (Cardiff, 2000), pp. 75–103.

——, 'Slander in early modern Wales', *The Bulletin of the Board of Celtic Studies* 39 (1992), pp. 119–53.

Glossary

Agweddi   The sum, determined by the status of the wife's father, from the matrimonial property to which the wife was entitled on a justified separation from the husband before their union had lasted seven years. The term was also used to describe the marital union during the first seven years before it was *priodas*.

Amercement   A fine.

Amobr fines   The fee payable to a woman's lord whenever she married or committed a sexual offence.

Argyfrau   The goods brought by a wife to the union. This became part of the common pool of matrimonial property only after seven years when the marriage became *priodas*.

Assythment   The process of arbitration and settlement to end a feud.

Branks   Scold's bridle.

Brewster   A woman who brews and sells ale.

Broken clan   A clan without land whose members were known as broken men or caterans.

Cateran   A member of a broken clan.

Chrisom   A white robe worn by a child at baptism and used as its shroud in the event of an early death.

Churching   A church service of purification or thanksgiving after a woman had been delivered of a child.

Conjunct fee   The term for jointure in Scotland.

Copyhold   Customary tenure of which the evidence was a copy from the lord's court roll.

Cowyll   The 'morning gift' made to a virgin bride by her husband.   The basic meaning of the word is a veil or head-covering as in English 'cowl'.

Cradle crown A fine paid by a cleric in Wales at the birth of his child.

Cuckold The husband of an adulteress.

Cuid oidhche A traditional render based on the obligation of tenants to provide food and hospitality for their chief and his men.

Custom of North Wales A custom according to which widows were entitled to half of the goods of their deceased husbands instead of the third that was customary in the rest of Wales.

Cynnwys A device developed to circumvent the prohibition in the Statute of Wales of inheritance by sons whom the Church regarded as illegitimate.

Cywydd A form of Welsh verse.

Dewin A highly revered male prophet whose insights were thought to derive from divine inspiration.

Dower The life interest of a widow in part of her late husband's land under English law.

Dowry The goods brought by a bride to her husband.

Ducking stool An instrument for the punishment of offenders, especially scolds. Also known as a cucking stool.

Endogamy The pattern of marriage in which brides are taken from within the group. The opposite of exogamy.

Feud A ritualised system of vengeance, conflict, dispute resolution and compensation involving kin groups.

Feu-ferm Land tenure in which an annual feu duty of money and grain are paid for heritable property instead of the old ward-duty.

Fine Clan elite.

Friendship, bonds of The simplest form of bond that established a common cause and often involved the whole kindred of the parties concerned, and a share of the land acquired, if any.

Galanas Blood price, which in the case of a married woman is not calculated according to her husband's status, but that of her father.

Goŵyn Insult payment.

Gyves Fetters, leg irons.

Hafodau Summer pasture on high ground in Wales.

Handfasting The exchange of consent by a prospective married couple, often witnessed by family and friends but not taking place within the church. A form of betrothal, but a process that could constitute a binding marriage if consent was expressed in the present tense, or was followed by sexual intercourse.

Hind A skilled farm worker, usually married and given a tied cottage.

Huckster A female pedlar or hawker.

Hudol   A type of male enchanter using acquired knowledge from books and other sources, which was gradually displaced by the *swynwyr* in the sixteenth century.

Jointure   An arrangement in which the bride and groom are put in joint possession of land. On the death of the husband the wife drew a fixed annuity from the jointure lands for her maintenance. In Scotland this was known as conjunct fee.

Jougs   An instrument of public punishment which consisted of a hinged iron collar placed around the offender's neck, attached to a wall or a post by a chain and locked.

Kindness   The claim to customary inheritance of land in Scotland on the basis of kinship with the previous holder.

Kirk session   The lowest level of court in the Protestant Church of Scotland (Kirk).

Letters of slains   A document, usually subscribed by the four branches of the dead man's kin, providing a guarantee to the killer that the blood-feud had been settled and was ended for ever.

Leyrwite   The payment owed to the lord in respect of a female villein's fornication in England.

Maleficium   The harm caused by the vengeful act of a witch.

Manrent, bond of   A more feudalised form of the bond of friendship in which protection and maintenance is offered in return for counsel, active military support, and payments of calp. It generally involved individuals and their kin.

Merchet   The payment owed to the lord in respect of a female villein's marriage in England.

Paraphernalia   Personal clothes and jewels which remained the property of the wife during and after marriage.

Penny bridals   A wedding celebration at which the financial contributions of the guests provide the economic wherewithal to establish the couple.

Priodas   The term used to describe a marital union which had lasted longer than seven years.

Regrator   A person who buys commodities to sell again, usually at a higher price.

Rentaller   A tenant who held his land from a lord for life, the written evidence of whose right was a rental.

Rheibwr (f = rheibes)   The only harmful type of native Welsh magical practitioner with powers associated with the evil eye.

Rhaith A group of oath swearers (compurgators) drawn in strict proportion from paternal and maternal relatives of the accused to try crimes such as theft in Welsh law.

Sarhaed Literally 'insult'. A term used to describe the offence and to describe the compensation payable to the victim which varies according to his or her status, and for a wife is calculated according to the status of her husband.

Shieling Summer pasture on high ground.

Sliochd A branch of a kin group.(pl. sliochdan)

Sorning The extraction of food and hospitality without proper right, often by raiding.

Swynwr (f = swynwraig) A charmer, male or female, who did good to man and beast by prayer, knowledge of herbs and charms. During the sixteenth century the *swynwyr* was resorted to more often than the *hudol* to ask for information or find lost things.

Tack A lease of lands by a tacksman in Scotland.

Tainistear The designated successor of the clan chief.

Tapster A woman who serves ale and/or beer in a tavern or alehouse.

Terce A one-third life interest in the heritable estates of a husband given to the wife as dower.

Tir prid A pledge (*prid*) of land, or a mortgage made for four-year renewable periods and used to circumvent the prohibition in Welsh law of alienating family land. The land could be recovered on repayment of the debt which it secured.

Tocher The goods brought by the bride to the marriage as a dowry in Scotland.

Vows per verba de futuro A promise of marriage made in the future tense often conditional on the consent of family and friends. Subsequent sexual relations or the exchange of vows in the present tense could make the marriage binding.

Index